ROB MATTISON

THE
DATA WAREHOUSING
HANDBOOK

Edited and illustrated by
Brigitte Kilger Mattison

XiT Press
Oakwood Hills, Illinois

Published by

XiT Press, Oakwood Hills, Illinois, USA - 2006

Originally published in 1996 as

Data Warehousing:
Strategies, Technologies, and Techniques

ISBN: 978-1-84728-665-9

Other Books by Rob Mattison:

The Telco Churn Handbook - 2005

The Telco Revenue Assurance Handbook - 2005

Web Warehousing and Knowledge Management - 1999

Winning Telco Customers Using Marketing Databases - 1999

Data Warehousing and Data Mining for Telecommunications - 1997

Data Warehousing: Strategies, Technologies and Techniques - 1996

The Object-Oriented Enterprise: Making Corporate Information Systems Work - 1994

Understanding Database Management Systems, 2nd Edition - 1998, 1993

To my darling wife, Brigitte, whose integrity, intelligence, faithfulness and courage have proven to me just how special she really is and caused me to love her more each day, and whose vigilant contribution to the preparation of this book has made it as good as it is.

Foreword

For someone who has spent the last 20 years working in the data processing industry, it is amazing to witness, first hand, the incredible impact the computer has had on business and on the lives of individuals. 20 years ago the computer was an extremely large, extremely complex, cumbersome piece of machinery, running with tubes, wires and punch cards. The principle means of programming was to rearrange the tubes or to rewire the guts of the machine. The effect of the computer on the individual's and business's lives was minimal. Only the largest, most sophisticated organizations could afford what the computer had to offer.

Since those early days, we have seen the computer and the micro-chip change, not only how we compute things, but the actual way we live and even the way we perceive reality. Wow! Think about it. The computer has changed how we look at things, what we think of as important, and what we consider to be "reality." The computer has changed our experience of life itself. Computers make it possible for us to do more kinds of work and enjoy more kinds of recreation than ever before imaginable. They have made it possible for us to land on the moon, create more fuel more efficient cars, and design and create buildings, bridges and basilicas that defy what used to be known as the world of physical reality. At the same time, computers have made it possible to cure diseases, perform surgery with laser beams and microscopic scalpels, and even to begin to manipulate the very genes that generate life so that we can now grow corn that is genetically resistant to insects and tomatoes that grow to the size of watermelons.

Of course, all of this incredible exponential increase in our capacity to do things has come with a cost. At this point, and for some time to come, the price we pay for this power confusion, disorientation and chaos. The reason for this is clear. As the computer continues to become more and more powerful, and as our sense of reality becomes challenged again and again, we find ourselves in a constant state of re-adjustment. As new things become possible, we must figure out how to make them fit into our already over-complicated lives.

One very critical component of this process of re-evaluating and re-creating our reality is information. Information is what we use in order to make decisions. Information is what we use to evaluate reality. The gathering of information, analyzing it, and making decisions because of it is, in one sense what life itself is all about. We are thinking animals and, thus, we process information.

In a very real sense, what the computer revolution has done, is provide us with the ability to collect, analyze and effect changes in the real world on a phenomenal scale. The computer is NOT a thinking machine, but an information storage and processing engine. We use computers to enhance our own capacity in that regard. Conceptually, the computer is an artificial extension of our own thinking process.

Of course, this explosion of information collection, storage and processing capacity has not occurred in a logical, well thought out manner. It is happening continuously and in a myriad of directions all at the same time. Our problem, is to try to figure out how to control this process of data collection, storage and analysis in a way which makes it manageable and versatile.

This is exactly the set of problems that the data warehousing approach attempts to address. Unfortunately, the process of figuring out how to harness all of this information and make it easy to examine and utilize is tied to a whole lot of rules of physical, economical, social and organizational realities. And it is these pre-existing conditions that make the job so incredibly difficult. We have physical laws of science which still limit us in what we can do. While computers are powerful, they are not omnipotent. They increase our capacities by leaps and bounds, but these leaps too have their limits.

Not only must we deal with the physical realities of what the computer can do, but we must constantly check with the economical realities of the process. While in the ideal world we would want to warehouse all of the data in the universe, the economic reality is that we cannot afford to.

No matter how hard we may try to make data stores a neutral and coldly logical kind of collection of information, the fact is that these stores are the product of a social and organizational system. These systems have rules of their own, and they also dictate what can and cannot be done with them.

Add to all of these conflicting conditions and frameworks the fact that the computer technology continues to grow in its capacity. Each time the capacity and capabilities are increased, we are forced, once again to re-evaluate all of the assumptions we made about all of our previous decisions.

This then is the real world of data warehousing.

The objective: to capture and make available oceans of information.

The constraints: chaos in the form of ever changing laws of physics, economics, social and organization.

It is the objective of this book to develop for the reader a set of tools, concepts and approaches which make the process of conceiving, designing and constructing the data warehouse a significantly less chaotic and frustrating experience than it has proven to be in the past.

What we cannot do, is provide you with a simple recipe book or to-do list where you can simply "follow the instructions" to successfully deliver the perfect data warehousing solution. That would be impossible.

What we can do, is provide you with a framework for understanding what a data warehouse is, what it takes to put one together, and how to understand and negotiate all of what it takes to make it a successful implementation.

Data Warehousing is complicated, but we can help make it less so.

Data Warehousing is challenging, but we can help you at least understand more clearly what the challenges are and how to address them.

Our primary objective in writing this book has been to provide the would-be-developer of a warehouse with a tool which fights the chaos so endemic to the undertaking of projects of this nature. We have tried to provide you with a framework for understanding what you are doing and why, and we have tried to give you a vocabulary and a problem solving paradigm set that should make it possible for you to attack the process of data warehousing with a clearer vision of what you are trying to do.

We have organized this book into two major sections:

The first section (chapters 1-3) deals with the concepts of data warehousing and the situational and environmental constraints and objectives that any project of this type entails.

The second section (chapters 4-12) gets into the detail of how to structure a data warehousing project, how to identify the different components of any data warehouse, and the detail about how to design and develop each of these components.

Table of Contents

CHAPTER 1

THE BIG DATABASE IN THE SKY

Los Angeles, 1994

After waiting around for a good 20 minutes, the maitre de', dressed in a Hawaiian print shirt and sandals showed us to our table. It was an incredible view; plate glass window walls on three sides. To the left was a building with a huge whale painted on it; to the left and straight ahead, the Pacific Ocean in all its tumultuous glory. We settled in, ordered drinks, and talked about the weather for a little while. Finally, our host (we will call him Preston) was ready to get down to business.

Preston is the CFO (Chief Financial Officer) for a major consumer goods manufacturer. He is well known in his industry, has many years of experience and has a reputation for being sharp, innovative and aggressive. Preston is no pushover. He is one bright businessman. Yet Preston felt that he needed to have this little "informal" meeting in order to share some of the concerns and visions that he has. By many standards, Preston could be considered to be among the brightest minds in business today. But despite his success, and apparent competence, he has come to the point of being completely overwhelmed with the problems he is currently experiencing in struggling with his information systems.

Oh, taken as individual systems, his information systems would probably be considered some of the best in the business. They are efficient, well run and dependable. These systems, without a doubt, keep the business running and are no small part of the reason why Preston's company enjoys the strong market and financial positions it currently enjoys. With all of these positive factors going for him, it would seem that the last place that Preston would be concerned would be in the area of computer systems operations. After all, Preston is a Financial specialist, not a systems specialist. Why is he even getting involved in these kinds of issues?

You see, Preston is stuck in a serious dilemma. On the one hand, he certainly would like to contain costs and keep the existing organization running as well as possible. On the other hand however, he sees all kinds of opportunities to make things two, five, or even ten times better than they are today, if only he could get those ugly, old Legacy computer systems to cooperate !!

So as the Pacific Ocean roared and crashed on the rocks outside our window, Preston roared on about his frustration over his current computer challenges. "Ultimately, it all comes down to my databases!" he raved. "No matter what we do, we always end up shackled by what these databases can or cannot do."

Preston then took a little time to educate us as to his understanding of what a database was. Of course, as an accounting type, the database to him was little more than a very large spreadsheet, but he failed to understand why he could not "have it his way," considering all of the time, money and energy that gets spent on these systems. "I have this vision in my head," he said, "of this huge database in the sky. A place where all of the information I need is stored for future reference. I mean, I understand about all the complexities and problems involved in working with my operational information in place, but why can't I just make a copy of it all and play with that?"

Preston, a person with no information systems background and no previous exposure to Data Warehousing conferences and seminars, has intuitively figured out that somehow, his imaginary Data Base in the sky (a Data Warehouse) is the solution to many of his problems.

And so, for whatever reason, we find that corporations are turning, en masse, to this intuitively obvious solution to the problem of trying to get more and better information for the development of better, more flexible information systems.

THE DATA WAREHOUSE PHENOMENON

If you're involved in information systems development in the corporate world today, then you have most probably been exposed to this, the most recent phenomenon to take the business by storm. Data Warehouses are the hottest new topics in the industry today.

Around the world, conferences geared to educating the masses on the how, what, where, when and why of data warehousing are springing up. These conferences espouse the many different benefits that a data warehouse can bring to your organization and feature speakers who are "expert" in the construction of such systems.

A typical brochure for such a conference includes headlines such as:

- Applying Client/Server, Object Technology, Open Systems and Relational / Multi-Dimensional DBMS to Provide Next Generation Decision Support Systems -- Proven Strategies and Fresh Insights from Industry Experts and Early Adopters
- The OLAP (On Line Analytical Processing) Forum -- How OLAP can benefit you and your organization

...and seminar topics like:

- Data Warehousing - The Competitive Advantage
- How to Build a Better Data Warehouse
- Critical Factors for Implementing Data Warehousing

...and dozens more.

Well, if you didn't think that data warehousing was a big deal with a solid discipline and thousands of backers with clearly established track records and construction disciplines in place; then a quick browse through any of these brochures would certainly convince you. Of course, these dozens of seminars are backed by an equally impressive onslaught of data warehousing exposure in the industry media.

The Media

Magazines are deluged with article after article of helpful hints and tips about how to build these data warehouses and how to manage them once they're built. Special issues, supplements and even Data Warehousing publications and newsletters are stuffing the mailboxes of corporate offices. A recent special supplement to a major industry weekly was entitled "Data Warehousing -- A Mandatory Initiative for IT Survival".

Data Warehousing Products

The manufacturers of computer hardware and software are equally committed to the advocacy of the Data Warehousing solution as the means to helping your organization meet its data processing needs. Almost without fail, hardware vendors are touting vast, expansive data warehousing support products and approaches, from the highly specialized data warehouse multi-CPU (SMP or MPP) platforms of the UNIX based hardware vendors, to the vaunted halls of IBM with its mainframe-based Data Warehouse solutions.

Many of the software vendors are getting into the act as well, from the "Data Warehouse Compatible" or "Data Warehouse Ready" stickers that show up on database products , to the grandiose Data Warehouse Management systems that claim to provide a complete data warehouse kit (just buy this product and add data). One software vendor recently announced plans to invest $45 million in the creation of a whole new line of Data Warehouse interface products, and new software companies are springing into existence daily, each claiming to meet some aspect of your data warehousing needs.

Business Planning and the Warehouse

As if all this clamor were not enough, recent surveys of several major corporations reveal that businesses are planning on spending big on the Data Warehouse as well. The sample survey consisted of organizations from the Manufacturing, Financial, Health, Retail, Utility, Government, Banking and Telecommunications Fields. The percentage of revenue spent on information systems averaged out to approximately five percent per year. Of those firms surveyed, a whopping 90 percent were involved in some stage of data warehousing system development.

Wow! If ninety percent of all businesses are building data warehouses in some shape or form, then it must be BIG. Some more information about these data warehouses might be helpful:

- Of the organizations working on data warehouse projects, over 60 percent are planning on storing data involving more that 20 Gigabytes of data, and over 10 percent are looking to build systems that involve more than 300 Gigabytes. Some are actually planning their systems in the Terrabyte range.

- Budgets for these systems range from a modest $250,000 at the low end to several millions of dollars at the high end.

- The number of users to be supported is measured in the tens, hundreds and sometimes even the thousands.

Well, these statistics would certainly seem to indicate that there is a data warehouse in just about everybody's future.

But with so much hype, and so much activity, what is by far the most perplexing thing, is that although everyone knows that data warehouses are good -- not essential to survival -- and although there are literally millions of pages and thousands of hours being spent on talking about how to build one, there is a definite lack of information about exactly what a data warehouse is.

What is a Data Warehouse Anyway?

So clearly, if a book is going to claim to tell you something about how to build a data warehouse, then it makes sense that we start with some kind of definition of what a data warehouse is. Coming up with a good definition for a data warehouse is actually going to be pretty difficult. Certainly not because of a lack of information about what people think it is, but more so because of an abundance of it. There is no force at work, no single authority, no regulating agency, that will establish a definition to which everyone can agree. As opposed to relational technology , who had its "inventor" Dr. Codd to act as the ultimate source of authority on the topic, and as opposed to Object Technology, whose definition is monitored and controlled by several standards groups and agencies, Data Warehousing *kind of just is.*

The closest we can come to an original source of information about data warehouses is a series of books written by Bill Inmon and Richard Hackathorn. These books represent the first time that the data warehouse was identified as such, and given the name "data warehouse." Unfortunately, as we will see after closer inspection, the underlying concepts and principles of the data warehouse can really be traced back to a much broader base, and much earlier roots.

The clearest "official" definition of a warehouse that we can derive therefore, is our best approximation of what the term means as it is used in the industry today. It is a combination of the foundational work done by Inmon/Hackathorn as modified by its practical use in business today.

A Data Warehouse is:

- a database
- organized to serve as a neutral data storage area
- used by Data Mining and other applications
- meets a specific set of business requirements
- uses data that meets a pre-defined set of business criteria

Obviously, we will need to be a little more specific before we can claim to have provided a useful definition of a data warehouse. So we will begin by coming to grips with exactly what we mean by the term database. Put into even simpler terms, a data warehouse is really nothing more than a big database that holds copies of data from other systems, that is then made available for use for other applications.

WHAT IS A DATABASE?

A Data Warehouse may be many things to many people, and may involve a lot of different parts, but everybody seems to agree that one of the critical components of any data warehouse is that it is some kind of a database. But before we can make such a bold statement, we will need first to examine just exactly how difficult it is to even come up with a definition of what a database is.

The term database, as well as the term data warehouse, is a name for a thing. But, because of the extremely complex nature of the world of data processing these days, they are names that can communicate very different things for different people. Let me provide you with some examples.

The Technician's View

My own personal background is extremely technical in nature. As an experienced COBOL programmer, I had several years experience working with programs and files before the term database ever came into existence.

Some time in the late 1960s and early 1970s, hardware and software vendors had found that they could create specialized data management software, called database products, which would handle a lot of the cumbersome data management tasks for the programmer. These original databases, with exciting names like IMS (Information Management System) , IDMS, ADABAS and Model 204 were the first generation of software, which made it possible for organizations to manage large amounts of data with ease.

So these were the first generation of database software products, known generically as "databases."

As the technology advanced, new generations of these products came out: Relational databases, object oriented databases and others. These databases were still databases in the classical sense. All they did was manage data for programs. The programs did the work and interfaced with the user, and the database simply managed the data.

In more recent years, a new type of database software product came on the scene. These "databases," mostly working on personal computers, managed the data for the programmer, but came included with programming languages and features all their own. The programming part of the database and the data management part became enmeshed. And so, when talking with someone about a database software product, you might get some very different answers about what they can or cannot do depending upon the experience of the person with whom you talk.

Now this little progression of the term database is one that makes sense from a technical perspective. But there is another use of the term, a business use, that has a very different meaning.

TheBusiness Person's View

A business person is completely unconcerned with the technical details about programming languages and database software. To the business person that is all just "technical stuff." From a system user's perspective, a database is the collection of all the information about a population of interest to them, regardless of where or how it is stored. For example, as far as a marketing person is concerned, all of the information about his or her customers that can be found within any of the computer systems run by the company are considered to be part of the corporate "database."

There is a customer database which consists of all of the information about who buys our products, a sales database with information about purchases, and a product inventory database. This "database" from the business persons perspective, is not part of any physical file or database software structure, and it is not even seen as being tied to any specific applications, screens or systems. It is simply all of the information that exists somewhere "in the system."

This more generalized application of the term database can actually be the cause of some pretty humorous exchanges. In fact, I'll never forget the hours-long discussion I had with a woman named Debbie, who worked for a marketing database company. We were both considered to be "database experts" and yet it took us over 30 minutes just to figure out that what she called a database was only remotely related to what I called a database. She didn't know what ORACLE was, and I couldn't figure out why a person who "built databases" would be concerned with the standard postal codes for zip codes.

So while at first, it might seem that telling you that a Data Warehouse is a type of database might be a useful bit of information, it turns out that this observation is only useful when made more specific. A Data Warehouse is a database in two senses, technical and business. In fact, one of the things that makes a Data Warehouse unique is that at the heart of a Data Warehouse is a clearly-defined physical database (technical understanding), which holds within it all information of interest to specific groups of business users (business understanding).

WHAT IS THE SPECIFIC SET OF BUSINESS REQUIREMENTS?

So we know that a data warehouse is a type of database. The next thing we need to know is what people want to do with them once they are built. Again, we are left with no solid set of criteria from which to work. What we can do, however, is point to a set of certain key assumptions that most people make when it comes to data warehouse construction.

In general, when people talk about making use of the information within a data warehouse, there are two uses to which it is to be put. First, they usually begin talking about "user friendly" query tools: Executive Information Systems (EIS), On Line Analytical Processing (OLAP) and Decision Support Systems (DSS). This impressive list of acronyms has become known generically in the industry as Data Mining Applications. Second, they often demand that the data stored in the data warehouse be formatted and exported for use by other systems; sometimes new systems, sometimes the information is shipped back to its sources in a validated form.

So, to be more specific, a Data Warehouse is a database, designed to be utilized by Data Mining products and applications and to serve as a staging area for the extraction of that data by other applications.

Data Mining Applications

There are several reasons why Data Mining applications have become as important that they have over recent years, and their application is so specialized and complex that we will be dedicating a fair portion of our book to their understanding and utilization.

By including Data Mining applications in our list of prerequisite components for a data warehouse we find that it becomes much easier to explain why people are interested in building a data warehouse in the first place. Data Mining applications have some very specific requirements for the data that they utilize. The data must be clearly defined, easily accessible, and stored in a specific format. The Data Warehousing approach makes that much easier to do.

For many organizations it might be said that a data warehouse is simply a database built to support the use of Data Mining technologies.

Staging Data for Use by Other Applications

There are also many reasons why organizations would find it useful to create a system to serve as a kind of data "clearing house" for other systems. With many different systems at work, and so many different versions of the same data floating around, it becomes impossible to coordinate them all without some kind of special staging area to get things organized.

While Data Mining applications and the desire to create a neutral storage area for data can result in a wide variety of approaches and applications, the format for the storage of the data that is needed must meet several specific characteristics. The data needed by these applications must, for operational and efficiency reasons, be stored in an area separate from the operational systems that created them.

In the case of data mining applications, this separate area is crucial because these applications tend to be very resource intensive when it comes to data, and attempts to share data between these applications and the Legacy systems that create the data have ended in performance disasters.

Characteristics of Data
Within the Data Warehouse

Our consideration of the primary purpose of a Data Warehouse to serve as a staging area for other applications leads us to the first of our observations about the nature of the data within the data warehouse itself. If the Data Warehouse is to function as this form of "neutral" data storage area, then we can conclude that: "A Data Warehouse produces no new raw information. It serves only as a storage area for the information produced by other systems." This is certainly consistent with its name, Data "Warehouse".

A Data Warehouse is not a data factory.

Historical Data

Not only do Data Mining and other types of applications require their own set of data in order to function, they usually require much more data than the amount legacy systems are used to carrying. Operational systems cannot afford to keep track of all the changes that occur to the data as time goes on. The systems would "choke" from the sheer volume of data needing to be managed. So in general, operational (Legacy) systems are designed to run "efficiently."

Data Mining operations, on the other hand, are meaningful only when they have access to a lot of the historical information that legacy systems have traditionally discarded. Therefore, the second characteristic of the data within the warehouse is that it will contain not only current copies of information, but historical copies as well.

For the most part, people do not build data warehouses for the sole purpose of supporting only one Data Mining application. Although certainly possible, it has been determined that it can be much more efficient to design the warehouse to hold data that several different applications can use simultaneously. In order to make this possible, the data warehouse must be designed in such a way that this "sharing" of data is simplified. The third characteristic of the data in the warehouse is it is organized in a way that makes it easy for people to find and manipulate.

While the definition proposed so far might seem a bit general, it needs to be, because the scope of data warehousing applications is so broad that it is difficult to define it in any more specific terms.

DIAGRAM OF A DATA WAREHOUSE

We can see, therefore, that a data warehouse project is really made up of three major components:

- The first component and the center of any Data Warehousing System is the Data Warehouse itself: A large, physical database, which holds a vast amount of information from a wide variety of sources. The data within it has been organized in a way that makes it easy to find and use and is updated frequently from its sources.

- The second component of the Data Warehouse System is the data importing and exporting component. This portion of the system includes all of the programs, applications, data staging areas and Legacy systems interfaces which are responsible for pulling the data out of the Legacy system, preparing it, loading it into the warehouse itself and exporting it out again, when required.

- The third and most important component of the system includes all of the different data mining applications that make use of the information stored in the warehouse.

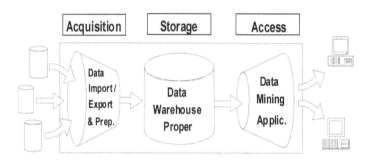

Figure 1.1: The three components fo the data warehouse system

This simple schema provides us with a basic overview of the make up of ANY Data Warehousing application.

Examples of Data Warehousing Applications

Businesses today are making use of the data warehousing approach to systems construction to solve a wide variety of problems and to meet a broad range of business needs. Some examples can help illustrate how this is being done.

Case 1: Quality control (petrochemicals)

This company is in the business of purchasing several different grades of "raw materials" and then subjecting those materials to a lengthy, complex series of refining steps, resulting in the ultimate production of several "grades" of end product.

Because of the intricate and specialized nature of these processing steps, and constant changes in the technology, the firm found itself in the position of needing to maintain dozens of independent quality control software packages, each measuring different things, and each working at a different phase of the manufacturing process.

Because these systems had each been developed at a different time, making use of different technologies and testing for different things, it was exceedingly difficult for production control to ever figure out exactly how well products were moving through the system or to anticipate what kinds of shortages they might find at a future date.

It was determined that the best solution would be a data warehouse. The design of the data warehouse was straightforward. Pertinent information about the progress of different "batches" through the factory was identified within each of the disparate quality control systems. The critical information from each system was copied daily to a centrally defined quality control tracking data warehouse. A selected set of data analysis tools was then used by production control in order to analyze the status of each batch, and to help anticipate raw materials requirements for the next week's production runs.

Case 2: Integrated marketing (telecommunications firm)

This firm, a large telecommunications provider, was having a lot of trouble keeping track of its relationships with customers. It seems that the company had several different systems, each managing different aspects of the customer management process. The billing system had one set of records. The direct mail department had their own customer list. The telemarketing group maintained yet another set of customer contact records and the service department maintained yet another.

The problem was that these systems did not communicate very well with each other. If a customer tried to tell someone about a change of address, depending upon who they talked to resulting in different copies of the customer information would be changed at different times.

In some situations, a customer might put in a call to customer service complaining about the service and demanding that the phones be removed. Two weeks later they would receive a letter stating "Thank you for being such a good customer." In other situations bad credit risks were given unlimited credit because of anomalies in the system.

The solution this organization opted for was a data warehouse which established a primary source of information for all customer information.

First, a customer master list was compiled. This was developed by extracting and comparing all the customer lists provided by each of the Legacy systems. These lists were consolidated into one master list. Then the critical information about these customers was identified. This information was extracted, "sanitized" and formatted for storage within the warehouse. Finally, applications were developed which could take advantage of this new consolidated customer view.

Case 3: Financial systems control (banking)

This organization found itself deluged with synchronization problems between dozens of different accounting systems. While each different division of this bank had accurate accounting, it was becoming increasingly difficult to create consolidated financial statements that made sense.

As part of an overall re-engineering of the bank's information systems, a financial systems data warehouse was constructed which would make it easy to balance one system against the others.

A Recognizable Pattern

The previously cited examples are only a few of the many different ways that organizations are trying to apply the data warehousing approach to their systems challenges. It can be informative at this point to note the similarities in the situations that are being faced.

In all of the situations cited, and in the vast majority of cases, businesses are turning to data warehouses in order to integrate of data across disparate Legacy systems. The subsequent goal is to use the consolidated data to better understand, coordinate and estimate their organizations.

The "classical" problem being addressed by data warehouses today is known as "vertical silos" of information.

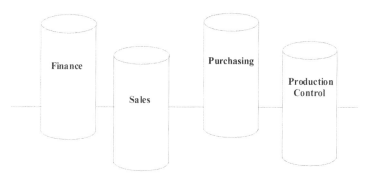

Figure 1.2: Silos of information

In this scenario, the operational systems that run the company are pictured as vertical stacks, each of which is dedicated to the efficient execution of some aspect of the business's operations. The

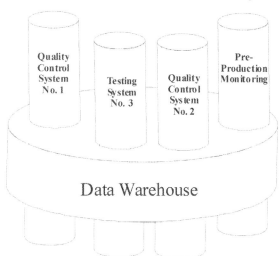

Figure

data warehouse is then utilized as a way to "bridge" these vertical silos, and to integrate the information that each holds into new, more synergistic and more meaningful ways. For example, in the case of our petrochemical company, each of the different testing and quality control applications represented a different vertical stack of information.

The data warehouse was created in order to integrate the information being collected and make it available to those people responsible for the overall process.

A Sense of Déja Vue ... Perhaps

By now, anyone that has been involved in the development of large scale information systems for any length of time is probably reeling. These veterans of systems integration are probably thinking: "Now wait a minute! Is that all there is to this Data Warehouse thing? Why, we've been building systems like this for years!" For the most part, these grizzled veterans would be correct.

The Data Warehouse concept is not new. It is almost as old as corporate data processing itself. I am aware of dozens of projects that attempted to do the same thing, years before the term "Data Warehouse" was even coined. In fact, I can even recall several articles in *Computerworld* and other industry publications as far back as 1985, which played with the Data Warehouse theme.

Therefore, the question that comes to mind is: Why all the fuss about Data Warehousing at this particular point in time. Why is this approach, which seems logical and which has been successfully utilized hundreds of times in the past, suddenly being treated like the greatest new approach to systems development.

While it may be impossible for anyone to believe how a phenomenon like this builds this kind of momentum, several factors have probably contributed significantly. To discover the roots of Data Warehousing mania, we can turn back to the days of the mainframe computer system.

A STORM ON THE HORIZON - 1975

Back before the wholesale incursion of UNIX servers and personal computers onto the data processing scene, the mainframe computer ruled as the unchallenged king of corporate computing. At that time, data processing was quickly becoming a well established, stable and dependable science. Business was in love with large, centralized computer systems, and corporate success could be gauged by how many mainframes you had and how many CICS terminals you had attached to them. As businesses continued to exploit this environment, it became clear that some limits were being reached in what could be accomplished.

It was obvious that the single largest limiting factor on the continud expansion of these corporate systems was the data that they managed, and the database software that managed it. The IMS, IDMS and other navigational databases could only hold so much data at one time. More importantly, in order to manage that data well, the data had to be pre-determined, pre-formatted and stored within a solid, hard coded database environment.

Visionaries Try to Prevent Impending Data Doom

Several people saw how large, unmanageable and inflexible these systems had become, and they began to try to figure out ways to break the bottleneck. They proposed approaches to the solution of the problem, and these proposals fell under two major categories:

- The first category concentrated on coming up with a different kind of database software product. The strongest case was made by Dr. E. F.. Codd with his relational database approach. Dr. Codd proposed that the main reason for this data intransigence was the software that managed it, and with his new, freer-formed database, the bottleneck could be broken.
- The other group of proposals to solve these problems came under the category of information engineering solutions. Advocates of these solutions said that the problems of data glut and over-utilization could be resolved by coming up with a way to identify and catalog all of the data, thereby making it easy to manage through the use of Data Dictionaries or Data Repositories.

So corporations dutifully went off attempting to get around their data problems by creating new relational databases, and/or by initiating different kinds of enterprise modeling excursions. The enterprise modeling advocates were quickly followed by a large group of CASE (computer aided software engineering) advocates, who claimed that once the data was successfully cataloged, that you would be able to automate even the software creation process through the use of their products.

Ultimately, despite many years of effort and millions of dollars, the information engineering approach has yet to yield any significant fruits. Most organizations have all but abandoned the enterprise modeling and CASE approaches to managing their data.

Relational databases however fared much better, but there is no way for us to know whether they would have ever reached their current level of acceptance without some help, because just as the relational databases began to reach acceptance, we found the halls of corporate computing being assaulted from several new sources.

Those were the days of the UNIX and Personal Computer revolutions. While corporate computing continued along its merry way, a new class of computer systems came onto the scene. Suddenly, there were hundreds and thousands of computers within the walls of the corporation that the computer departments knew nothing about. These systems landed on every desktop and in every department, supported by completely different groups of computer specialists, with a completely different perspective on data processing, and riding on the crest of this wave, was the relational database.

Relational databases were the only databases that anyone knew about in these environments, and as the acceptance of the personal computer and UNIX server grew, so did the acceptance of relational databases Today, almost every major new system, on any platform, is built using relational technology.

Unfortunately, with the rise of the non-traditional (non-mainframe) computer platforms, and the more free- form relational databases came the breakdown of something else. The biggest fatality of the relational and personal computer revolutions was a process known as the Systems Development Life Cycle. This process, a process perfected over many years of experience, was the road map, the template, the instruction manual for the way that people were supposed to build computer systems. For all its weaknesses, the SDLC gave people a set of guidelines, which when followed, allowed them to develop large, complex computer systems with some predictability. But with the explosion of non-SDLC-based hardware products and databases, came the ultimate breakdown of the methodology. We lost the instruction book for how to put systems like this together. The net result was that people continued to build newer, bigger and more expansive systems, but these systems were less integrated with the previous systems than ever before. More and more data got duplicated across more and more systems, with less control.

The Impended Doom has Arrived

So the problems that were cited as major concerns back in the 1970s, have become problems that are hundreds of times worse than any of those people could have imagined. Organizations are literally buried in data that they cannot use, because it is stored in so many different places. Not only is the data scattered all over the place, but no one is sure what it all means. Because of the failure of the information engineering disciplines to take hold, no one has created any kind of catalog of where data is or how it is being used.

And so, corporations are desperate. Desperate to get control of their data. Desperate to make better use of it. Desperate to figure out where it is, what it is and what they can do with it. Coupled with this lack of control, is a tremendous amount of pressure to do more things with the data. New approaches to marketing, just in time manufacturing techniques and sophisticated statistical analysis and projection software give business people the potential to make their businesses more efficient and profitable then ever before; but of course, they need data to do it. They need more data then ever before, from more sources then ever before. They need it and they need it now. They cannot wait three years or even three months.

Coupled with the power and potential of these new tools has come the latest of the revolutions: Client/server. Now all of these disparate personal computers, UNIX servers and mainframe computers can be tied together into a huge, network of computers. The physical barriers that used to isolate all of these systems have broken down. Every computer is now physically tied to every other computer. But of course, it is still unclear as to why this should be done; since no one can figure out where all the data is, and how it should be used.

DATA WAREHOUSES:
THE ONLY VIABLE SOLUTION

Only the bravest, boldest and more trusting of corporations will even attempt to get control of their data through the necessary investment in far reaching, long term enterprise planning and modeling programs. The track record of these initiatives is abysmal, and no short term benefits are likely.

Some of the bravest have begun to embrace object-oriented approaches, and while these at least have a chance of long term pay back, the start up cost is very high. For the most part, businesses cannot afford to continue to re-engineer their existing systems anymore. Those systems, some of them currently housing 20 years worth of 'fiddling", simply cannot be modified cost effectively and yet, businesses cannot afford to replace them they are too critical to their operations and too delicate to mess with.

So, ultimately, most corporations are stuck. Data Warehousing, at this point in time, seems to be the only viable option if they are to continue to expand their systems capabilities without taking a major setback in their budgets and time tables.

The Future of Data Warehousing

Given the alternatives, Data Warehousing, no matter how ineloquent a solution, provides a viable alternative to the continued, less than cost effective alternatives. If we carry this trend to its logical conclusion, we can see that what we are doing, through the wholesale creation of data warehouses, is creating a new, artificial baseline of data, against which whole new generations of software can be written. Ultimately, these new data warehouses will probably become the foundations for the next generation of business applications.

This more relaxed vision of the data warehouse, as the solution to the many of the problems of data management faced by organizations today has a lot of merit to it. Under this more liberal interpretation of the term, we can actually envision the warehouse as supporting not only simply decision support and query intensive kinds of applications in a direct access manner. We can also see how the data warehouse could be used as the provider of input into a whole new

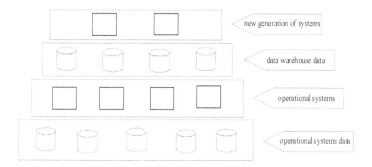

new generation of systems

data warehouse data

operational systems

operational systems data

Figure 1.4: the data warehosue pyramid

generation of operational systems. It is this broader perspective of the warehouse that holds more excitement and potential for the future than the "warehouse as decision support delivery vehicle" view.

In the pages to come we will be exploring the possibilities provided by this not so new approach to data and systems management, and provide the reader with some insights into the issues and approaches that can make data warehousing a viable alternative to systems development problems.

Chapter 2

The Immutable Laws of Systems Development

Detroit, 1993: The client was not pleased, to say the least. We were sitting around a conference table behind the movable walls of a makeshift conference room that had been plopped into the middle of a renovated factory building. The client, an executive with several year's experience, had called this meeting to check on the status of our "audit" of her company's latest data warehousing initiative.

"Would you repeat that, please," she said slowly in an exaggeratedly calm voice.

I cleared my throat, looked around nervously and said, "Yes, our initial findings are that you would be better off scrapping this project and starting over again."

She grimaced, "Do you mean to say that the hundreds of thousands of dollars we have sunk into this project so far have been wasted?"

I managed a strained smile before I replied, "Well, certainly there are some things that can be salvaged and re-used, but for the most part the answer is, yes."

The scene we have just described is not a pretty one. Sadly, it is actually representative of the fate of most major computer systems initiatives in business today. The records show that if a corporation undertakes a major systems development initiative, chances are good it will fail completely or, at the very least, end up costing considerably more, taking much longer, and doing a lot less than initially envisioned. Statistics indicate failure rates as high as 60 percent for even small to medium sized initiatives. As the projects get larger, so does the likelihood of failure. Some sources suggest that the failure rate for multi-million dollar, multi-year projects may be in the 90 percent range.

It is critical, for several reasons, that we address these issues at the onset of our investigation into the construction of data warehouse projects. The main objective is simply to establish validity. Anyone who claims to tell you how to build something as large and complex as a data warehouse should also be able to tell you why the approach being submitted would not result in the kind of scene we described earlier. In fact, in this author's opinion, a discussion about how to avoid these failure traps is a prerequisite to any proposed project.

Unfortunately, it is in the very nature of systems development theory and practice today to try to ignore these sobering statistics at almost any cost. The industry and the press are deluged with experts, opinions, products and approaches to systems development which either fail to address the issue at all, or allude to grandiose schemes which claim to provide a safe, predictable path for systems development, but in the final analysis fall just as short as any of its predecessors.

Clearly, what is needed before we begin to talk about how you should approach the building of a data warehouse, is a much better understanding of some the fundamental forces that drive people to participate in failed project after failed project.

In fact, there are two questions that I would want answered before going any further:

- First, I would want to know why corporations continue to participate in systems development initiatives that are clearly (based on experience) very high risk ventures. Why does a company choose to risk so much in the pursuit of a data warehouse, or any other kind of system for that matter?
- Second, I would want to know how the proposed approach to data warehouse construction is going to give me some sense of assurance that the results will be successful.

In order to create a framework for this investigation, we will consider the problem through the identification and explanation of several of the "immutable laws" that seem to govern and drive the corporate systems development process today. These laws, some well known and some simply implied, should provide us with some valuable insight into the how and why of building a data warehouse in today's high risk environment.

MURPHY'S LAW

The first law that seems to apply in the world of computer systems development would clearly seem to be Murphy's Law. "If anything can go wrong, it will." Unfortunately though I have certainly seen Murphy's Law at work on almost every project that I have participated in or audited, the law in and of itself provides us with very little insight into what we can do about it.

Response to Murphy's Law

One obvious conclusion that we can draw from our continued exposure to the consequences of Murphy's Law as we continue to build computer systems, is that we are participating in a high risk endeavor, and that we should exercise as much caution, and reduce as much risk as possible. While we will attempt to apply this rule of conservatism to our approach whenever possible, we will see that in many cases it is simply not possible to do so.

WHY DO PEOPLE TAKE THE RISKS?

Our first objective then, is to try to why people continue figure out to participate in a seemingly endless parade of disastrous systems development projects.

In order to understand this superficially obvious need of major corporations to invest, willy-nilly in a wide range of high risk, low success projects, we need to take a step back and try to understand this process from a larger perspective. We need to understand something about the relationship between businesses and their computers.

THE INTRODUCTION OF THE COMPUTER TO BUSINESS

Back in the early days of business, before the introduction of the first Burrough's or IBM mainframes, businesses were run by people and by paper. In fact, the bigger the organization got, the more paper needed to be created, and the more people were required to take care of it. Take a simple function like accounting. Corporations needed dozens of payroll clerks, who spent their time adding, subtracting, journaling and ledgering all the different financial transactions that drove the business along its merry way.

Then came the first computers; large, sensitive and very expensive, but these computers, with their simple punch cards as input and output, provided the business with the opportunity to process a lot more paper, a lot more quickly, and with a lot more accuracy then they could with human computing. And so, the first mainframes made their appearance.

The result was staggering. Corporations got an incredibly lucrative return on the investment that they made in these systems.

Of course, since it worked so well the first time, they did it again, and again and again.

Soon, as computers became bigger and better, smart corporate executives were able to capitalize on those capabilities too. Each new generation of computer capability enabled large corporations to gain efficiency, reduce costs and grow larger.

This pattern has continued to this day. As computers become faster, more powerful and more efficient, opportunistic business people take advantage of those capabilities.

The next law that we therefore consider, is Moore's Law. Moore examined the relationship between computer power and cost, and found them to be inversely related. In fact he identified a pattern. The details of the pattern vary depending upon the variables that you include, but generally, it states that every few years, the power of computers increases exponentially with a corresponding drop in the cost to provide that power.

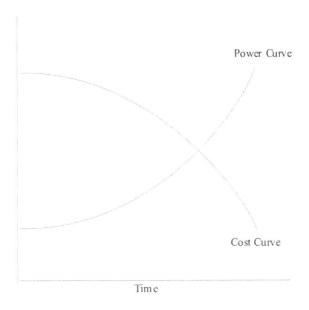

Figure 2-1. Moore's curve. As the power of computers increases, the cost of that power decreases.

MOORE'S LAW

Moore's law tells us, that until some kind of wall is reached in the current progression of computer capabilities, there will continue to be drastic growth in the computer capabilities area.

While Moore's Law provides us with the ability to understand what has been happening with computer technology itself, it does not explain the relationship of business to that capability. In order to understand that , we will make an application of Darwin's Law of evolution.

DARWIN'S LAW

Charles Darwin was the first to propose the theory of evolution. We will be able to draw many parallels between Darwin's observations about how living systems change and grow over time and help us understand how business systems do the same thing. The first application of this law is Darwin's basic observation that the species that survive are the ones best able to take advantage of the opportunities presented to them. Darwin's "survival of the fittest" theory.

In the same way that different kinds of animals were able to survive by capitalizing on their environment better than others, so too does this rule apply to business.

Since the wholesale acceptance of the computer as an integral part of business, it has become clear that the businesses that thrive and survive are those that are best able to take advantage of computer capabilities.

No major business organization could survive today without its computer systems. And the companies with the better systems do better. Just look at any industry: Transportation, Finance, Manufacturing. All are driven by the computer technologies that hold them together.

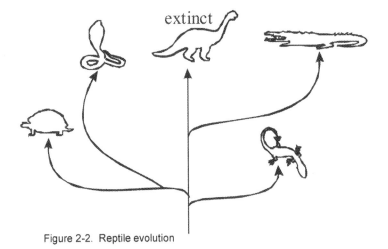

Figure 2-2. Reptile evolution

So, the answer to the question about why businesses keep taking on these high risk computer systems projects is clear. They do so because they must in order to survive in a highly competitive marketplace.

And just as evolution has shown that species evolve through a process of trial and error, so to do computer systems.

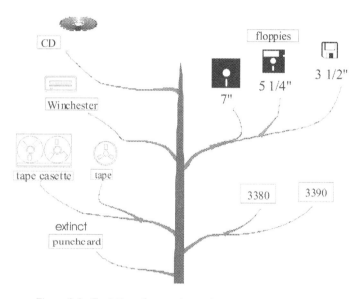

Figure 2-3. Evolution of computer systems

Just as the palentological history of each species is peppered with dozens of "dead end" evolutionary adjustments that failed (causing the extinction of the species), businesses must experiment with untested, risky, systems development projects if they hope to beat their competition to the next plane of existence.

Going back to the computer power/cost curve proposed by Moore's Law, that we can in fact draw a parallel curve, to indicate the progression of corporate computer systems. The corporations that survive will be the organizations exploit their systems' capabilities along the ever changing computer power/cost curve.

This analysis provides us with some valuable ground work for developing a better understanding of why organizations are spending the kind of money that they are, and taking the risks that they take. The trick, of course, is to figure out how to keep your company on the curve. To spend too much money, or to invest in dead end approaches can mean the end of the business, but so can being too conservative and allowing the competition to gain an irretrievable advantage by moving along the curve faster or better.

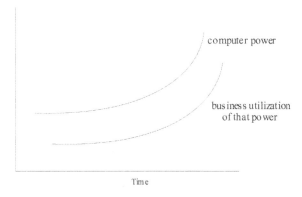

Figure 2-4. In order to survive, a business must strive to keep up with the computer power available.

MOORE'S COMPLEMENT

Armed with the insights provided by Moore's and Darwin's laws we can begin to develop an appreciation for why things are done the way they are. Business people know that they need to continue to improve their computer systems in order to survive. They also know that the process will be risky, and that they will have to take some leaps of faith in order to move along the evolutionary scale. Yet this need to change, in and of itself does not fully explain the chaotic and tumultuous environment that surrounds most projects of this nature. In order to understand that, we need to gain access to a couple more of the laws that seem to drive this industry and a more detailed understanding of the process of systems development.

The building of any large computer system for business these days is an incredibly large and complex exercise. The deployment of a large system can involve the concentrated efforts of dozens and sometimes hundreds of people, all working in order to make the vision of the new proposed system a reality.

Given this foundation, we can begin to develop an appreciation for what some of the underlying pressures are to drive organizations to undertake these projects. To get an even better picture, we turn once again to some of the fundamental laws that drive the process.

While Moore's curve allows us to anticipate the progression of computer systems capabilities, there is a hidden aspect of this curve. Moore's law tells us about the raw processing power that improved capabilities provide, but says nothing about the complexity of the processing that is being done. As businesses learn to exploit each new generation of technology, they do so with ever more complicated sets of processing tasks.

In the early days of computer processing, computer capability was measured in simple terms. A computer could execute only so many instructions per second. Because of the limitations that those capabilities imposed, processing was very simple, focused and linear. A certain number of cards were read and written per hour.

As more computer power became available, and as the ability to share data through disk packs and databases developed, the complexity of the systems increased tremendously.

In other words, in the early days, the computer could do little more than compute percentages and store the totals for a payroll. With improved capabilities, systems could perform comparisons of different salaries, operating efficiencies and so forth.

In today's world, these simple tasks are taken for granted, and the computer is expected to extrapolate, interpolate and perform sophisticated statistical analysis, linear algebra and other extremely complex processing.

In other words, the increase in computer power that is attained is not simply applied to the tasks that were previously being done. The new power available with the second generation of computers was not utilized in order to get those computers to read tapes faster and enhance the overall batch processing approach. Instead, the newly available power was used to create a new more complicated type of processing: real time, direct disk access.

At the same time, the amount of information that needs to be processed is continuously increasing. While the original computer systems were expected to keep track of all the most recent transactions, many of today's systems are expected to "remember" everything that ever happened.

Not only is each new generation more complex and makes use of more data than previous generations, but in order to provide new, improved value over previous systems, they must be bigger and work with more of the processes and data collected by earlier systems than ever before.

By definition, a new system that provides a new kind of value must make use of the things done by the earlier generations of systems.

We can again identify parallels in the natural world. If you were to take a look at the different components of the human brain, you would find that it is organized in many layers. At the core is a small area of the brain that takes care of only the most basic and rudimentary of

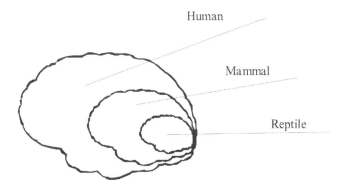

Figure 2-5. Layers of the brain.

processes. This core area makes sure that we breathe, that our heart pumps, etc. The next layer, which surrounds this core, and interfaces with it, takes care of a second more complex set of functions. The process continues until we reach the outermost layer, which is the largest and the most complex, and which handles all of the higher functions: thinking, creating, organizing and communicating.

What evolutionary biologists have found is a correlation between each of these layers of the brain, and the evolutionary progress of different forms of lower animals. In fact, we find that we can attribute the construction and functionality of each layer to the full thinking capability of our lower level cousins on the evolutionary ladder.

In the same way, each new generation of computer systems is built upon the foundations of the systems that came before it. Those systems are never eliminated, but are simply re-integrated in new ways to feed and support the higher functions.

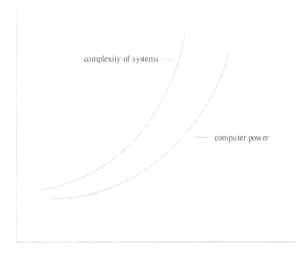

Figure 2-6. As computer power increases, complexity increases.

So, what is not obvious from the Moore Curve, is the assumption that as computer capabilities increase, and costs go down, and as businesses fight to stay as close to the curve as possible, that there is a corresponding increase in the complexity of what the systems are expected to do, in the volume of information that they must process in order to do it and in the interdependencies with older systems that must be integrated.

These lessons of the biological world provide us with some valuable insight into the reasonableness of what we may or may not try to accomplish. It is clear that mother nature wastes little, and systems that get the job done are kept. By contrast, our experience to date has shown that organizations are finding it impossible to eliminate old antiquated systems. While this observation appears obvious, it forces us to turn to yet another of our basic truth's and that is the one proposed by Frederick P Brooks, Jr.

BROOKS' LAW

Frederick P. Brooks, Jr. was the author of a book, back in 1975, called "The Mythical Man-Month". In this book, Brooks, a project manager for a very large computer operating systems development project, cited many of the inconsistencies and counter-intuitive forces that seemed to be at work in the development of computer

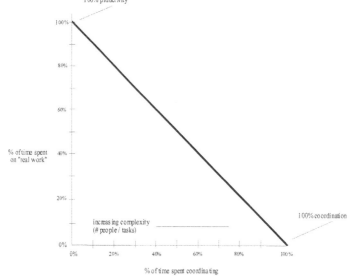

Figure 2-7.   Percent of time spent on "real work" as complexity increases.

software. These observations were incredibly insightful and are more valid in the systems development world today, than they were in the 1970's. In his book, Brooks observed that the bigger a project got, and the more complicated it became, the more time would be required just to keep all of the system developers in synch with each other as the system grew.

Again, it only makes sense that as more people become involved in the process, it will take more of the energy of each resource to stay coordinated with the others.

But what does this mean when we combine this insight with the conclusions drawn from Moore's Complement? It means that by

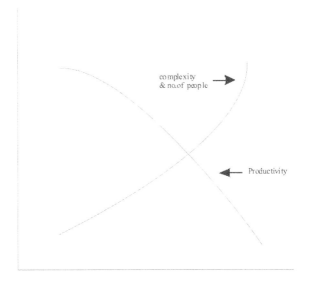

Figure 2-8. As the complexity of the systems goes up, the productivity of participants goes down.

definition, each new generation of system will be harder to build, will take longer and will dedicate more and more of its resources to figuring out what has been done by previous systems. It means that systems will get more expensive, more coordination-dependent and more subject to failure, based not upon technical problems, but upon the inability to coordinate and synchronize the activities of hundreds of people and dozens of other computer systems.

Nobody needs to develop a new system to process purchase orders twice as quickly as the previous system. You can fix that with a simple upgrade to you computer's memory. Nobody needs a system that does what an earlier generation of system did, using the latest and greatest Windows-based, mouse driven screen. It provides no new value to the company and therefore does not make economic sense.

What people need, to continue the climb up the evolutionary scale of computer systems, are systems that coordinate and mediate better.

THE CONSEQUENCES

Up until this point, our exploration of the laws that drive computer systems development has proceeded along a basically logical line of reasoning that no one could argue with. The observations and applications are clear, logical and easily supported by a huge body of evidence. But it is at this point that we can begin to uncover some of the insidious counter-assumptions and counter-claims that make the world of computer systems development as risky as it is.

THE HUMAN NEED FOR SIMPLICITY AND CATEGORIZATION

While no one could argue with the assumptions we have made so far, you will find an incredible amount of discord when asking people what we are supposed to do about it. It is here that the rubber meets the road and we will provide you, the reader, with some viable approaches to undertaking data warehouse construction.

In the past several pages, we have provided you with a basic understanding of the underlying forces that motivate people to do the things that they do when it comes to systems development. What we have not yet done is provide you with the detail about the complexities that underlie each of these observations. It is this complexity and the very human desire to simplify complexity that sets us up for most of the problems that when encounter when trying to build a system.

Let's face it, computer systems and businesses today are extremely complex animals. A typical corporate computer system today involves the use of thousands of computers (from mainframes, to minis to personal computers), billions of lines of computer code, and billions upon billions of bytes of stored data.

It is not even humanly possible for anyone to understand it all. You would have to be an accounting genius, marketing guru, manufacturing maven, have years of experience in dozens of disciplines and be technically competent in dozens of languages, operating systems, applications and network technologies. No one can take it all in. And this is where the real problems begin.

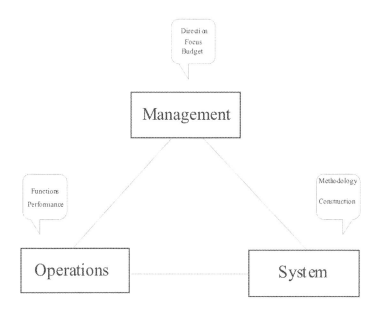

Figure 2-9.

THE PARTICIPANTS IN THE SYSTEMS DEVELOPMENT PROCESS

In order to help us understand the process a little better, we will attempt to oversimplify the case, and say that there are basically three groups of participants in any systems development initiative. Management, Operations and Systems.

Management defines all the people involved in the control and direction setting functions of the business. They are usually executives and are commissioned with responsibility for setting the direction of the business, monitoring its progress and approving its major initiatives and expenditures. Management is always involved whenever large sums of money or major operational modifications are concerned.

We will use the term Operations to identify those people within the business who are commissioned with the day-to-day execution of the duties that make the business run. We usually identify different operational units as divisions or departments. Each is commissioned to perform some set of tasks that help the corporation get its job done.

The final group involved in systems development are the people that work on computer systems themselves. These are the people that run the systems, write the programs and make the computer systems vision a reality.

In order to effectively deploy a new, major computer system, these three groups each have a vital role to play.

In general, it is the job of management to be aware of the marketplace, to know what the competition is doing and is likely to do, and to set the agenda for operational enhancement that will help the organization grow or at least survive.

It is the job of the operational group, to provide systems developers with the knowledge and experience necessary to deploy a new system that will be effective.

It is the job of the systems group to take the direction provided by management and the input provided by the operational group in order to build a system that meets the requirements of both groups.

This model provides us with the starting point for the development of a better understanding of what goes wrong when large systems are built.

THE SYSTEMS DEVELOPMENT LIFE CYCLE

Given that new technology systems are going to, by definition, be extremely large and complex, will involve individuals from management, operations and systems, and will provide new levels of functionality and interdependency than ever before attempted, we are faced with our next problem, which is figuring out who should have input to the decision-making process.

Historically, we find that most large systems initiatives have been proposed and are sponsored by individuals from any of the three groups, or jointly between them all. In other words, sometimes it is management's idea, sometimes operations, and sometimes, the driving force to build a system comes from the systems group itself. As the systems development cycle continues however, it is clear that participation from all three groups will be mandatory. And since it is not possible for anyone to really understand all of the consequences of what will be involved in the systems development, people assume trust that those things that do not make sense to them, have reasons that members of the other groups do understand. It is this tendency to have faith that leads us to the last law that we will consider. Ultimately, the process is driven by the systems people. They are the people charged with responsibility for the delivery of the software and hardware, so ultimately they must orchestrate the development. So in the final analysis it is systems developers and their systems development methodologies that are relied upon to coordinate the systems development cycle.

Unfortunately, it is here that we find the application of our last and most insidious law.

BARNUM'S LAW

P.T. Barnum was considered by many to be the greatest showman of all time. He was responsible for creating the "Greatest Show on Earth" and really revolutionized the entertainment industry in the days before movies, radio, television and video games. Probably the most famous statement that Barnum ever made about people and their seeming willingness to believe any kind of atrocious nonsense that he created, was that "There's a sucker born every minute."

We place Barnum's law at the top of our list of laws to take into account when considering this topic. For wherever you have chaos, high risk, and a large group of people who do not know what needs to happen, but trust that somebody else does, you create the opportunity for all manner of circus acts to dominate your planning horizon.

Barnum's Law in Action

Let me begin by saying that I truly believe that the vast majority of the people involved in computer systems development are hardworking, honest people with a high degree of intelligence and integrity. But these characteristics notwithstanding, what seems to be happening again and again is that people, on an industry-wide basis, are making decisions that involve the dedication of billions of dollars and millions of man hours of effort, with almost no assurance that what they are doing will yield anything remotely resembling tangible, usable results.

Our industry has been plagued by generation after generation of dead ends along the evolutionary scale. And while some organizations have been able to avoid doing themselves any serious damage, many have found the experience to be painful and frustrating.

It is precisely because the environment we are in is so complex, confusing and chaotic that organizations try so desperately to place their bets on approach after approach.

This tendency for people to "set themselves up" in this way was best identified by the Ancient Greek philosopher Demosthenes when he observed that "A man is his own easiest dupe, for what he wishes to be true he generally believes to be true."

In more modern times Samuel Johnson stated that "We are inclined to believe those whom we do not know because they have never deceived us before."

While these approaches vary in their assumptions and solutions, they all have the same basic set of claims associated with them, and as shall be evident, these claims themselves, mark the approaches as doomed to failure.

CLAIMS

It is intrinsic in the way that the computer systems industry works, or at least how it has worked up until this point, that people are looking for ways to make the process easier to live with. Because of this, we are bombarded with generation after generation of magic solutions that are guaranteed to:

- Simplify the development process
- Reduce the cost of systems development
- Make is possible to maintain and modify code for less
- Develop systems very rapidly

In other words, no matter what the claim happens to be, whether it be:

- CASE
- Relational Databases
- Client/Server
- Object Oriented
- Repository
- Enterprise Modeling

or, of course

- Data Warehousing

All claim that if you simply do it their way, all of the problems you are experiencing with your new systems development process will magically go away.

Now the fact of the matter is that each of these approaches has merit. Each can, and has, contributed to the progression of organizations up the evolutionary scale of computer utilization.

Equally true is the fact that:

- None of them has simplified anything. Each has added another layer of complexity on top of what was already there.

- None of them has resulted in the ability to build large, complex systems more quickly or for less money or effort.

- None of them has managed to reduce the risk involved in undertaking new systems projects (in fact, most of them add significantly to the risk, time and expense).

The reasons should be obvious. As we have already discovered, it is within the very nature of what we are trying to accomplish, to continuously add to the cost, complexity and time. There is simply no way to get around that.

We refer to these approaches under the section on Barnum's law, not because they have no value, but because, people, people in the management, operational and systems side, are all too likely to embrace these new approaches based upon their promises, without considering the consequences.

At least when P.T. Barnum introduced you to the three-headed dog boy from Mars, you were amazed and entertained for your trouble. In our case, the results are anything but amusing.

When you take all of the different factors that are simultaneously working against the builder of a new system, it is actually quite amazing that anything gets done at all. By combining the ever increasing capabilities as indicated by Moore's Law, and the concomitant complexity demanded by the entrepreneurial "survival of the fittest" approach that business takes to computers, add a few dashes of Brooks' Law and Barnum's and you have all the makings of a first class fiasco.

Any proposal which claims to provide you with a road map which can help you successfully a build data warehouse had better include in its very core, the ways and means to address the many weaknesses that we have so far expounded.

There are certain assumptions about any systems development approach that we dismiss immediately as being infeasible, and there are certain characteristics of the process that, by definition, must be included in the planning if the system is going to be successful

SURVIVAL OF THE FITTEST FOR COMPUTER SYSTEMS

At first glance, it will seem that the effect of all of these laws on our attempt to develop a new computer system would result in nothing but chaos and failed systems. And yet, computer systems do get built, and businesses do function by making use of them. Somehow, yet another law would seem to be in effect.

In order to understand how this law works, we will need to take a few steps back and take a brief look at the history of computer systems and the business.

THE INTRODUCTION OF THE COMPUTER TO BUSINESS

If we go back to the early days of computers in the business, we can begin to gain some insight into how this law was originally established, and see how it still is at work today. In the days of business before computers, the corporation was driven and managed by paper. Accounting, sales records, production control, everything was managed by people and paper. Obviously, this resulted in a lot of paper, and in the need to have very large staffs of people who simply managed that paper. Not only were these businesses driven by paper but they were also driven by computation. Big companies has scores of accounting personnel, whose jobs it was to add, subtract and tally all of the different transactions that had to take place.

A good mental image of any large, pre-computer business would have to include the existence of incredibly large buildings, whose only purpose was to house filing cabinets full of records and large rooms full of accountants with adding machines on their desks. Peoples' jobs involved scurrying about gathering up papers, adding things up, creating new papers and passing them on to the next group.

Into this paper and manually intensive environment were introduced the first business computer systems. When the first computers were brought into the business world, the people involved had no idea just how big and complicated this whole process would get. The business people of those days were looking at very specific, tactical business problems and expenses, and the early computers provided good, simple tactical solutions.

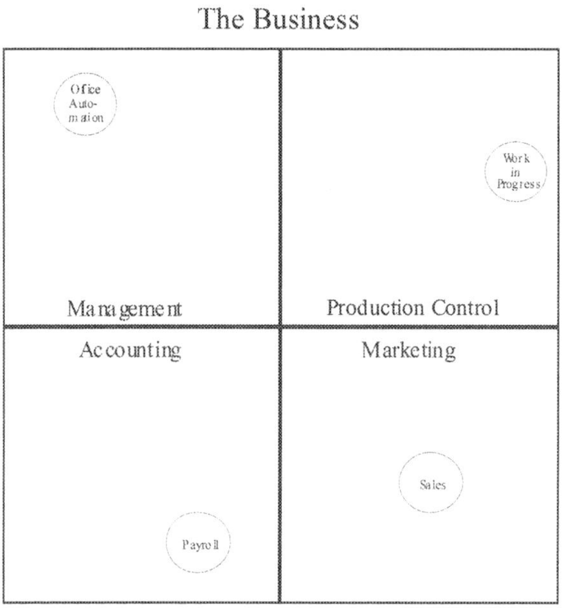

The Business

Figure 2-10. Initial deployment of computer systems. Specific, tactical, high return on investment.

We began to see large, bulky, punch card driven computers being introduced to the business. These early applications were very simple (by today's standards) and very limited in scope. For many businesses, the payroll system was the first one to be introduced. Payroll was a perfect application for the computer. It was simple, straightforward, repetitive and time consuming. So the payroll systems moved in and the payroll clerks moved out. The same kind of pattern occurred in other operational areas at other times.

Although these early computer systems were very expensive, the businesses that brought them in did not seem to mind. The reason? Simple; the deployment of these systems resulted in a very good return on the initial investment. The money saved was far greater than the money spent, and usually within a very short time frame.

The Business

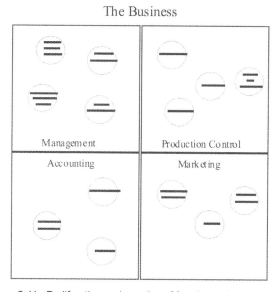

Figure 2-11. Proliferation and creation of functional clusters.

And so business' love affair with the computer was started. Of course, as the technology became more mature and it became obvious that even more savings and efficiencies could be gained, businesses brought in more systems.

Of course, these applications were brought in one at a time and always on a good return on investment basis.

At some point in this process, it became obvious to someone that a new kind of efficiency could be accomplished. People found that if you took the data from one system, and fed it into another one, that

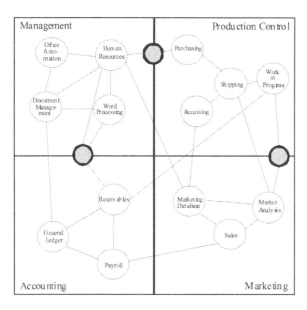

Figure 2-12. Integration Phase. Cross cluster data sharing.

these new kinds of "dependent" systems also yielded great returns, and so the next phase, the data integration phase began.

The integration of data also created value. In fact, new kinds of systems that did nothing but integrate data from other sources began to be popular.

We will return to this history of the proliferation of computers in the business environment within a later chapter to consider some of the other implications of this approach. But for now, the important thing to realize is that since the earliest days of computer systems, the one thing that has always been true is that the driving force behind business' decisions to deploy computer technology has been to use it in order to address short term, tactical kinds of problems.

We do not mean by this statement that long term computer systems strategies are undesirable. On the contrary, the history of most successful corporations today include the presence of a sound, long term strategic computer systems vision. We also do not mean that businesses are unwilling to spend large amounts of money on large scale applications.

What we do mean is that history has shown repeatedly, that the only computer systems strategies that have stood the test of time have been based upon the business' need to address specific, tactical problems.

THE DRIVE TO ACHIEVE TACTICAL / OPERATIONAL EFFICIENCY

The entire history of data processing has been based upon the application of systems to the solving of specific problems. You could say that it is the fundamental principle upon which the entire business / computer relationship is based.

What this means is that no matter how hard we try to do otherwise, we are going to ultimately end up favoring those solutions which get us the best short term benefit, no matter how good the longer term benefits may sound.

OPPOSITION FORCES AT WORK

What we have seen with this historical perspective is that there are two forces at work within the data processing environment. First, the drive on the part of each business area to make their own internal processes more and more efficient. Second, the drive on the part of the overall business to attempt to integrate more and more of this information in order to accomplish greater overall efficiencies.

In the long run, what this means is that people will continue to build more isolated, highly specialized applications while at the same time achieving greater integration.

In both cases, only those solutions which provide the most value to the overall organization will survive.

THE DEATH MARCH OF STRATEGIC INITIATIVES

The history of data processing is full of strategic visions and initiatives which claimed to provide the solution to a lot of business' computer system problems: CASE, structured programming, enterprise modeling and a host of others. Each of these disciplines claimed that if the business could only take a "strategic" view of their corporate resources, and develop a long term vision that treated the data as a precious corporate resource, they could eventually get to a higher level of efficiency within their systems overall.

Unfortunately, regardless of the theoretical merit of these approaches, the end result has been failure after failure. At first glance, this may not seem to make a lot of sense. It would seem that if you approached the problems of data processing from a scientific perspective, as opposed to the rather short term driven, almost random perspective that the systems have been based upon up until this point, that efficiencies could result. But alas, that never seems to happen.

ECONOMIC CYCLES

Unfortunately, when people begin to operate their business off of visions that are far removed from the day to day tactical realities of the business, they tend to take on initiatives that cannot stand the test of time.

One way to look at this, is to consider the fact that every business undergoes business cycles. For certain periods of time, the business will be forced to be "lean and mean" under the pressure of intense competition, shifting markets and the need to change their means of production. At other times, the business will be very prosperous. High revenue, high growth, bright future.

When the business is at one of the high points of the cycle, it has the time, available resources and keen interest in the development of long term strategic kinds of solutions. It is during this time that the business is most subject to the workings of Barnum's Law.

On the other hand, no matter how well the strategic vision has been set up, eventually the economic profile of the business shifts, and suddenly everyone is forced back into "lean and mean" mode. When this happens, the strategic implementations are the first to go.

The long term effect of this cycle is that the only systems that end up standing the test of time are those that meet specific tactical objectives. These applications form the basis of the corporate information systems infrastructure, not the more strategic, "big picture" kinds of approaches.

Ultimately, therefore, our law states that:

The only strategic system initiatives that will stand the test of time are those tied to the solution of specific tactical problems.

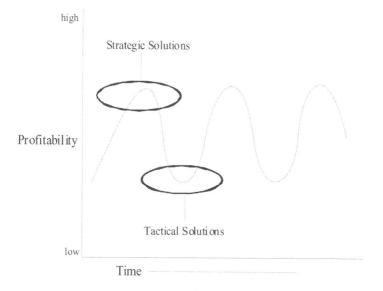

Figure 2-13. Economic cycles and systems.

like this

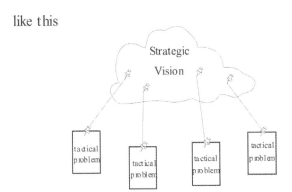

... not this

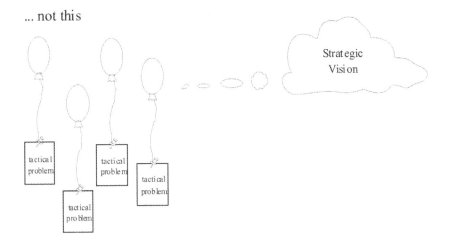

Figure 2-14.   Tactical problems.   Successful strategies - tactical relevance.

In other words, only those systems with tactical relevance will make any sense. This law will certainly make sense to any manager of computer systems in the business environment. Everyone is hearing the same story these days: don't offer me solutions that do not solve today's problems.

Applicability of the Law of Tactical Relevance to Data Warehousing

The implications of this law for the developer of a data warehouse should be clear, and the role of the warehouse defined in terms of this model.

A data warehouse is the ideal approach to take when trying to integrate information between disparate systems. The warehouse can easily meet many of the data integration demands of the business on a strategic and tactical level.

On the other hand, warehouse developers should stay away from any attempts to subrogate the role of already efficiently running tactical, operational systems. These systems need to be left alone as much as possible.

The greatest implication for the developer of the warehouse, however, is that he needs to stay sensitive to the tactical implications of what is being built, and base its construction upon that foundational strategy.

Conclusions

Our discussion about the immutable laws of systems development, have provided us with the ability to make certain assumptions about what we will and will not be able to accomplish with the process of data warehouse development.

To start with, we will assume that the Data Warehouse Project will be:

- Large
- Financially risky
- Difficult to manage
- Complex

- Resource intensive
- Time intensive

In response to these known and accepted characteristics, we will build the following safeguards into our approach:

- We will manage the problems and risks associated with its large size, by developing a approach that allows us to partition the job of building one into a collection of smaller, more manageable tasks. These tasks will be autonomous of each other, and will involve the production of tangible, functional deliverables.

- We will manage the financial risk by tying the finances of the project to each of the individual pieces of the process.

- We will manage the problems and risks associated with its unmanageability, by organizing a structure which holds management, operational and systems personnel responsible for different aspects of its construction, and we will tie that accountability to each of the deliverables and tasks identified.

- We will manage the problems created by overwhelming complexity by designing a structure that allows people to maintain their focus and direction. We must create a blueprint for a way to build a data warehouse that makes it possible for people to concentrate on discreet pieces of the whole while being assured that the system will work when completed.

- We will manage the risks associated with underestimating the complexity, financial cost or time required to get the job done by being thorough in our understanding of what it will actually take to get the job done.

To say the least, these objectives are not easily met. But it is our hope that in the next few chapters, we will be able to deliver on the promises.

CHAPTER 3

DATA WAREHOUSE DEVELOPMENT LIFE CYCLE

Boston , 1995 : The scene is the cafeteria of a major financial services firm. The people sitting around the table are enjoying a break from their work day. They are all involved in different aspects of the construction of a financial data warehouse for their firm.

"So, how's the programming progressing on that new Data Warehouse system?" an innocent bystander asks.

"Don't ask," replies the disgruntled programmer, sipping a cappuccino and snorting in disgust. "I've never seen such a screwed up project in all my life. Here we are, four weeks into the development of the screens and it turns out that the database people don't have requirements for any of the data that we need. I don't know what they expect my programs to work with. And to top it off, we just found out that it doesn't really matter because the users have just changed their minds about what we're supposed to be doing anyway. We just got word that half of the screens we've been working on are going to be changed so much that we have to just start over."

The resident database person then chimes in "Yeah, well, we would've had what you wanted if the people writing the programs that take the stuff out of the Legacy system had gone after the right data in the first place! What they got for us is all wrong. Bad dates, missing fields, it's just about all garbage... why, did you know that, by the time we got through with those name and address files, we found out that only about 100,000 of the 1 million records had usable state codes. And there's no way to fix it. Someone is going to have to go in and change all those records manually. "

"So when do you think this project is going to be finished?" asks our clueless bystander.

"How about in say, five more years" replies the programmer.

"But the project is scheduled to be done by November." he persists.

"It will never happen," responds everyone at the table, in unison.

This little snippet of a discussion is typical of the conversations that occur daily within the ranks of people building Data Warehousing projects (and most systems development projects). This conversation does little more then echo the sobering findings we cited earlier: That most large data warehousing projects turn into organizational and financial disasters. If we try to develop a strategy for how to build a successful data warehouse, we must first map out a plan to prevent this scenario.

At this point, the more traditional writer might jump into yet another tirade about "How to build a data warehouse the right way." And indeed, it is tempting. We could quite easily slip into a rhetoric here whereby we describe the different phases of a data warehousing project (don't worry, we will get to that, but not quite yet). We could then proceed to give you all sorts of technical detail about how to build this feature and what not to do with this or that situation.

All of the information would be useful and I am sure that a lot of it would help you in the process of building your own system. But, by diving into that level of detail right away, we will be missing the forest for the trees. We will end up making the mistake that so many books trying to tell people how to build systems have made in the past. We will basically be describing how to use a screwdriver without telling you anything about when, where, how or why to use one. And the results will most likely be the same. You will end up trying to use a screwdriver when you should be using a hammer and vice versa.

And so, before we begin expounding on the way a data warehouse should look after it has been built, we will invest some time in understanding how they get built, and how we approach building them in a better way.

What's Wrong with the Way we Build Systems?

The first step in this process will be for us to get a basic understanding of how people go about the process of building large scale business computer systems in general and data warehouses specifically. We will approach this exploration, not from within the confines of any predefined methodology or belief system or by regurgitating thousands of pages of diatribe which dictate how things should be done, but by considering how things really happen in the business world today.

We will, however, use the traditional systems development life cycle as a starting point. This process describes the process of systems development as:

- Development of Concept
- Feasibility Study
- Analysis
- Design
- Construction

Starting with this framework will be useful for many reasons. First, it makes logical sense to do things this way; second, it is a framework with which everyone can identify and therefore can serve as a common point of reference; third, it allows us to better understand how the process can go awry so often.

In our examination of the way things really get done, we will be especially sensitive to those situations which support the observations and rules we have discussed in previous chapters. We will try to identify the ways the approach actually seems to be designed to create failed system after failed system.

1. We will try to identify the major factors which contribute to the demise of so many warehouse projects. Mainly, these include: Failure to control the scope of the project (focus)

2. Failure to assign responsibility for the varied aspects of the construction process (accountability)

3. Failure to accurately estimate the many different costs of system development including the:
   a   Financial cost

  b Time investment of systems, management and operational personnel

  c Time required to complete each phase

Specifically, we will look for the different ways that people:

1. Fail to plan for the time necessary to coordinate and integrate business information

2. Fail to plan for the time necessary to develop complex technical solutions

3. Fail to coordinate the phases of the actual construction process

We will then propose an approach that will allow us to avoid many of these pitfalls. What we will find is that, in general, these failures occur because of the way we approach the building of warehouse systems themselves. Therefore, if we want to build a successful data warehouse, then we had better figure out how to get around those problems.

An Approach Specific to Data Warehouse Construction

At this point, the reader may be wondering if this topic might be more appropriate for a book which is focused not specifically on Data Warehouse building. Isn't this topic better suited for a book on how to build computer systems in general?

My response to that is simple.

Although many of the reasons for the failure of Data Warehouse projects are the same reasons for the failure of so many other systems development projects, the solutions for them will be unique to the Data Warehouse construction process. The approach we will propose here will provide a good solid framework from which people can undertake the construction of a good system, but the solutions that we consider will not work to help in the construction of other types of systems. It is only possible to develop this kind of solution because Data Warehousing applications have a large number of characteristics that are similar, no matter where they are being built or for what reason. We can therefore leverage what we know about this process and assist the developer in the process of building similar systems. The insights and approaches we propose can certainly be useful in trying to develop approaches for the construction of other types of systems, but that is beyond the scope of what we are trying to accomplish.

How are systems built today? The process of building a system is started long before the first analyst sits down and begins mapping out specifications.

Phase One - The Concept is Born

The first phase in the life of any system occurs when someone, somewhere has an idea about how a computerized, automated process can help the business make more money or run more efficiently. This idea is then bantered about, and if enough people think that it is a good idea and enough momentum builds up, eventually, someone proposes that the system should be built. In our case, that idea will be an idea for a Data Warehouse.

One of the first things to take note of is, who has proposed the system in the first place. Depending upon the corporate culture and the specific situation , it might be a person from either the management, operational or systems group.

Phase Two - Feeble or Feasble? - System Justification

In many cases, if enough people think that the idea for a Data Warehouse is sound, the next thing that will happen is that some kind of feasibility study will be commissioned. Unfortunately, the quality of most such studies leaves much to be desired, and in fact, it is here that the seeds of failure are sown for the majority of the future warehouse development projects.

Feasibility studies can be done by the internal systems people or by the operational people. Often an outside consulting firm will be commissioned to do it. The objective of this study is to determine whether or not the building of the warehouse makes sense.

What actually happens more often than not, is that the half developed concepts and unsubstantiated beliefs of the project sponsors are simply regurgitated and formalized through the process. The net result is a decision to move ahead on the construction process based upon very weak business justification, if any.

A well executed feasibility study will tell people:

- What the system is supposed to do
- How much it will cost
- What the benefit will be when it is done

Probably the biggest shortcoming of most feasibility studies is that they are much too general in their scope and not nearly specific enough in their claims.

If an idea sounds "good enough," or if the momentum is simply high enough, organizations will not even bother with the feasibility phase at all.

Phase Three - Consensus Building

Phase three is a new phase, one not part of the SDLC. The reason this phase has been added is because the way businesses run has changed since it was first developed. In the "olden days" organizations were extremely hierarchical in nature. There was a chain of command. Different people had responsibility for different things and you knew who could approve what.

Today's business world does not work that way. Businesses are much more democratic and decentralized. The lines of demarcation have blurred considerably, and everyone has a say in decisions that affect their area. Therefore, if you want to get a system built these days, you need the buy-in of all the different people that will be affected.

A good example of this autonomy and democracy in action can be found in the process of computer systems development itself. Within most organizations, any department can, if it has the money, buy its own UNIX server and basically create its own mini data center. Individual departments and individuals all have their own personal computers and it is common business practice for these departments to commission their own systems, independent of the larger corporate information systems staff. So if you want to build a large data warehouse, then you are going to need everyone's approval and participation.

It is here that the process becomes particularly interesting because a data warehouse is a pretty flexible kind of a thing. The whole objective of building the warehouse is to store a lot of data so that a lot of people can "do their own thing" with it.

The temptation with a project like this, therefore, is to begin promising everybody that everything they want can be "piggy-backed" onto the system, either now or later. As a consequence, the original "vision" of the warehouse becomes more and more blurred as more and more "future promises" are traded for buy-in and funding approval today.

At this point it becomes very difficult to control the direction in which the data warehouse will ultimately go. There is very little written documentation and, usually, the "vision" is in a constant state of flux as more and more things are added and the vision grows larger and larger.

Of course, feasibility studies are generally not done on any of these alternative realities. If a study was done, everyone assumes that their little extra piece is not going to change the baseline numbers. The reality is that the warehouse concept has usually become so large by the time it gets out of the consensus building phase that it is unrecognizable.

Another damaging aspect of this informal consensus building process is that, since it is informal, no real, formal consensus gets reached. At best, everyone involved has agreed that you can proceed with the next phase, but the process does little to appraise the level of commitment that each party makes to the process. The danger here, of course, is that the implicit buy-in of many individuals can easily be misinterpreted and considered to be an explicit buy-in. Sometimes, this comes back to sabotage the system development process when a party chooses to pull out its support at a later date. It also can cause the advocates of the system to assume that their informal extrapolations about the benefits the new system will provide are valid, when in fact they are speculative.

At this point in time, no one has seriously looked at any of the real operational parameters upon which the system is going to be based. If you are lucky, there may be some diagrams of some screens and maybe some lists of anticipated benefits. But in general, no rigor has yet been applied.

Phase Four - Getting Some Estimates - The Pandemonium Stage

It is at this stage that most organizations make their biggest tactical blunder. It is at this stage that the seeds for the destruction of the vast majority (probably over ninety percent) of projects are planted.

Our organization has decided that it makes sense to find out about what it will cost to build a system of this kind. Of course, at this stage we have very little information about the details of how the system will work, and a significant investment of time and energy will be necessary to work out these details.

Unfortunately, corporate computer systems development culture has a pat solution to that problem. It is time to put the system out for bid.

The process of developing cost estimates for large scale systems projects has got to be the sorriest excuse for a "discipline" that anyone has ever invented. There is simply NO WAY for someone to tell you how much it is going to cost to build a huge system, one that involves hundreds of users, thousands of system components with dozens of operational business details to re-engineer, based upon the haphazard collection of screen layouts and benefits statements that most people start out with. And yet, that pretty much describes what most people expect.

I have participated in the process of responding to hundreds of corporate RFP's (Request For Proposals) for all manner of different systems development initiatives, and I have yet to see one that contained enough information to develop a conscientious bid.

At this point, organizations will invite different people to participate in the bidding process. Sometimes they invite the "Big Six" consulting firms or the big name system integrators. Sometimes they involve the specialty consulting firms or independents. Often, the RFP is used as the "honey" to attract hardware and software vendors to participate in the process. In some cases, the systems people are simply asked to "put some numbers together."

In all cases, people are being asked to estimate when they have no real way of knowing what it will take to build the system.

The reasons for this have nothing to do with the ability, integrity or veracity of the people developing the estimates. They have everything to do with the false assumptions that people make about the integrity of the systems development life cycle.

It is here that our immutable laws of data processing come to full bloom.

The system being developed must, by definition, be more complex and involve more components than any system developed before it, but for some reason everyone seems to feel that "this one will be different" or that "this will be an easy one" .

The Data Warehousing project is a typical example of a system that ends up becoming oversimplified in people's minds. "How hard can it be?" the thinking goes. "Just copy the data and go to town!" This kind of thinking dooms the systems' sponsors to typically disastrous conclusions.

COMPLEXITIES AND DEPENDENCIES

We know, based on our application of Darwin's Law and Moore's Complement, that the new system will most likely involve the coordination of people's activities in ways never before accomplished. If it didn't, then people either didn't need it or didn't think of it before. You cannot count on people being able to draw on past experience. This means that you will have to spend a lot of time figuring it out and that you are going to have to take up a lot of those people's time to help you do it. It also means that you really cannot be sure of what the system is going to do until after that has been done.

In addition to the unworked-out details about what the system needs to do, we will also get into problems based upon unanticipated technical complexities. Building the new system is going to involve making use of the latest technologies. This means that,, by definition there is no track record upon which to base a history of how long it takes to do things. It also means that there is no depth of expertise available to build the system. It even means that no one can predict what kind of hardware or software you will need to buy and, of course, you also need to know, in specific detail, what the system is going to do. In the old days of data processing it was much easier. You had fewer variables than today and the business itself was much more stable.

So how can we estimate what it will cost when we are not sure what it is going to do?

Ultimately, we end up with the classic chicken and egg scenario. We cannot develop a reasonable estimate of the cost without knowing what the system needs to do and how we are going to build it. But we cannot decide whether we actually want to build it or not until we know what it will cost.

Many times, the people who have agreed to provide estimates for the project agree to take on this dilemma. The big question is, how do they do it? The easiest way to solve this dilemma is to use several of the scientifically sound estimation techniques and the old standby technical solutions that have been developed over the years in the data processing industry. These are known as the WAG technique for estimating and the PFM technique for answering the question of how will it work.

The acronym WAG stands for Wild Absolute Guess. In other words, when you don't have anything to base an estimate on, make something up. It works like a charm. You get an answer every time. Unfortunately, you also live with the consequences further down the road. The second acronym, PFM, stands for Pure Freaking Magic is the answer to any technical question that you can't answer any other way. How will you do it? PFM will take care of that problem!

For the most part, there is nothing wrong with a little application of PFM or WAG to an estimating situation. Obviously, you are going to have to do some guessing and make some assumptions about how the system is going to fit together. The problem is that, over time, as systems have become more and more complex and as technical information has become more and more diverse and obscure, the level of PFM and WAG has reached astronomical proportions. In fact, the numbers they usually come up with are pretty close to meaningless.

How Much Will it Cost? - How Much Have you Got?

By far the most common estimation technique is for the bidder (internal I/S department or outside consultant) to base the bid amount on their best guess estimate of how much the organization will be willing to spend. The rationale goes something like this: "First we will get the project awarded, then we will figure out what it will do", or even more blatantly "How much you pay us determines how much we will get done. We will simply keep building until the money runs out. Then you can either ask us to stop, or you can give us some more to finish."

Of course, estimates of this nature can lead to all kinds of abusive situations. There are firms that will get a contract awarded and then continue to push out the scope of the project further and further, just to avoid actually having to do anything. Such projects become perpetual analysis and design projects which are halted only when the sponsors cannot stand it anymore.

But blatantly abusive situations not withstanding, even in the best of cases, we establish a situation where a serious disconnect is set to occur between the systems, operational and management people.

Imagine the situation. A group of managers has agreed to a "vision" for the new system based upon early investigations and payback scenarios. Over the course of time, as the consensus building process continues, this "vision" has turned into several mini visions held by the different people who have been involved in the discussions. Finally, when systems or a vendor is asked to come up with an estimate, it is based upon a WAG which is based upon a little bit of each.

A Touch of Reality?

If you were to accept that the preceding scenario is accurate, how would you try to inject some reality into the situation? It is extremely difficult because of the way the stage has been set.

First of all, if the bidder wants to get the work, then the last thing they are going to admit is that they cannot come up with an estimate because their understanding is unclear or that not enough information is available. What about all the other bidders? Internal systems people, consulting firms, vendors -- there are plenty of people willing to stand up and say "I'll do it for this much." A kind of a high stakes version of "Name That Tune." If you can't bid on this, it is a reflection of your ability, not a reflection of the vision.

And if the sponsors of the project were to actually listen and believe that there is not enough information to develop a good estimate, they must then go back to management and say, basically, "In order to get an estimate for this project, we have to figure out what it is going to do in better detail first." In other words, you have to invest a sizable amount of money in the execution of the analysis and design phases before it can be estimated. Pay for half of it up front and then we will tell you how much it is going to cost!

This is not an easy proposition to sell to anyone, no matter how trusting or farsighted they are. The irony of this situation is that the "How do we build the Data Warehouse game" is actually rigged to favor the building of systems with low returns on investment or even none, simply because they are much easier to estimate and control.

But we digress. Let us continue with our examination of how system building is approached today. After the sponsors of the project have examined all of the proposals, there are several things they can recommend:

1. Walk away from the project because it will cost too much
2. Award the building of the system to a bidder, or in some cases
3. Sponsor a study to figure out more of the detail

We will ignore the first and third options as these are rare occurrences. In the case of option three, the study may or may not end up being enough to prevent the problems cited. If the job that is done is not thorough, and the project is commissioned anyway, we still find ourselves in the same position.

Phase Five - Catch Up - The Application of a "Customized" SDLC

Assuming that someone (internal systems or a contractor) has been awarded the Data Warehouse contract, the pandemonium begins to really take hold. Since the bidder is aware that a whole lot of up front analysis and design needs to be done before they can really figure out how to build the system, they propose the execution of some kind of modified SDLC. This customized approach will, in theory at least, attempt to involve all of the parties required from management, operational and systems areas, in order to determine the details of the vision.

Of course, at this point, management and the operational group assume that their participation is over. They have approved the project, the systems people that are building it must be aware of what they wanted, so now they can go on to other business.

Now the operational and management people begin being drawn into an endless death march of JAD, RAD and in general very SAD analysis and design sessions. Despite whatever window dressing of hype that has been associated with these methodologies, the reality is that these sessions are conducted for one reason: to try to figure out what the system is really supposed to do.

It is at this time that all of those "pesky little details" about how the system is going to work, how the operational people will do their job differently, how the system is going to impact existing systems and where the data is to support the vision that people had of the system begins to unravel. For the most part, as people participate in more and more of these sessions, the original vision gets foggier and foggier. It is at this time that people begin to discover the real cost of the system in terms of their investment of time and energy in the coordination of activities and the changing of their work environment. It is also at this time that the systems people begin to realize just how complicated and thorny the design, loading and delivery of the Data Warehouse is really going to be.

Of course, by now it is too late. Commitments have been made. No one wants to take the bull by the horns and go back to the project sponsors and management and say "Boy, were we off! It is clearly going to take four times longer, and cost five times more than we agreed to!"

No, no one wants to do that, and usually no one does. Usually, they try to defer the inevitable as long as possible and simply hope that something will happen to salvage the situation. It hardly ever does.

There are several symptoms of a project that indicate that this kind of stall-out has occurred. First, the users who are supporting the design process find less and less reason to participate in the process. They would much rather go without the system then continue with the painstaking, back breaking work of constantly revising their visions over and over again while the necessary interchange between systems, operational groups and management takes place. In general, people would rather do anything than participate in the grueling process of trying to figure out how to rectify literally hundreds of discrepancies between what people thought they were going to get, and what they are going to have to live with.

Eventually, the project gets to the point where everyone involved in the process of building it knows that the objectives that were set will never be met. Severe frustration and de-motivation sets in and the whole process gets even harder to move along.

Phase Six - Compromise and Surrender

After things have gotten bad enough, and enough has gone wrong, and enough excuses have been made for enough mistakes and enough people have been blamed, management steps in and declares a compromise. If anything at all is going to be delivered, then clearly the scope of the vision is going to have to be severely trimmed and the delivery schedule will be greatly lengthened. This is the first sign of compromise, the extending of deadlines and the cutting of what the system is to deliver.

In the more adroit corporate culture, this will be disguised via the creation of new "Phases". "Oh yes, of course the system will do that; it was just moved over into phase two." If the company is committed enough to the project, then the addition of phases will become the camouflage which hides the infusion of fresh budget into the project. With persistence, and very deep pockets, a company may actually get the system it went after, but never on time or on budget.

ALTERNATIVE APPROACHES TO THE PROCESS

First of all, let me assure you that the systems building life cycle I have just described is accurate. It is a cycle that has been repeated hundreds of times at corporations around the world. The question we must ask ourselves is whether or not we care.

If you simply accept this as the way things are done, then you can certainly skip the next section of this book.

If, on the other hand, you would like to consider some approaches that will allow you to build a data warehouse, avoiding a lot of the waste, frustration and false expectation setting that accompanies projects of this kind, then read on.

We will not be able to prevent all of these problems, but we can certainly come up with a game plan that minimizes them.

Our initial premise then will be that, if you want to build a Data Warehouse effectively, you must develop an approach that avoids a lot of these problems. While an explanation about how all of the different pieces should work with the system is certainly useful, it is actually quite meaningless if there is no way for you to reasonably expect that you can actually get there.

The approach we consider, therefore, will be much broader in its scope than most discussions. We will actually take responsibility for helping you figure out, not only how the data warehouse will work, but also how you will build it.

This approach will, therefore, include the following:

1. It will be based on a set of assumptions about how systems really get built. It will not be based upon any kind of false reliance on typical systems development life cycle approaches.

2. It will include the definition of specific areas of accountability and responsibility for management, operational and systems participants, and will attempt to fill in many of the gaps that most approaches leave between these groups.

3. All phases will be tied off to specific deliverables. We have little tolerance for endless analysis and design adventures which yield no tangible benefit.

4. It will certainly include techniques for guaranteeing that all of the different parties (management, operations and systems) and all of the different components of the computer system itself will be coordinated and integrated . Computer component integration includes all of the issues relating to the hardware, software, network and application development within all three areas of the warehouse - the Legacy systems interface, data warehouse proper and data mining front end.

5. It will most importantly be an approach specifically laid out to assist in the construction of Data Warehouses. We will in fact leverage our extensive experience and the relatively consistent nature of such projects to tie down a lot of the variables that make large scale systems development difficult.

ORGANIZING THE DATA WAREHOUSE CONSTRUCTION TEAMS

As we have previously stated, the Data Warehouse is made up of three major components:

1 The Acquisitions Component - a "back end" - which consists of the Legacy system interfaces.

2. The Storage Component - the Warehouse itself - which usually consists of a specially identified hardware platform that runs a specific database software product. Into this environment we will load and store all of the information of interest.

3. The Access Component - the "front end" - which will consist of any number of different custom built Data Warehouse applications and any Data Mining tools.

What is especially useful about this breakdown of the system is that the skills and experience required to support construction in these three areas corresponds to three different personnel.

The people designated to work in the Legacy systems interface area will, in fact, need to have a good business understanding of the way those Legacy systems work. Additionally, for most organizations they will have to be familiar with all the different facets of working in a basically older, mainframe type environment.

To be effective in the construction of the new Data Warehouse, team participants will need to be experts in the database software product and the hardware that is being utilized. The skills of a relational database DBA and data analyst are far removed from the skills required in the Legacy systems interface area.

Developers and designers assisting with the construction of the Data Mining and Data Warehouse Applications need to be specialists in the actual business environments within which these tools will be used. The level of business and technological sophistication necessary to effectively build these super-charged front end applications is pretty high and the technical and design issues faced are very different from those in the other areas.

Experience has shown that, when putting together the Data Warehouse construction team, it is a very bad idea to try to get the same person to work on more than one of these three areas (except in the case of three special roles that we call the "cross component specialists" -- data mapping, infrastructure and architecture). The amount of work and the amount of detail in each area is quite different. It has been tried to "cross pollinate" people in order to reduce costs or to increase coordination between the groups and have paid the consequences. Ultimately, the person ends up concentrating on one area of the three, and the other two suffer for it.

If you are going to build a Data Warehouse, then you might as well accept from the outset that you are going to need three different, autonomous types of people, each commissioned to execute a different part of the construction process.

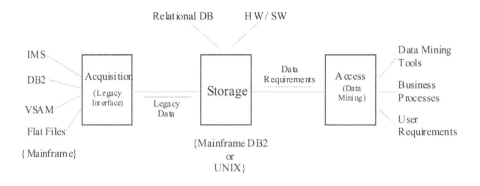

Figure 3-1. Data warehouse teams

THE TRADITIONAL DATA WAREHOUSE CONSTRUCTION APPROACH

Okay, so having accepted the need for three autonomous, specialized development teams, lets begin to consider how we are going to set this project up. Let's begin by returning to our model of how the "typical" Data Warehouse project gets set up so that we can draw some comparisons.

Our Data Warehousing project has been awarded to a consulting company, software vendor or to the internal systems department. The next thing they are going to do is map out a development plan. While there may be many variations on the theme, the plan will look something like this:

1. Analysis - (four weeks) - recruit users into JAD sessions to develop data requirements and screen layouts

2. Design - (two weeks) - normalize the data, generate DDL, build tables

3. Identify Sources -(one week) - identify where the data should come from

4. Data Extraction - (three months) - find some programmers to read the data out of the old system for loading into the new

5. Load- (one week) - load the extracted into the tables
6. Install Data Mining Product - (one month) - install the Data Mining product and point it towards the right tables
7. User Training - (one week) - send the users to a one week training class in how to use the tool
8. Project Done

What a great plan! It makes sense, it puts everything in the right order (according to the systems development life cycle anyway) and it creates a nice, short, easy to understand 13 week project timeline.

Unfortunately, this project plan will never work!

We have already considered, at a higher level, why this kind of plan is doomed to failure, but now let's dig right down to the detail level and see how those principles work in reality.

False Assumptions

We will consider this project plan one phase at a time and try to figure out what the false assumptions are that lead us to making these mistakes.

False assumption one - serial project plans

The first place where we will get into problems is that this project plan assumes that each phase will go to completion before the next phase begins. A basically serial plan. First we will do analysis and then, if we do a really good job, we will be able to stop the analysis process and begin the design. After design, we can begin construction, etc.

Well, unfortunately it doesn't work that way. In order to help develop a better understanding of why this linear approach to building data warehouses in this kind of environment cannot work, we will take a moment to track one of the many processes involved in construction to see just how complicated and inter-dependent things can get.

FOLLOWING THE LIFE OF A SINGLE DATA ELEMENT

For our first example we will try to follow the life of a single data element from the time it is first conceived until that element actually shows up on an actual personal computer screen.

Operational users usually have a pretty good idea about the kinds of data they want or need. It is not very difficult to get them to tell what these things are and what they are for. Many times they'll even have some ideas about where it can be found in the Legacy systems. However, there are problems that will arise after we have gathered this information.

Data Mining Analysis - Multiple Meanings for the Same Thing

The first problem will be that the users' ideas about the information they want are usually not in sync with the information that other users want. Take a relatively simple element, like "sales." A user will say that they want to see the daily, weekly, monthly and annual sales numbers for a given product line. Seems simple enough. But when we go and talk to a different user who also wants to see product sales information, there is a chance that they may not mean the same thing.

For one person, the periodic sales number they want to see is gross sales before expenses. Another may want to see a net sales number where the amount has been adjusted for variable sales expenses (take out commissions and sales overhead) while another may want to see the sales number with an additional adjustment, removing a percentage of the fixed costs. Sometimes people want the sales amount adjusted to reflect returns, sometimes they don't. The first challenge, therefore, is to get everyone to agree on exactly what it is they want to see, and that is not easy. It takes a lot of time and discussion to sort through all of the disagreements.

Data Warehouse Analysis

After you get all the users to agree on what needs to be in the warehouse, you are ready to create a data model which maps each of these data elements into a proposed collection of data tables. During this phase a number of inconsistencies will be found between the individual pieces and the big picture. The way to resolve these things is to go back to the users and, once again, develop a consensus.

Legacy Systems Analysis

So we have mapped the users' wishes into the warehouse. Now we must develop a map that tells us where all the data is going to come from.

MULTIPLE POTENTIAL SOURCES

Let's assume that the users have all gotten together and agreed upon the one, true meaning for each of the data elements they want to see. Now we get into the next set of problems, figuring out where to get it from.

It is in the nature of most Legacy systems that information is duplicated many times. The number for sales may be carried in dozens of systems and each system may or may not apply some minor adjustments to it based on what they are trying to accomplish. The challenge we must face is deciding which one of those numbers to use for the warehouse.

In order to do this, we often end up backtracking through a number of systems, trying to figure out which number we want. An arduous and time consuming task not only for the people investigating the Legacy system, but for the data modelers working on the warehouse itself and for the users who originally developed the requirements.

Every time we run into these inconsistencies, we must go back to the ultimate users of the data "You said you wanted the data from here, but that was no good because of this reason. We can get what we think you want from here instead. Is that okay?"

At this point you either get approval, or you get sent back to keep looking.

PROBLEMS WITH HISTORY

Another problem is getting historical information. Unless you are very lucky, it is unlikely that the system has kept track of all the history. In many cases no history is available at all. In others, you find that your primary, preferred source of the most accurate data holds no history, but other, less accurate systems do. You end up either having no history, or needing to blend data from several sources.

Again, every deviation from the plan requires the involvement of data warehouse modelers and the original operational users.

PROBLEMS WITH POST EXTRACTION LEGACY SYSTEM COORDINATION

While the previously cited cases define the worst of what it is going to take to get your data loaded into the warehouse, you still have several additional things to consider. After pulling the data into the system for the first time, how are you going to keep it updated and in synch with the original systems? And when you begin blending different sources of data, how do you get them to "unblend" for auditing and validation purposes?

Data Sanitation

So you've located the data, mapped it back to the warehouse, and you even found it where you were told it would be. Now comes the next problem: "How "clean" is the data?"

We use the term data cleanliness to identify how accurate and consistent the data stored in the Legacy system actually is. It may come as a surprise to many, but just because a file or database has a field called "Sales" for example, and just because the users and the programs say that this is the correct value for their purposes, does not mean you can be sure that all of the sales information you want is in there, or that all the sales information you don't want can be excluded.

Legacy systems tend to do interesting things with data over time. Fields are bridged, recycled, dummied-up and in general fudged by any number of Legacy system programs. The fact is that nobody really knows what is in the underlying files that make up these systems until you actually dump them out and start trying to use them. If you are smart, you will check these things out early and head off some problems. If not, you will find out at the last minute and panic. Of course, when the data files are dumped and dirty data is found, you have no choice but to once again go back to the users and find out what they want to do about it.

The Case of the Missing Data

It is not uncommon to find users requesting information that doesn't exist anywhere. Remember, to an operational user the "database" is this big, amorphous thing that holds all the information they think they need. It is not uncommon to have to scrap fifty percent of a data warehouse model because no valid, clean, accurate source for the desired data could be found. These are only a few of the dozens of data issues that crop up when building a warehouse.

As you can see, the process of identifying and pulling data into the data warehouse is not a linear process. It requires the continuous interaction of operational user, data mining people, data warehouse people and Legacy systems people in order to validate, map and sanitize the thousands of elements that make up a typical warehouse.

THE DUMP AND RUN MODEL OF DATA WAREHOUSE BUILDING

Now, if all this checking, validating, cleaning and fussing about individual data elements seems like a terribly tedious and painful process, you are absolutely correct. But what is even more interesting is the way a great many advocates of data warehouse construction believe you can avoid these problems by using what we will call the "Dump and Run" model.

According to this model, the best way to build a data warehouse is to simply dump everything you possibly can into it, and then let the users sort it all out at their leisure. Under this plan, a team of highly trained data analysts "attack" the Legacy systems files, identify the elements and derive the nature of the tables being built within the

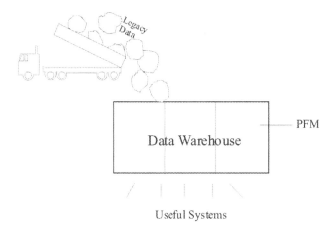

Figure 3-2. The "dump and run" model

warehouse based on what they discover. The thinking goes that, since you have dumped everything into the warehouse, you don't need to be so selective. Let the users figure it out.

Anyone attempting to build a warehouse in this manner is naive to say the least. There is no way anyone can look at a bunch of data file layouts and systems documentation and "derive" what the data contained therein really means. It is simply impossible. Systems documentation is never accurate (if it exists at all) and the programs will be no better off. The only way an approach like this could work, is if the users were asked to participate in every decision about every field being pulled. Not likely.

MULTIPLE LEVELS OF COMPLEXITY AND MULTIPLE DEPENDENCIES

The whole problem here is that, in order to make the warehouse work, you have got to go through the painful, detailed process of mapping each and every element against a plethora of dependencies and then you have to map those against a barrage of technical and operational issues before you ultimately deliver a system.

There are certain realities here, and one of them is that people can only keep track of so much detail and so much interdependency at one time. When the load gets too great they go on overload and begin assuming, guessing and filling in the blanks with inaccuracies. It is this information overload which really brings large systems to their knees. It is simply not humanly possible to manage that much complexity.

Going back to the Brooke's Law curve we can see that when projects get to a certain size, everyone has to spend all their time coordinating and no work can get done. In the computer hardware world we call this condition "thrashing".

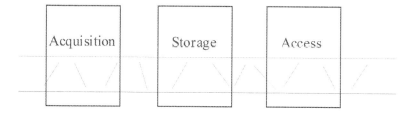

Figure 3-3. Minimizing and controlling the thrashing

THE AUTONOMOUS VALUE BASED SEGMENTATION APPROACH (AVBS)

Our proposal will be to approach the construction of the data warehouse in such a way that we can avoid the problems caused by this kind of thrashing. Our principle assumptions will be that the data warehouse must provide real value to the corporation during each stage of its development, and that there is no way this can be done all at once. Our second assumption, therefore, will be that the data warehouse project will be made up of several smaller sub-projects and that each of these sub-projects must be:

- Autonomous - meaning that it can be built without benefit of any other sub-projects except for those which have already been completed.

- Value Based - meaning that, with the exception of the first two sub-projects (the Project Planning and Infrastructure/ Prototype sub-projects), each sub-project will provide a real value to the corporation in and of itself. In other words, each sub-project can be cost-justified based on what it will deliver to the business in added value.

While the traditional and popularly held approach to warehouse construction view the project in terms of the systems development life cycle, the Autonomous Value Based Segmentation (AVBS) approach views the project as a series of smaller, more manageable, self contained mini-projects, each of which can build on the work done in mini-projects before it.

Under the AVBS approach there is no investment in large, drawn out, unfocused development efforts. The project is divided up into several mini-projects. Each project must then be justified to management as having its own inherent pay back. Each sub-project, therefore, requires very little "sell job" at all since it is clearly understood by everyone how much benefit will be derived when it is completed.

This kind of approach puts an entirely different perspective on Data Warehouse construction for everyone. We are no longer going to ask management to try to figure out how to "justify" a multi-million dollar budget in order to get the delivery of an unknown or immeasurable system at the other end. Instead, we are going to present management with a menu list of sub-project options, each of which should deliver a different, tangible, economic benefit to the corporation in its own right.

The question is no longer one of needing to take one tremendous leap of faith and hoping that things will work out as we planned. Instead, it becomes a process of allowing management to approve the construction of each piece of the warehouse, and withholding commitment on future pieces until the pieces that have been completed are delivering as promised.

SEVERAL TYPES OF PROJECTS

Of course, the pay back from different kinds of sub projects is going to be different. In fact, there will be four kinds of projects that need to be developed:

1. Planning and Evaluation Projects - Projects whose objective is to define what needs to be done, estimate the effort to develop it and assess the benefit it will yield.

2. Validation Projects - Projects whose sole purpose is to validate the assumptions made by a planning project. These projects exist to help minimize the risk of subsequent development steps and help clarify everyone's understanding of what is to be done.

3. Infrastructure Development Projects - Projects designed to create an environment within which the warehouse functions can be executed.

4. Warehouse Applications - The "real" applications that make the warehouse useful.

THE OVERALL WAREHOUSE DEVELOPMENT PROJECT

The first project we propose is one which we will use to actually develop the specifications for the overall data warehouse itself. It is the one that takes all of the "pre-bid" aspects of traditional data warehouse construction into account. As we shall see, this project is actually the most important one for many reasons.

The output of the first project should be several items. The first set of output from the warehouse development process will be the identification of a collection of value propositions. Each of these value propositions represents a different business application that will be developed through the use of the warehouse. The second output of the process will be a plan for the development of these applications and the warehouse itself. The third output will be the specifications for the infrastructure upon which the warehouse will run.

The most important single deliverable out of the first project is a plan that clearly identifies a series of subsequent projects, each of which will result in the construction of one, and only one, piece of the data warehouse. No project should take longer than six months to deliver and each project should do something and provide some real value. Each should be cost justifiable as a stand-alone project and should make sense from a business perspective outside the context of the

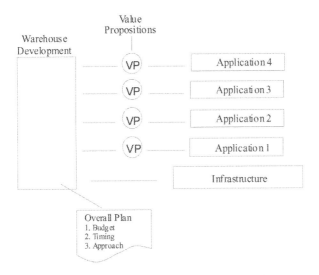

Figure 3-4. The warehouse development process

bigger data warehouse. In other words, it should be a real, viable project in and of itself.

Not only do we want to have our project divided into a series of smaller, autonomous projects, we are actually going to demand that they be done serially for the most part. Get the first project done before starting the second. If the projects in question are not related to each other they could, obviously, be done in parallel, but if they must be tied together, then they must be done separately and one

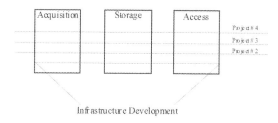

Figure 3-5. Subsequent projects

before the other.

There are many reasons for recommending this kind of approach. One of the biggest is that, by forcing the developers of the system to focus on a much narrower deliverable, you allow them to concentrate on the delivery of that piece. More importantly, this kind of "scope boxing" allows you to manage the amount of thrashing that can occur.

The art and science of figuring out how to "box" the scope of these projects is something we will consider later. Suffice it to say that determining the right scope is not easy.

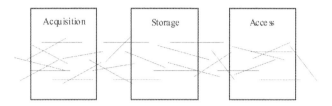

Figure 3-6. Systems development thrashing

Examples

To help illustrate the difference between these two approaches a little more clearly, we will develop a case study for a fictitious company that we will continue to use throughout this book. We'll call our company XYZ Motors and assume that they make automobiles. Of course, we will draw upon our experience building data warehouses for financial institutions, insurance companies and other types of organizations as well as the many automotive warehouses that have been built, but the examples will help us make the topic easier to relate to.

The XYZ Motors Data Warehouse Project Plan

The project plan originally proposed for XYZ fit perfectly into the model of what we have described as a "dump and run" or "traditional " construction approach. When the Warehouse was put out for bid, the "vision statement" associated with it read as follows:

"The XYZ Motors data warehouse is being built to serve as a common location to house information about customers, sales and vehicle information, and will make use of information from over 25 Legacy systems, in addition to rented customer lists from a half dozen name providers. The information contained within the system will be used to help coordinate sales and marketing efforts, and provide the Marketing and Customer Service departments with more accurate, timely and robust sets of information in order to do their jobs better."

What a wonderful vision of a warehouse! But, what does it really tell us? Not much. What it tells us is that a lot of data is going to somehow be dumped together in a common location and that a lot of people are going to somehow make good things happen when they access it. We can see the ear marks of a disaster in the works just by reading through this statement. There is simply nohing truly tangible, accountable or measurable about the way it is being defined.

Let's take a look at the vision and subsequent plan as detailed under the autonomous value based segmentation approach. First, our vision statement will be a lot more specific. It will include within it a brief summary of what each of the sub-projects intend to deliver. Second, our vision statement will include a series of value propositions, one for each sub-project. (A value proposition is a statement which specifies what the new sub-project is supposed to do and what economic or operational value it will bring to the company when it is complete.)

By preparing our pre-bid project plan in this way we guarantee that everyone understands what each sub-project is supposed to accomplish and we assure that everyone knows how to tell whether the sub-project is worth doing or not. The vision statement for XYZ Motors, using this approach, might read as follows:

The data warehouse project for XYZ Motors is being designed to serve the needs of the Marketing and Customer Service departments in the execution of their responsibilities. The Warehouse itself will consist of the information necessary to support the following business functionalities:

1. A customer tracking system which will provide the cus-tomer service agent with up-to-date information about customer transactions over the past five years. Included in this history will be information from the Warrantee, Sales and Customer Service databases. The system will allow the Customer Service department to provide better and more timely responses to problems that customers may have. Research has indicated that this increased level of support should result in an improvement in the retention rate of our current customer base, resulting in the firm's ability to hold on to ten percent of those customers who might otherwise defect to other manufacturers. This would result in a pro-jected 10 year increase in sales of over $7.5 million, while at the same time allowing us to reduce up front, traditional marketing expenses by $100,000 per year.

2. A marketing database engine which will house the firm's current population of over 20 million "prospect names" in the support of direct mail campaigns. it is estimated that the development of this capability will allow the firm to eliminate $2 million a year in fees to outside service bureaus who provide that service at this time.

As can clearly be seen, these vision statements provide the reader with a much better idea of exactly what it is the system is supposed to provide. It also breaks the whole data warehouse down into its subsequent parts and provides us with a basic cost justification for each piece.

THE INFRASTRUCTURE DEVELOPMENT PHASE

We stated earlier that the Data Warehouse project would be made up of a collection of autonomous, cost justified, value based sub-projects - except for the first two. The first one, the sub-project which ultimately delivers a plan, makes perfect sense and in many ways fits right in with the traditional SDLC. The second sub-project, however, is a little more difficult to justify and is immeasurably more difficult to do.

After we havedetermined the different sub-projects which will eventually contribute to our data warehouse, we still have one barricade to really figuring out what all is going to be involved in the construction and execution. In the vast majority of cases we will need to sponsor a small project, to be done before the others, which allows us to establish the infrastructure and architecture for all of the projects to come.

You will recall that earlier we established that we will need three teams of people to build the warehouse, one associated with each component: a Legacy systems interface team, a data warehouse team, and a front-end data mining and application development team. If we are going to expect people to build small, short lived, high impact data warehouse sub-projects, then we are going to have to provide them with a framework within which to do it.

Working out the Details Before you Begin

The Data Warehouse that we are talking about building here is not a one-shot deal kind of a system. It is large, complex and expensive. It is not as if we can simply tell a bunch of strangers to go off and build it and expect that anything but chaos can result. What we need to do is create an environment within which each of these teams can get themselves organized and figure out how they are going to work together.

Roles and Responsibilities Issues

We said that the biggest drain on the resources of any project team is the number of variables they must deal with and the number of details they must try to reconcile at the same time. One of the major investments by a new project team is the time it takes to figure out who will be responsible for doing what and how they will "hand off" things to each other. The time spent figuring this out is "wasted time" as far as the individual sub-projects and their value propositions are concerned. The sub-project cost estimates will be based on the assumption that everybody working on this project has already figured out these organizational fundamentals before the real work begins.

If we create a straw man project, one which is very simple in scope, but which forces all participants to work together and iron out these details, we can shave months off the duration of future projects.

Among the most important roles and responsibilities to work out are those of the three types of cross-component specialist. These individuals will concentrate their efforts on guaranteeing that what happens across the boundaries between components happens smoothly and accurately. These specialties include:

1. Data Disciplines Expert - Who is responsible for tracking the identity of data from the user workstation all the way back to the source Legacy system, making sure that the values the users see are acually the values they think they are seeing.

2. The Infrastructure Expert - This is the person who makes sure that the we have built into the data warehouse everything to make it a smoothly running production environment, as opposed to the slip-shod, thrown togeth-

er collection of isolated functions that plague most large warehouses.

3. The Architecture Expert - Who makes sure that all of the hardware, network and software components are working together as a cohesive whole.

Data Discipline Issues

We have already considered, in some detail, exactly how complicated and tedious the process of mapping data back to its origins can be. If you do not make one person or group of people responsible for this, then you are going to end up with a lot of disconnects from one end of the system to the other.

Infrastructure Issues

In addition to all of the organizational issues that must be worked out between the data warehouse builders and users, there are a plethora of system and project reporting, software management, environmental support and other types of infrastructure issues that must be solved. One of the biggest pieces of this component of the system is the development of the software that will eventually manage the warehouse itself, and provide information to the users about the data within it. These aspects of the system are also "overhead" type characteristics, and it would not be reasonable to burden any one sub-project with the cost.

Architecture Issues

Finally, there are an unbelievable number of architectural issues which involve the computer hardware, network and software environment that must also be established. The best and most efficient way to do this is to create some kind of small project which allows the members of each team to run their pieces of the system through its paces. Most warehouse projects involve the integration of personal computers (over several sizes and types), one or more LANs, a warehouse platform, and however many Legacy system platforms you may have to deal with. Setting things up for the huge volumes of data you want to transport from one platform to the next can be quite challenging.

PAY NOW OR PAY LATER
AND LATER AND LATER

Undoubtedly, people are going to have their biggest problem with this aspect of our proposed approach. All of the other pieces will fit very nicely into the pre-conceived fantasies which are supported by the traditional SDLC. But, the irony is that the traditional SDLC was developed at a time when people did not need to spend all extra time figuring out their organizational and operational relationships, building a project infrastructure from the ground up and creating a computer systems architecture. During the days when the SDLC was invented all these things were a "given" for most organizations. There was a stability and track record in place back then which does not exist today. And there is simply no way of getting around the fact that it must be done.

If you were to diagnose dozens of the failed data warehousing projects over the past few years (and I have), you would find that more often than not it is the failure of people to take these issues into account at the front end that led to the project's ultimate demise. Unfortunately, the other major cause, the failure to realistically account for what it will really take to execute an individual sub-project, is also present, making for a truly disasters undertaking.

Rationale

There are several ways we can rationalize the demand that the first sub-project to be one which has no "hard value" except to get the organization, infrastructure and architecture in place for the subsequent sub-projects.

The first is that this work should only be done once for everyone. It is incredibly wasteful to start five project teams, each working in parallel, and then forcing each of the five to invent their own brand of infrastructure, procedures and architecture. This should be done once, first and for all.

The second is that it really is not fair to place the burden for figuring these things out on any single, tactical sub-project. This cost should rightfully be spread across the lifetime of the warehouse and all business units that will eventually use it.

Objections

Our first and most important recommendation then, for data warehouse construction, is that you break the overall data warehouse project into a series of smaller mini-projects, each of which will provide, on it's own, some deliverable value to the organization (in other words, the mini-project should have a return on investment profile which cost justifies its existence) and which can be delivered without the benefit of all of the other pieces.

This is actually a pretty revolutionary proposal and it flies in the face of a lot of the "seasoned logic" that drives computer systems development today. In fact, this approach defies the vast majority of the "understood rules" that drive the industry, and challenges many of the "sacred cows" (like the SDLC, Case, Enterprise modeling and many data warehousing approaches) as well. The first thing you are going to hear when you propose an approach like this, is all of the reasons why it can't or shouldn't be done that way. The more polite individuals will say "Wow, this all makes perfect sense in theory, but it will never work!" The more intransigent will simply dismiss what we are saying as heretical and ignore it completely.

There is certainly cause for skepticism when anyone proposes that we change the accepted logic of how things are done, especially in this industry at this time. It is clear that the ways we have approached data warehouse building in the past have not worked too well, and a radical departure like this will raise everyone's eyebrows.

Let's consider some of the more obvious objections that are going to come up as the result of this proposal and consider them for their merit.

1. It can't be done - To those that say this approach cannot be done, and will not work, all we can say in response is that variations of this approach have been successfully utilized many times in the past.

2. It's inefficient - For those who cringe at the supposed waste that an approach like this fosters (with the thinking that it is more efficient to do all of the analysis first, and then do all of the design etc.) we simply point to the abysmal track record that approach has left in its wake.

3. It's too complicated - too many interdependencies - For those who feel that such an approach makes the building of the data warehouse overly complicated, our only reply

is that our model reflects the "true" complexities involved much better than any other we have seen (except maybe for RAD). The fact of the matter is that a data warehouse is very complicated, and trying to pretend and structure it into something simpler, more easy to understand is NOT going to make it so.

Our approach does one thing to make the process a lot less complex: We concentrate on stabilizing one piece at a time before moving on to the next. First we stabilize the team itself, the infrastructure and the hardware, then we build one narrowly defined component, get all of its Legacy systems coordination issues and user utilization issues stable, and then move on to the next level of complexity.

Our response to the first three objections was to basically refute the claims they made, showing that the approach actually produces the opposite of the effect they fear. On the other hand, our response to the next three objections is different.

4. It will cost more than the "big bang" approach - Our response to this is simple. Although the proposed plan for a project run in this way is indeed much more expensive, the reality of what this will cost versus what the others will eventually cost is not even an issue, since the odds are very good that the "traditionally" run project has a very good chance of failing and never being delivered. At least, with our approach you can stop at any time after the first real sub-project is complete and have something to show for it. You can stop at any time with a minimal investment at risk.

5. It will take longer than the other way - The argument here is pretty much as it was for the cost issue. It may show up on the drawing board as taking longer, but how confident are you that the other way will work at all?

6. It's not the way we do it! - What can one say to this kind of argument?

Ultimately, our response to objections numbers four, five, and six is one word: Tough.

Yes, it will take a long time. Yes, it will be expensive. And, yes, it is a different way of doing things. But it is our belief that this approach much more accurately and equitably appraises the situation as it really stands. Up until this point we have been able to establish several of the fundamental concepts which we feel are key to understanding and effectively building data warehouses. We have spent some time in considering the basic principles which underlie the warehouses construction. We have also presented several arguments regarding what the best approach to building that warehouse should be.

We have also begun to propose a very specific data warehouse system development life cycle. Now we are actually ready to define and formalize this cycle and to begin describing the different phases.

ITERATIVE AUTONOMOUS PROJECT DEVELOPMENT

Only after we have developed a clear vision of the role that the warehouse is going to play within the business and an equally clear vision of how it is going to work should we begin to actually make use of the warehouse by populating it with real data and providing that data to end users.

The last phase of the process is the continuous construction and deployment of discrete applications within the warehouse framework.

The Data Warehouse Development Life Cycle

We have established as our basic set of premises regarding system construction that...

1. The construction of a data warehouse in the corporate environment today will, in the vast majority of cases involve the development of extremely large, complex systems.
2. The abysmal record of failures that haunt most large systems development projects requires that we develop some kind of understanding of why those failures occur and that we develop an approach that greatly reduces the risk that our warehousing project will suffer the same fate.
3. The root cause of most large systems failures could be

traced back to three fundamental areas of concern, complexity, coordination and cost justification.

a. Systems are becoming more and more complex. In most cases, the sponsors and directors of these projects fail to take that complexity into account. When a system reaches a certain level of complexity, all of the people involved in the project end up spending all their time trying to coordinate and resolve issues, and have no time left for actual system construction. We also proposed that in most cases they will be so complex that, even under the best of conditions, could not be done given the specified time frames and resource availability. (Brooke's Law)

b. Even when the complexity of the system is simplified, we are going to have an equally difficult time keeping the people from different areas of the business in synch about what the system can and should do. The systems development life cycle methodologies have broken down and no clear "game plan" exists for developers to follow. Somehow, we must come up with an approach that allows management, operational and systems people to all understand what their roles are in the process and how they are to inter-relate.

c. The computer systems industry in general and data warehouse construction specifically is a discipline void of any meaningful cost justification criteria. Gnerally, people build systems based on whether they think it is a good idea or not, not on hard numbers that indicate the relationship between cost and benefit.

4. The best way to try to ameliorate these circumstances, decrease our risk and increase our chances of success, was to develop an approach to warehouse construction that forced everyone to limit their scope to a reasonable level, while at the same time providing all participants with the means to coordinate their activities. Included in this approach, we need to ingrain a solid directive which states that all utilization of the data warehouse needs to be justified on a into account the issues of complexity containment.

We have identified three levels of complexity that must be dealt with.

First, we must deal with the complexity which comes when a large group of people struggle with trying to develop a common vision of what the warehouse is supposed to do.

Second, we must deal with the technical and procedural complexities that a data warehouse itself must deal with.

Third, we must address the specific complexity of each of the individual applications that are added to the warehouse.

In all cases, we will attempt to manage this complexity by ...

breaking big problems down into smaller parts,

providing everyone involved in the process (management, operational groups and systems development) with a clear understanding of their roles and responsibilities within the process,

providing a clear focus, tangible objective and measurable deliverables for each step,

equiring that managerial and fiscal responsibility be assigned for each stage.

We have defined the data warehouse development life cycle as being made up of the following phases:

Phase 1 - Overall warehouse development

Phase 2 - Infrastructure development

Phase 3 - The development of applications

The Overall Warehouse Development Phase

One of the first and biggest challenges that the builders of a warehouse face is presented by the incredible amount of miscommunication and misunderstanding that develops as people go through the creative idea development process. Without doubt, the failure to get everyone to agree to a common vision at the outset of what the warehouse should be will cause innumerable problems as the system develops. During the overall warehouse development phase we can arrive at a consensus between all participants regarding the size, scope, complexity, approach to construction and value of the warehouse project.

The Infrastructure Development Phase

After we have determined how big the warehouse will beand what will be included within it, our next challenge is to figure out how it will be technically delivered. In the past it was relatively easy to determine the appropriate infrastructure for a system (since that infrastructure relied heavily upon an already stable and functioning mainframe environment). In today's world of object oriented, client/server, relational databases, and personal computer based data mining tools, this technical environment can easily turn into a nightmare of tremendous proportion.

During the infrastructure development phase all the technical, managerial and system support issues are resolved. The physical infrastructure is built and tested and it is staffed with the appropriate support personnel. Only after the infrastructure has been stabilized will we begin to actually try to use the warehouse.

The Application Development Phase(s)

The last phase of warehouse development is actually an iterative phase that never ends. During this phase we begin to add usable applications to the warehouse, one application at a time. This is the part of the warehouse development process that most people associate with systems development. During this phase tables are designed, programs are written and specific business needs for information are met.

In future chapters we will provide much of the detail that goes into each of these phases, as well as a lot of the rationale for using this particular approach.

While this approach may not seem to be the most efficient or logical, when considered against the backdrop of how things really work in the systems development world today, it should quickly become apparent that it is the only approach that has a good chance of success.

CHAPTER 4

THE COMPONENTS AND CONSTRUCTION

April, 1994, (excerpt from an RFP for a Data Warehouse)

The data warehouse will consist of an Oracle database, running on an HP9000 platform. The existing customer, sales, warrantee and tracking data will be loaded into the database, and the users will make use of Excel to process the warehouse data.

While the diagram and description provided above might give all the appearances of being a complete physical specification (it does describe the input, processing and output mechanisms), it clearly falls short of providing the builders of the system with any idea of the complexity and challenges this project will eventually entail.

Before we can continue with our discussion of how to set up and manage the individual sub-projects within our data warehouse project, we will have to develop a better understanding, in much greater depth, of exactly what issues and challenges we will really be facing when we undertake to build one.

In this chapter we will attempt to provide this requisite background information. First, we will set the stage for further discussion by dissecting a little more of the detail surrounding the workings and techniques for building each of the three major data Warehouse components (The import/export [acquisition], data warehouse proper [storage], and applications front end [access] components). Then we will take an introductory look at the construction of the data warehouse itself, and the structural layers upon which it is based (the infrastructure and data disciplines layers) and see how those will make it possible for our warehouse to function smoothly.

We need this information before we begin discussing the details of how to set up the warehouse project, because once we start this setup work, we will immediately create expectations in the minds of management, the users and the builders of the system. It is critical that, as we establish those expectations, people have a clear understanding of what they are going to get, how it is going to work, and how much it is going to cost in time and effort. Errant expectations at the early stages will lead to nothing but disappointment, mis-coordination and other kinds of problems at the later stages.

THE STORAGE COMPONENT

Let's consider for a moment just exactly what we mean by the data warehouse itself. What is it? What are its component parts and what are the tricks to building it correctly?

Tables

For the vast majority of data warehouses built today, the structure which underlies the label "data warehouse storage area " is a collection of relational database tables. Each of these tables will hold a different subset of the information which people want to have access to.

Of course, just because data is in a relational database does not make it a data warehouse by default. There are certain characteristics that data warehouse tables share which are not common to other types of systems.

The Characteristics of Data Warehouse Data

In general, if you are building a data warehouse, your data will meet the following criteria:

1. The tables will be extremely large.
2. The data in those tables will have a high degree of interdependency with the data in other tables.

3. The principle means of accessing these tables will be ad hoc (as opposed to pre-defined) access.

4. Not only will the tables within the warehouse be large, but there will be a large number of tables available to access.

5. The data is accessed in a read-only mode from the user's perspective.

6. The data will need to be refreshed periodically from multiple sources.

7. Much of the data collected will be historical (therefore time-dependent).

We can group these characteristics into three categories of concern, each of which will require us to consider some specific organizational assumptions as we proceed with the construction process.

1. High-volume/ad hoc access
2. Complexity of the environment
3. Time sensitivity (one aspect of the complexity)

High Volume / Ad hoc Access

Anyone with any experience at all dealing with relational database systems knows that the combination of high volumes and a lot of ad hoc access can be toxic to the performance of any kind of database. The paradox is that, while relational databases can make it easy for a user to ask for any kind of combination of data that they want, it is also true that the user can therefore put in any number of requests which can tax the capabilities of the largest machine and bring the system's performance to a screeching halt. Simply stated, there is a tradeoff between flexibility and system performance. The more power you give to users to do things, the more opportunities you create for that user to bring the system to its knees.

ADDRESSING THE PERFORMANCE/ FLEXIBILITY TRADEOFF

From the very outset of data warehouse construction, therefore, we must be sensitive to this tradeoff and come prepared with some approaches to managing the consequences.

One of the ways we can try to head off these kinds of problems is to anticipate the worst possible case, and engineer the system to take that into account (i.e. get a computer with ten times as much power as you think it will need). This is obviously the weakest kind of solution we can come up with, as experience has shown that users will always find ways to max out any hardware configuration you can imagine.

Therefore, it is incumbent upon the data warehouse builder to develop some restriction or structuring strategies that will allow the users some considerable freedom in their activities withoutletting them become too ad hoc.

Some organizations have tried to create this kind of structure by simply training the users in the proper use of SQL and making them responsible for monitoring the performance of what they do. In some rare cases this can work, but the users are usually not interested in becoming relational database experts.

Some of the more useful structuring approaches have included:

1. The use of query regulators which monitor the work load an individual user is putting on the system, and can cancel the activity if it gets out of control.

2. The creation of query templates which are pre-defined SQL commands They accomplish the major navigational aspects of a query, but allow the user to change certain parameters within it. These queries are also ad hoc but within the confines of the templates that are provided to the user.

3. Staged tables, another solution to the problem, are for the manufacturers of the data warehouse to pre-execute and store parts of queries, thereby identifying and isolating a subset of data which the user can then access in a true ad hoc fashion.

The deployment of any of these techniques requires that we construct the warehouse differently, and that we allocate a certain amount of time, energy, computer power and disk space to each. Each has consequences for the ultimate user of the warehouse as well.

For example, a query regulator solution implies that the major burden for SQL query generation will fall upon the user. This can be good or bad depending on how those users feel about SQL.

The query template solution, takes a lot of the burden off the users, but requires that we allocate time and resources for someone to actually go through the process of identifying, building, storing and making the templates available to the user.

The staged tables solution has the same consequences as the query template solution, with the additional need to allocate a lot of extra disk space and management time to include the extra tables in the warehouse itself.

Managing the Complexity of the Environment

One of the biggest traps data warehouse builders fall into is that they fail to appreciate how complicated the management of the ongoing environment will really turn out to be. This false confidence in the ease of complexity management is supported by the prototype development approach.

The most common ways for people to kick off a warehousing project is to take a few critical data tables, put them into the warehouse, and let a select group of expert users have access to it. These projects are usually considered to be great successes by everyone involved.

Unfortunately, because we started with a small number of tables and a small number of users, we managed to avoid much of the impending complexity issues that we will have to face at a later time.

It is easy for three users to keep track of twelve tables. It is a much different matter to expect hundreds of users to keep track of hundreds or even thousands of tables.

Many Layers of Complexity

Let's consider some of the different kinds of complexity that we will need to manage within this full blown warehouse solution:

1. The sheer number of tables - A full scale data warehouse will involve hundreds of data tables. As the number of tables grows it becomes more and more difficult for people to know what each one contains. A catalog of tables must,

therefore, be developedthat is not simply a list of contents. It must be organized in a way that makes it extremely easy for people to zero in on what they need to find.

2.   Table interdependencies - Besides the problems of simple table inventory management, we will also need to find a way to allow users to understand what the relationships between those tables are. This can raise the level of sophistication required from our catalog many times over.

Solutions to table identification and cataloging problems:

In general, a large number of the data warehousing products that flood the market today concentrate on, or at least provide the purchaser with a lot of the capabilities for catalog management that we have been talking about. The key word associated with these capabilities is "meta data" management. (Meta data is information about your information.)

3.   Timing - An additional set of complexities arise around the issues of timing. The data warehouse is not time stagnant by any means. We will have to keep track of hundreds of tables being refreshed at different times. The time frame which applies to a given population of data is critical to the user's analysis, and the time at which each table is refreshed is also key. Therefore, we must develop the means to track and report on these time and synchronization complexities, for the sake of the users and for the administrators of the warehouse.

The solution to these problems, again, will vary upon the system. But some kind of software will need to be developed or purchased to help keep track of it all. Some data warehousing products include data synchronization and timing monitoring as part of their offering as well as the meta data management capabilities. However, a lot of organizations end up building their own customized solutions.

However it is identified and delivered, the software that manages these things is critical to the ongoing efficient operation of the warehouse. When we tie these kinds of data warehouse support capabilities with their complementary functions in the data mining and Legacy systems interface area, we begin to have an idea of exactly what the data warehouse infrastructure is all about.

LEGACY SYSTEMS INTERFACE - THE ACQUISITIONS COMPONENT

The second component of the warehouse we will consider will be the "back end" or the data import and extract facilities that we formally dub the acquisition component.

While some of the issues that were apparent in our dissection of the data warehouse itself will create complementary issues on this side, there are additional problems we will need to track.

We will begin by developing an understanding of the steps required for us to make the data available.

The Phases of the Data Extraction and Preparation Process.

When looking at this process from a high level perspective, the premise seems very simple. Identify the data you want to load into the data warehouse, unload it and then load it into the warehouse table. Unfortunately, it is never that simple.

Whether we are pulling data into our warehouse from a mainframe DB2 system, a VSAM file, from a UNIX database, or from someone's Excel spreadsheet on a personal computer, experience has shown that several things are going to have to happen before that data is ready to be loaded.

1. Data Extraction - The actual removal of data from its source (purchased or rented tape, mainframe file structure, personal computer etc.) and the placement of that data within the processing area.

   There are actually two types of data extraction that we need to be concerned about. First, there is the process of initially extracting the data and making it suitable for the initial load. Then there is the establishment of a regularized data extraction procedure which will be executed again and again throughout the life time of the warehouse, as we constantly refresh it.

2. Data Cleansing - Most people have no appreciation for exactly how "dirty" most data is. Dirty data occurs when the

values stored in individual fields are inconsistent, missing, unreadable or wrong. There are many ways that stored data values can be wrong. They can be plain inaccurate (wrong address, wrong color), they can be wrong in the way they relate to other fields (a customer key that does not match up with customer file), or they might not fall within an acceptable value range (i.e. a person who is 200 years old).

The Data Cleansing process also comes in two forms. The first, and most grueling process occurs after we have made our initial data extraction. At this time we will want to spend a considerable amount of time figuring out what is not clean about the data, and then getting it cleaned up.

The second form occurs when we take the basically manual cleansing process which we performed the first time and turn it into a regularly scheduled integrity checking and data cleansing routine, which re-cleans the data each time we make a fresh extraction.

3. Data Formatting - Just because we have extracted and cleaned the data does not mean that it is ready to load. The next challenge we face is how to format the data so that it is laid out in a way the warehouse will accept. Included in the list of formatting issues are:

    •   The sizes of fields

    •   The data types for those fields

    •   The order in which fields are positioned in the record

and others...

4. Merge Processing - Sometimes, if you are very lucky, all of the data that you want to load into a data warehouse table will come from the same source file or database. Often, however, the data for one warehouse table actually comes from many different sources. In these cases, we must pre-process each of the disparate partial sources of the data and then merge the files together to get the population we need.

5. Key processing: A primary reasons for building a data warehouse is to provide the organization with a more coordinated, consolidated view of their information. One major obstacle to this ability to have a "common view" is that disparate systems and sub-systems tend to use different sets of keys to uniquely identify the core data groups upon which the rest of the system is based.

Some examples of core data groups would include customer records and the subsequent customer numbers for a marketing system or parts and their part numbers in a manufacturing system. It is not uncommon to find corporations with dozens of different customer numbering key systems, or half a dozen part-numbering schemes.

In organizations fraught with these kinds of situations, the ability to cross reference all the different keying schemes into one consolidated keying structure can have immense value. It is, therefore, not uncommon to find incredibly large and complex key synchronization and merge processing steps as a critical piece of the data extraction and loading process.

5. Purge Processing - Not only do we end up needing to merge different files together to get the right collection of fields for a table, but many times we will also need to do some form of processing which compares the values in two files and eliminates certain records from the ultimate warehouse population.

For example, we may want to load up our customer table, but decide that we do not want to include the customers that have failed to pay their bills for the past three months in the mix. In this case, we will run a purge process that compares a late payment customer list to a list of all customers. The customers which match up with the first list are then purged from our data warehouse load.

6. Stage - The last step is the staging process, which is the moving of all the data (in the form that the data warehouse wants to load it) to the place from where the warehouse will ultimately read it.

Some Observations About the Extract Process

It is important to note that, while we have identified several distinct steps in the data extraction and preparation processes, there is no reason that they must be done in any set order or that they must even be done as separate steps. Many people have successfully incorporated many of the steps into the execution of a single, extract/cleanse/format/merge/purge/stage program. Others have done merge/purge first, then cleanse, then format and finally stage.

The actual order and nature of these steps depends on the nature of the data being extracted and processed.

Back Flush Capabilities

In many situations, the fact that we have actually cleaned up the data and standardized the keys across all the organization's different subsystems makes the output of the data extraction process much too valuable to simply pass on to the warehouse and leave.

In those situations, organizations will want to build in a "back flush" capability where the end products of the sanitation and preparation process are actually fed back into the Legacy systems that originally provided them, in order to help cleanse and consolidate the Legacy systems themselves. (For example, if we clean up all the names and addresses for customers, we will want to return those accurate addresses to the source systems so that they can benefit from the best available information also.)

It is therefore important that we plan for and develop fully functional data back-flush capabilities with the same degree of thoroughness and manageability as we build the forward directed process.

Complexity and Tracking in the Import/Export Component

This brief exploration into the workings of the data extraction process (we will spend significantly more time later) presents us with a set of complexity management issues similar to those explored in the area of management in the data warehouse itself.

While it would be a simple matter for us to build a data warehousing system which involves the extract and load of a dozen or so files without too much of a problem, it will be an entirely different matter to try to manage such an environment when we are trying to keep track of the simultaneous processing of hundreds of these job streams, all at the same time.

What will be sorely needed in this environment, is the means to track and manage the progress of each and every extract file as it moves through these steps. For the most part, we will need to BUILD this management and tracking capability for ourselves, but it will become a critical facet of our successful, full blown data warehousing system.

DATA MINING AND DELIVERY - THE ACCESS COMPONENT

The last component of the data warehouse to be considered is the "front end." Included in this component are all of the data mining access techniques utilized by the end user to make the data warehouse usable. As with the other components, we shall see that even this area is not as simple as it first seems.

Different Means of Access

When most people think about data warehousing, one of the first images that come into their minds is a specific set of data mining or warehouse access tools. These tools, in many cases, are very high powered data analysis and executive information system kinds of products which provide the user with all sorts of new ways to view, analyze and explore the information that runs their business.

These flashy front end products are not the only data mining tools to be considered, and usually only represent a small percentage of the tool sets that will be utilized to view and explore the information that the data warehouse provides. In the vast majority of cases, the real payoff that can be gained from the warehouse will come from the more mundane, day to day, simple query kinds of operations that allow people to do their jobs better.

We will, therefore, define the class of data mining and warehouse access products and tools into the following major categories:

1. Simple ad hoc query interfaces
   - Traditional query managers (QMF, QBE, MS-Query)
   - Query Management Facilities embedded in other products (Excel, Access etc.)
   - Traditional report generators

2. Custom warehouse access applications
3. Sophisticated data mining applications
    •   Visualization facilities
    •   Advanced traditional statistical analysis packages
    •   Data surfing facilities
    •   Quasi-artificial intelligence
    •   Simulations
4. Autonomous business packages

With such a wide variety of products and data access approaches to choose from, it is difficult to develop any kind of generalized view of how the front end of the data warehouse is going to have to be built. However, since in most cases we are going to have to assume that some of the approaches from each of the categories are going to end up being included, we can say something about how we will have to structure and manage this "hybrid-ized" type of environment.

Feedback Mechanisms

Just as the acquisition components need to feed information back to the Legacy systems that feed it, there will be situations where the access component will need to provide the same kind of capability. These feedback mechanisms must be planned for and built into the infrastructure of the system itself.

Data and Architectural
Characteristics of Each Category

While it does not make sense at this point to get into the details about how each of the possible products that might work with our warehouse will need to interface with it, we can draw some conclusions about each of these categories, to set the stage for that discussion at a later time.

Simple Ad hoc Interfaces

At first glance it might appear that we have finally found a portion of the warehouse construction process that is going to be relatively easy to implement. We will simply install the query manager type product, hook it up to the warehouse, tell the users which data to go after and then move on to the next part of the project. Of course, it is never that simple. There are several reasons that the implementation of even the simplest of query or report manager packages is going to present us with challenges.

The first set of challenges revolves around those issues we identified under the section about the data warehouse itself. You will remember that we said that the data that needed to be accessed was going to be of a high volume in nature and the ad hoc access, by definition, was going to present some problems. We offered many solutions to those problems (query regulators, 'paramater-ized" queries (templates) and pre-staged tables). At no time did we talk about how those would be managed and implemented. That is because the management of these solutions must be tied to the many different access techniques that users are going to be employing.

However we decide to protect the integrity of the system's performance, we are going to have to implement it in such a way that access to the users is easy. The user should not care about how we are going to improve the performance of their systems, they should only care about finding the information they need.

Therefore, what we will need to do is provide the user with a way to gain access to the catalog and data management environment that we talked about building as a part of the data warehouse itself, and incorporate its use into the functionality of whatever query management type of tool they might employ.

In addition to the need to make the process of finding their data easy for the users, in most cases we are also going to have to make the process of accessing all of the different data access tools as easy as possible. A typical user might end up needing to use Excel, Access, Q&E, Lotus, Forest and Trees and any number of other data accessing tools depending upon the work they are trying to accomplish. It does not make sense to simply leave them on their own to figure out how to get all of these products to work together.

A third area of complexity will come about when users begin to want to save the results of those queries in their own private data storage areas. No user wants to execute a simple query. What they really want is to extract several different pieces, and then combine those results in order to create yet another set. It is not practical to expect the warehouse itself to provide all of that capability. Therefore, we must incorporate a personal data storage and retrieval area into the user's desktop, and provide them with the means to manage that as well.

Sophisticated Statistical Analysis and Visual Packages

The users of the more sophisticated data mining tools, like SAS, DSS Agent, S-Base or a long list of others, is going to run into all the same problems as the simple query tool users and then some. Most of these products are built to force people to pull in different subsets of data, and then perform multiple recursions of processing against that self contained subset of data, before yielding the results they want.

If the providers of the data warehouse services expect to be in business for very long, then they are going to have to help the users figure out how to use these as well.

Custom Warehouse Access Applications

Ultimately, most organizations end up building their own customized applications to work with different specific parts of the warehouse. For example, most marketing or customer information warehouses include a customer look up facility, which allows a customer service or sales person to page through all of the different kinds of historical information about the customer that is available.

The data access and management challenges that are created when you begin to tie these kinds of applications into the warehouse are entirely different than those in the previous two cases.

Autonomous Applications

In some situations, people will actually purchase fully functional applications systems (i.e. human resources, financial accounting etc.) and expect these systems to make use of warehouse information input. Again, another set of criteria to consider.

User View of the "Back room" Warehouse Processes

In addition to all of the explicitly defined warehouse access methods that users will incorporate into their work stations, it will eventually become incumbent upon the warehouse managers to provide those end users with access to the "back room" warehouse information. The information that users are looking at is usually very time sensitive. And before they can do a good job of using that information, they will need to know exactly how up to date each of the tables they are using really are.

For example, a user trying to make a report which tells them about the current balances in each of a customer's various checking, savings and investment accounts, will need to know how recently each of those was refreshed. If the savings account table is refreshed only once a month, and the checking account table is refreshed once a week, then that user will need to know both, when the last refresh occurred, and maybe even when the next one is scheduled.

The user's need for information about how timely their information is goes even deeper than that. No matter how much we would like to fool ourselves into believing that computer systems are these large, dependable as clockwork machines, the reality is that computer systems, especially very large, very complex ones, have failures all the time. What if the user is desperate to finish some end-of-month reports? The user checks and finds out that two of the files have not been refreshed as they should be. The next set of questions that the user is going to have are:

"What went wrong?", "Is it being fixed?" and the big question, "When do I get my data? "

The people responsible for managing the warehouse will have to make a choice. You can either put yourself in the business of constantly needing to respond to questions and researching the answer for the users, or you can provide them with the means to find out for themselves. With a system of any size and complexity, the latter option makes infinitely more sense.

The User Workbench Environment

The long range solution that many people develop in order to address all of these issues is to create an integrated user workstation application that ties together all of these disparate pieces. A user workbench of this kind will usually start out with some kind of a menu or icon driven interface that allows the user to easily and seamlessly navigate through the catalog, select tables to work on, tie their identity over to the reporting or query tool of choice, and then allow them to schedule, execute, store and continue to process the results. At the same time, this workbench can create an environment where this same user can check on the status of the updating of each of the tables they have targeted, and to inquire as to the next scheduled refresh time.

Tying the Components Together

In the previous three sections we attempted to summarize some of the issues and complexities that the builder of the data warehouse is going to face, within each of the components of the system. With this information in hand, we are now ready to consider the many layers of issues that are going to crop up when we try to actually build the warehouse and coordinate the construction of each of the components.

Comparing the Data Warehouse to a Real Warehouse

It should come as no surprise that the three components of the warehouse we have described are roughly analogous to the three major functions that any real world warehouse would perform.

Every warehouse has a receiving function where goods are accepted, checked for damage, broken down into storable chunks, and placed within the warehouse itself. Every warehouse also has an inventory management function, whereby the locations of goods are tracked, and their storage organization kept optimized. And every warehouse has an inventory check out, packaging and shipping function. We will continue to develop this analogy to help us understand how the data warehouse needs to be built.

BUILDING A WAREHOUSE

A commonly asked question is, "If you're going to build a data warehouse, where should you begin?" Most people think that you should start with the data itself. These "data driven" advocates believe that you must first develop a logical model of all of the data that the warehouse will hold, before you begin figuring anything else out. Well, in some ways, this is correct, but for the most part it is not.

When a company decides that they need to build a new warehouse for their inventory, they do not start out by developing a list of everything they want to keep in it. That would be silly. A warehouse is a transient thing. Materials move into and out of the warehouse at a rapid pace, and what we store in the warehouse is going to change over time.

Step One - Figuring out Whether you Need a Warehouse or Not

Before any business person would begin to build a real warehouse, they would have first determined whether the company in fact needed one or not. It would be senseless to go out and buy a new building if you didn't need one. How does a company decide that a warehouse is needed? It's simple. Companies build warehouses when they are having trouble managing their inventory. There are actually several ways that this "inventory management pain" can manifest itself.

Inventory Overload

Some companies find that they simply no longer have enough room to keep products and files. Their manufacturing facilities take up more and more space of storage, while their retail outlets cram the back rooms full of items they don't need. Both sides of the supply chain eventually find that they are spending more and more of their time managing inventory, and less and less time doing their jobs. Manufacturers want to make products and retailers want to sell them. Neither of them want to manage the inventory of the other.

Break Down and Consolidation Services

In other situations, the company may find that they need to set up a facility which can "pre-process" inventory before forwarding it to its destination. For example, a clothing store chain found that they could save money on women's jeans by purchasing them by the train car load from a manufacturer. Unfortunately, after they purchased it, they had to send it somewhere to get the load broken down into the different smaller sized packages for each of their stores. Other organizations put warehouses in place so that multiple, smaller orders for disparate goods can be consolidated into larger, more efficient shipments.

Prudent Reserve

Another reason to build a warehouse is to create a storage area where you can store production overruns, or simply allow the factory to run at a higher volume, higher level of efficiency. The warehouse serves as an inventory buffer, allowing the company to have a prudent reserve of their goods in between production runs.

The Bottomless Inventory Pit

Despite the presence of so many good rationalizations for building a warehouse, the manager will always approach the decision to build a new one with care. The reason is simple. There are many organizations that have built warehouses which turned into bottomless inventory pits. These inventory pits become places where worthless inventory accumulates for extended periods of time, taking up more and more space and becoming a large liability to the company instead of being an asset. Data warehouses can easily turn into the same kind of thing.

Searching for Alternatives

The decision to build a data warehouse is a big one. It should not be approached with any less analysis or caution than the building of a real warehouse. There are always alternatives to warehousing, and the sponsor of a warehousing project must be convinced that the alternatives are worse than the cure before advocating this kind of solution.

Step Two - Criteria for Evaluating the Data Warehouse

Ultimately, the value of the data warehouse needs to be measured with the same criteria as a real warehouse. How do companies decide whether a warehouse has value or not? There are several criteria, but the most prevalent is a measurement called "turns."

Turns

In a real warehouse, the term Turns refers to the measurement of how many times a sopecific cargo moves into and out of the warehouse over a given period of time, or how many turns per time period. A high number of turns means that items of the category being measured have moved into and out of the warehouse several times for the given time period. A low number of turns means that it moved in and out very few times.

For example, when you are warehousing fresh vegetables, you need to have a high turn rate. Vegetables should "turn" every few days or they will rot. On the other hand, expensive jewelry moves at a much lower "turn rate." If you move one a week, you are doing well.

The data wrehouse also needs to be measured in turns. Data with a very low turn rate should probably not be warehoused at all. (For example, it has happened in the past that people have dumped millions of records into a data warehouse and never looked at it at all). Data with a very high turn rate may more appropriately be handled via some other mechanism. (For instance, if millions of rows of data are completely refreshed daily, it would be prudent to question the process.) Of course, figuring out what kinds of turn rates are acceptable, and developing the infrastructure to measure that, is a different story.

Step Three - Legacy Systems Inventory

Along with needing to know how much the warehouse will hold, we will need to know what the different sources of goods for the warehouse will be.

Step Four - Accessibility Requirements

Of course, we also need to know where goods are going to be shipped.

Step Five - Sizing

When a manager decides to put a warehouse together, it is because he or she knows that they have some items that need to be stored, processed (unbundle, rebundle etc.) and forwarded to another location. This manager will begin by deciding exactly how big the warehouse will need to be. To make this decision, he or she will need to know what kinds of products will be stored and what kinds of volumes of this item to expect. In other words, the first thing we do is size the warehouse.

Just as the manager will size the warehouse by getting some rough estimates from the different departments that will be the intended users of the building once it is completed, so too, must the data warehouse manager get some rough estimates as to the size, shape, quantity and throughput of data to be managed.

Step Six - Determining the Type of Warehouse

The manager does not need to know what brand of microwave ovens, or which designer's clothing will be kept in the warehouse. He or she only needs to know if the warehouse is for appliances, clothing, electronic parts or maybe a combination of all three.

As a part of this decision will come obvious conclusions about the kinds of turns we expect. In general, the more valuable or complicated the product, the fewer turns to expect while, conversely, the less valuable the product, the more frequent the turns. Early on in the process, these criteria must be explored.

Step Seven - Determine the Location

After figuring out approximately how big the warehouse needs to be, and what types of things will be kept in it, the next step will be to determine where the warehouse should be located. Obviously, placing a warehouse in Hong Kong, when all of your distributors are in Kokomo, Indiana is not a real good idea.

The physical location of the data warehouse is going to be important for several reasons. The first and most obvious location issue will have to do with the warehouse's proximity to either the users or the sources of data or both. Despite the perceived notion that with

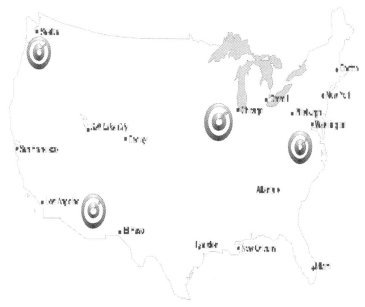

Figure 4-1. Location, location, location

modern computer equipment location is not an issue, the reality is that it can still have a big impact on the effectiveness of the warehouse.

A second, more nefarious, but equally important issue revolving around location has to do with determining where the warehouse will physically reside from a political and organizational perspective.

For example, should the warehouse be located in the computer room on the mainframe with the other Legacy systems? Should it be located in the user area? This decision will determine a lot about how people will perceive it, and will also influence the decisions about who is going to be responsible for supporting it.

Step Eight - Build, Modify or Buy?

Now that we know where the warehouse should be, and some of the requirements for its construction, it is time to make a decision about where to get it. Maybe we can take an existing building, or a part of one of our other facilities and turn them into a warehouse. Maybe we can buy something that already meets our needs. Perhaps we just have to build our own.

The build/modify/buy decision is a tough one. And it is especially tough for the data warehouse procurer. Just as the business person must weigh a vast number of variables in order to make this determination, so too must the data warehouse advocate.

Step Nine - Build the Warehouse Itself

Assume for whatever political, physical, capacity or requirements reasons that we have decided to build a new warehouse and that we are ready to begin the specifications process. This is the point where our analogy to the physical warehouse construction process begins to diverge. In the real world our manager can simply call architects who specialize in warehouse construction, give them the requirements and wait for some blueprints to review.

In the computer systems world, this process is complicated by several factors. First, there is no such thing as a set of blue prints for a computer system. People have tried, but they have consistently failed to spec out the process anywhere near as well as the construction planner. Second, the entire design and construction industry is based upon a series of well established principles and guidelines for how to make use of those plans. The odds of a group of programmers following the specifications given to them is actually pretty rare for a large number of reasons.

In the pages to come, however, we will propose a set of blueprint documents that can be used to accomplish the same thing as the architect's drawings.

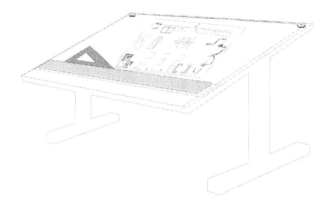

Figure 4-2. The blue print

Specify Hardware and Network Architecture

During the previous steps, the manager in charge of the warehouse project has collected a significant number of starting points for us. Because this homework has been done in advance, we can begin immediately to specify the critical components of the system.

Because we know where the warehouse will be, approximately how big it will be, the number of turns to expect, the people that will use it and the places the output will go, we will be in a position to specify all the hardware and networking components necessary to support what has been proposed.

It is critical that this be specified as soon as possible because every subsequent decision is dependent upon these decisions. In other words, if we change one of these decisions later on, it is going to force us to re-do a lot of our planning and construction work, with the subsequent complete loss of anything that has been accomplished.

Determine the Data Architecture

After we have laid our foundation, built the walls and created all access roads, we will be in a position to actually begin to lay the warehouse out. We need to figure out where the different kinds of goods are going to be stored, we need to figure out where people will walk, where they will drive fork lifts, where and how they will inventory little things, big things, fragile things, expensive things.

Laying out the data warehouse is no different. Before we begin to actually try to manage data, we had better have thought through all of the same kinds of issues. Where will I place big tables? How will I manage little ones?

Determine Staffing Requirements

When we know how the warehouse is going to be laid out, we can then determine how many people it will take to support it. How many office people? How many people in receiving? How many in shipping?

Who will manage the warehouse? You cannot expect it to run itself. It is actually amazing how many people think that they can simply skip this step when it comes to building a data warehouse. It is a fatal mistake to ignore this issue.

Develop and Install Warehouse Management Policies and Procedures

In tandem with the development of personnel requirements comes the need to determine the rules for how the warehouse will be used. In the real warehouse, people are given roles and they fulfill them. In the data warehousing world, we create software (the infrastructure management software) that fulfills this same need.

Install bins, paint, lines, bring in the forklifts

Finally, we are ready to bring in the equipment and tools and begin making the warehouse functional.

Step Ten - Begin the Inventory Management Process

Only now should we actually consider bringing product into the warehouse. Have you ever heard of people trying to use a warehouse before it was finished? Have many people been pleased with the

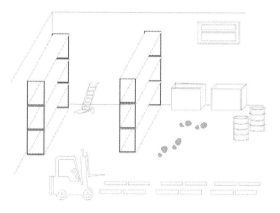

Figure 4-3. The real warehouse

results when they sent valuable merchandise to an incomplete warehouse and lost the goods because they were stolen, or got wet because the warehouse had no roof yet? Unlikely.

So too, must we fight the urge to use the warehouse before it is ready.

CHAPTER 5

A MODEL FOR THE DATA WAREHOUSE

Webster's Dictionary - 1995: model (mod'l) -n 1. a standard or example for imitation or comparison 2. a representation, generally in miniature, to show the construction or appearance of something.

Up until this point in our consideration of the data warehouse we have remained very general in nature. Now, we are ready to get more specific about how our warehouse will actually be put together and start to develop a model.

Acquisition	Staging Area	Storage	Work Space	Access
Infrastructure {		Operational Infrastructure		
		Physical Infrastructure		

Figure 5-1. The core data warehouse

To begin with, we have already established that the warehouse can be viewed as consisting of three major "vertical" components.

1. The Acquisitions Component, responsible for the extraction of data from a variety of sources as well as for the

cleansing, validation, formatting and staging of that data for loading into the warehouse.

2. The Storage Component, consisting of a collection of relational database tables.

3. The Access Component, made up of an assortment of analysis, query, visualization and manipulation tools that make the warehouse useful to the business.

We have also established that we could further dissect the warehouse in terms of its horizontal layers. The lowest level, the one which forms the foundation for the entire warehouse structure, represents the physical infrastructure, or systems architecture.

Specifically, we will identify the following as being part of the physical infrastructure:

*   The computer hardware which hosts the acquisitions, storage and access components

*   The network configuration that will ties the pieces together and ties the system itself to the outside world (Legacy systems at the acquisitions end and end users on the access side).

*   The operating system (OS), network operating system (NOS)

*   The systems level utilities and procedures that work in this environment (i.e. copy programs, sort programs, file management systems, database software etc.)

*   The support staff that keeps this environment running

*   The roles, responsibilities and procedures that make the environment manageable

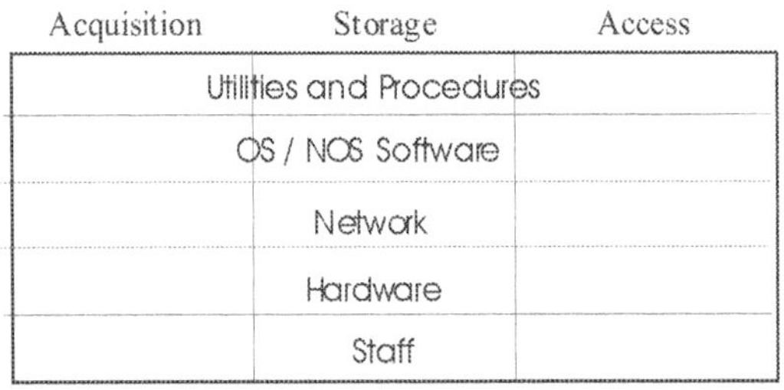

Acquisition	Storage	Access
Utilities and Procedures		
OS / NOS Software		
Network		
Hardware		
Staff		

Figure 5-2. Components of the physical infrastructure

- The management structure that define who will be responsible for keeping all of the parts working and communicating with each other.

Overlaying the physical infrastructure layer of the system is the operational infrastructure. While the physical infrastructure is concerned with the mechanical, fundamental functionality of the computer systems' aspect of the system, the operational infrastructure defines how the warehouse itself is going to run.

We can use our real warehouse analogy to help explain the difference. The first layer of the real warehouse is the physical building itself. The concrete floors, the walls, the ceiling (the computer hardware), and the roads, railway accesses and loading docks (the network aspects). Within our real world warehouse, we must build this infrastructure before we can do anything.

After we have gotten the "physical plant" in order, however, we must figure out how the warehouse is going to be run. We need to know what the flow of material through the warehouse will be. Which docks are for loading? Which are for unloading? Where will we park the trucks that are waiting to pull up to the door? We need to draw lines on the floors so that fork lift truck drivers know where to drive. We need to install bins and shelving units, and stock up on an inventory of pallets. We also need to figure out how many dock workers we will have, how we will check-in and check-out merchandise and, in general, figure out how the warehouse will work. We need to have completed all of this before we begin receiving merchandise.

In the same way, we need to have all the "how will this warehouse work" issues settled before we can begin using the data warehouse. We call this collection of assorted warehouse management requirements the operational infrastructure. It consists of:

- The staff who will support the operation of the warehouse itself (DBAs, Data Analysts, Job Schedulers, etc.)
- The rules and procedures that will govern warehouse operation
- A customized set of software which will be responsible for keeping track of our data warehouse "inventory" and the progress of data through the different components
- Feedback Mechanisms that send warehouse data back to the Legacy systems

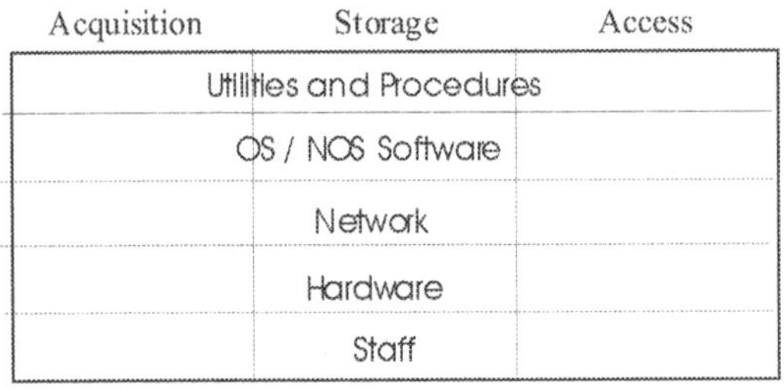

Acquisition	Storage	Access
Utilities and Procedures		
OS / NOS Software		
Network		
Hardware		
Staff		

Figure 5-3. The operational infrastructure

FEEDBACK MECHANISMS

In addition to the data disciplines, we have one other set of responsibilities that are considered to be part of the operational infrastructure, and those are related to the problems presented by feedback mechanisms.

Inadvertently, no matter how hard we try to avoid it, it will become necessary for the builder of the warehouse to feed information back into the system which sent the information in the first place. Although it will be necessary, it is important that we have a clear set of rules for how and where this kind of feedback will occur, otherwise we jeopardize the very foundations upon which our warehouse has been built.

The dangers involved in allowing feedback mechanisms into the warehouse are diverse. First of all, the warehouse has been built in a certain way in order to optimize certain characteristics. In general, we want the warehouse to be a read-only operation so that we can optimize the storage of data for access, query and analysis. By burdening the system with backwards moving data (data that moves from the user to the warehouse to the Legacy systems), we make it impossible to tune the system for optimum query performance.

Second of all, we have designed the warehouse to serve as a neutral data storage area which insulates end users and analysts from the idiosyncrasies and requirements of operational Legacy systems performance. If we allow our warehouse to work directly with those systems, we tie them to those systems in violation of the fundamental principles upon which we based the reason for the warehouse in the first place. In effect we would turn the warehouse into an extension of whatever Legacy system for which we are providing feedback.

In general, if we allow any but the most severely restricted type of feedback mechanism into the warehouse, we risk turning the warehouse into an operational system.

One might think of the data moving through the warehouse as creating a current, or a flow.

Figure 5-4. "Flow" through the data warehouse

The entire purpose of the warehouse is to optimize the process of moving data from the one end to the other as efficiently as possible. Any attempts to push data "against" the flow are going to slow it down and muddle its efficiency and operational focus.

Despite our best intentions, people are going to insist that some kinds of feedback mechanisms to the warehouse exist. There are just too many situations where it makes sense. We must, therefore, from the outset define what kinds of feedback mechanisms will and will not be allowed, and build from there. What we can do, however, is limit the ways we will allow these kinds of feedback mechanisms to be worked into the warehouse.

We will propose three feedback mechanisms to build into the warehouse infrastructure: the backflush mechanism, feedback loop and the workspace area. Experience has shown that these approaches can protect the warehouse from too much "dilution" of function, while allowing people to do the things they need to do.

BACK FLUSH MECHANISMS

The first type of feedback mechanism we will consider is the one we call a back flush mechanism. A back flush occurs when it becomes apparent that the data which the acquisitions component of the warehouse has prepared for loading, has been cleaned, prepared and validated in a way that will be of value to the Legacy systems which sent the data in the first place.

An example from the development of a typical customer database should help explain this situation. In the building of customer data warehouses it is often necessary to do quite a bit of cleaning up of the names and addresses. This is known as name and address hygiene. When Legacy systems store name and address information, it is not uncommon to find that the information has become inaccurate or was never quite complete. In order to make this information useful to our warehouse, we will need to go through the process of getting all of that information correct.

At this point, the people using the Legacy system will end up having worse information than the warehouse. So what they usually require is that the now sanitized name and address information be fed back into the Legacy system so that the users of the operational systems have the benefit of the latest and most accurate information.

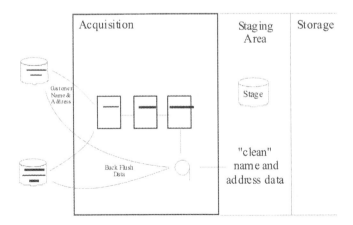

Figure 5-5. Back flush mechanism

Back flush mechanisms usually consist of nothing more than the creation of a special additional file which is written at the same time that the data being loaded is sent to the staging area. This file can then be picked up and applied to the Legacy systems by the managers of the Legacy systems themselves.

LOOPS AND WORKSPACE AREAS

The other types of situations where feedback is required are a lot trickier. When our warehoused information is accessed by users there is always the chance, and often the requirement, that the users will need to update that information. In some situations people will want to make changes to the information and then send those changes back to the Legacy systems at the same time. For example, suppose a customer calls, advising the customer service person of a change in address. The natural assumption is that the user should simply make the appropriate changes to the warehouse itself. Unfortunately, this could create a disaster. We would then have some information in the warehouse that we do not have in the Legacy systems. Somehow, we need to figure out how to get the new address information back to all of the Legacy systems that need it too.

The second situation is even more complex. In some cases, people will want to make changes to the warehouse data, and then immediately allow other users to be aware of those changes. For instance, in the execution of mailing list scoring algorithms it is critical that people assign relative "weights" to each potential mail recipient and then make a selection of only those customers with a high enough score.

There are no easy solutions to these kinds of problems. Any attempt to read the warehouse backwards, back into the Legacy systems, is going to result in an operational and performance nightmare. At the same time, you do not want to ignore the convenience of simply allowing the user to make the change in place and move on to the next problem.

We provide two solutions to these feedback challenges.

In the first case, our solution will be to create mechanisms which capture the changes to the warehouse data and send them back to the acquisitions component for processing. Specifically, we must capture all changes made to the warehouse storage area at the point they are created and send copies of those changes to a "holding file" that will be utilized by the acquisitions component for the next full warehouse load/refresh cycle. This is akin to making a rule for our real warehouse which says that, if you want to check things back into the warehouse, you must send it to the receiving dock, not the shipping dock.

While the logistics of building this kind of feedback loop can be inconvenient and complicated, establishing this discipline is going to save us from dozens of complexities and inconveniences later on in the life of the warehouse. We call this solution a feedback loop.

In situations where we must allow people to drastically change the nature of the warehouse data, it does not make sense to allow all of these in-place changes to the warehouse to occur. We will make use

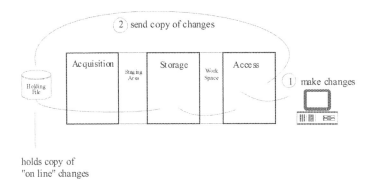

Figure 5-6. A feedback loop

of workspace areas instead.

In these cases, the subset of data which the users want to manipulate are copied into a temporary workspace (either database tables or flat files). The users can then manipulate, change, share and alter the

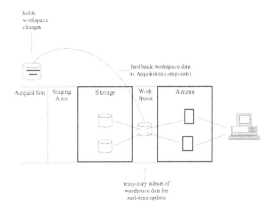

Figure 5-7. The workspace solution

contents of the workspace as much as they want without endangering the integrity of the warehouse storage area itself.

At key points in the process, the workspace area can be cleaned up and the changes sent back to the acquisitions component for loading into a hold file, and for eventual inclusion in the acquisition and warehouse loading process.

Infrastructure Conclusions

Taken as a whole, this collection of procedures and approaches defines our operational infrastructure. When we combine this operational infrastructure with the physical infrastructure we will have defined the overall warehouse infrastructure that will be pre-requisite to our being able to actually use the warehouse to do any real work.

It is critical at this point to note that no one would try to utilize a real warehouse until all of the grounds, building, personnel and storage areas were defined. No one would dream of using a warehouse where the storage locations weren't cataloged and the part numbers of the goods being managed weren't clearly displayed and understood by the warehouse support staff.

In the same way, it will be critical in our construction of a data warehouse that we build this infrastructure before we start trying to do any warehousing work.

Data Warehousing Applications

Assuming that we have developed our infrastructure, we will now be in the position to begin entertaining the thought of taking on some real warehousing work.

The next issue we face when deciding how to construct the data warehouse, is how to manage the process of putting real, usable data into the warehouse. We have a very specific set of recommendations and they do not correspond to the approaches that many people try to take. Before we go into details about our recommended approach, let us consider some of the alternatives.

Building up the Warehouse Inventory

Returning to our real world warehouse example, we know that, when someone starts up a new warehouse, they do not simply open the doors on day one, fill it up with materials on day two, and then start using it. That approach is too simplistic and doesn't take the realities of logistics and utilization into account. The view we want to take of our data warehouse is not so much of a big storage locker where things are placed and then forgotten, but more of a merchandise conduit through which things pass. A viable, well run warehouse is measured, not by how much it holds, but by how much passes through it. Looking at it from this perspective, it doesn't make any sense to think of our warehouse as being loaded up all at once.

Therefore, the advocates of data warehousing all have their own recommended approaches for how to structure the warehouse construction process While we could identify an endless array of variations on the basic themes, in general, these approaches are either model driven or application driven.

The Model Driven Approach
to Warehouse Construction

The basic operational assumption of the model driven approach to warehouse construction states that we need to develop a data model which defines what the warehouse should hold first, fill it up with data, and then allow people to use it. This approach bases most of its assumptions on the validity of data modeling, enterprise modeling and the data engineering disciplines in general.

Proponents of this approach believe it should be possible to develop a logical model of all the data that the warehouse should need, and only after this model has been perfected, should you consider loading and making use of it. Of course, if you were to carry this logic out to its natural conclusion, you would find that you needed to model all of the data within the organization before you could start construction. (Any organization participating in the development of enterprise models knows how long that can take.)

In recognition of this inconvenience, most model driven practitioners begin by saying that you do not have to model everything at once, but that you can break down the task of global modeling into smaller pieces and build the warehouse one section at a time, by logical subject area . (For example, you might build a warehousing component in support of accounting first, then take on production control data and after that personnel information.)

While this approach certainly makes some sense, it unfortunately ignores several key practical considerations.

First, no enterprise level mapping scheme to date has ever been successfully completed. There are a number of reasons for this; the main one being that no organization stays stagnant long enough for the modeling effort to near completion. While people are busily trying to figure out the information in existing systems, new systems are being built simultaneously. You can never catch up.

Second, the practical value of databases and data models, developed in a vacuum without the benefit of the knowledge of what people want to do with it and why, is to be seriously questioned. Experience in the development of hundreds of systems has shown that you cannot model useful databases without knowing what they will be used for.

Third, and most importantly, an approach like this makes it incredibly difficult for the builders of the system to focus on what they are to deliver, and scope management becomes the biggest concern. Those projects which have taken the model-driven approach to warehouse construction have met with failure more times than not. If we look upon our data warehouse as we would look upon a real world warehouse, instead of as an exercise in data processing theory, we would see very quickly why these approaches do not make sense.

The people who build real world warehouses do not begin by figuring out how many screws, nails, nuts, bolts and other items the warehouse will hold. They know that the actual contents of the warehouse are going to vary constantly and often quite dramatically. No company plans on needing vast amounts of inventory. If you could predict what you were going to need to store, you would head off the problems and eliminate the need for the warehouse in the first place.

We propose taking the same attitude toward the data warehouse. It is not something to be planned out and forgotten. It is a necessary evil, a stop gap measure. When we condescend to build a data warehouse, what we are really saying is that we cannot predict where the ups and downs in inventory are going to be, but that with a warehouse we can smooth out the spikes and valleys and provide our customers with a more dependable flow of information.

Another good analogy for the data warehouse is to think of it as a library. We want to store all of the information that people might need and simply provide them with an inventory of books, a Dewey Decimal system, a card catalog to help them find information and some librarians to keep order. When we view the data warehouse as a service, instead of as an application, we begin to create an entirely new paradigm for figuring out how to approach it.

The Application Based Approach

We advocate an entirely different approach to warehouse construction, one which is logical, intuitively obvious, but which flies in the face of what is considered the "right way to do things" in the data processing world.

Instead of looking at our data warehousing project as a stagnant one which is built, turned over to production and ignored, we view the process of providing a warehouse to the organization as the development of a new support service yhat will continually be upgraded, changed and tuned to meet the needs of the organization. In other words, we will view the data warehouse as a critical component of the organization's overall information systems infrastructure. We see it not as a tactical application to meet a specific set of short term needs, but as a facility through which we can build dozens, or even hundreds of low cost, rapidly deployed tactical applications. The managers of our warehouse will eventually become the managers of an extensive inventory of small, high impact, highly sophisticated applications, each designed to meet a specific set of tactical business objectives.

This view of a data warehouse, not as an application, but as a vehicle for the mass production of applications, provides us with a totally different framework from which to consider the whole construction process. If we are going to accept this second, much broader vision of the warehouse as being valid, then we are going to have to rethink some of the traditional assumptions about system construction and support.

Acquisition	Storage	Access
	"Application 3"	
	"Application 2"	
	"Application 1"	
	Infrastructure	
	Architecture	

Figure 5-8. Data warehouse "applications"

We cannot afford to approach the data warehouse project as a one time deal. We cannot plan on one analysis phase, one design phase, onc data model etc. We must assume that the warehouse itself, and the warehouse support team will be in a continual state of mapping data, cleaning, loading and delivering it to end users.

Once we accept the premise that this will not be a one shot project, then we must rethink our assumptions about how the system is going to be staffed and built from the very start. Taken from this perspective, we can see that the warehouse is not a monolithic block of data attached to another monolithic block of end user access mechanisms, but is instead a collection of discrete applications, each of which provides a different set of functionalities to end users. We can view each of these discrete applications as adding another layer to the warehouse. And we can see that, as we add more and more of these layers, the warehouse becomes more and more robust.

By changing our perspective to this more incremental kind of approach we create an environment that will allow us to increase the probabilities of success for each of the subsequent applications, while still building up a synergy which allows us to eventually benefit from having a critical mass of data within the warehouse itself.

THE NEED FOR A DATA DISCIPLINE

Just because we claim that an application driven approach to warehouse construction makes more sense than a model driven approach does not mean that we intend to build the warehouse without the benefits of data modeling and the other data management and data architecture disciplines. Far from it. Indeed, the process of building each application must be driven entirely by a collection of disciplines that we refer to as the data disciplines.

Just as you would never dream of trying to run a real warehouse without some kind of method for identifying individual parts as well as all of the different storage locations within the warehouse so that you could keep track of what comes in and where it gets stored, so too must we have a similar inventory management approach in order to run our data warehouse.

In the real warehouse environment, everything that needs to be managed already has some kind of identifier. The process of building the data warehouse is, of course, a little more complicated. Part of the job of running this warehouse is actually finding the data that people need, tagging it appropriately and then bringing it into the warehouse for their use.

We call the overall approach to the problems of data management in the warehouse the "data disciplines," and there are several that must be in place. The list of these disciplines includes:

Data Analysis Processes

- Data Sourcing - Identifying where the data people want currently exists and validating that what they think they will find is really there.

- Data Integrity Validation - Verifying that the data extracted is accurate, valid and usable.

- Data Synchronization - Making sure that the multiple sources of data synch up with each other

  (including the development of back flush mechanisms).

- Data Transform Mapping - Verifying the identify and applicability of the data as it travels from one end of the data warehouse to the other.

- Data Modeling - Cataloging an inventory of all the data within the warehouse.

- Data Design - Fguring out how the data will be arranged in the new warehouse relational tables (including the development of a data architecture).

- Data Metrics Gathering - Determining how much data will be managed and at what access rate

Data Transformation Processes

- Data Extraction - Pulling the data out of its source and into a warehouse-usable form.

- Data Cleansing - Correcting errors in the accuracy, validity and usability of extracted data, including merge, purge and formatting programs.

- Data Loading and Storage - Loading data into tables and data chains.

We refer to this collection of responsibilities and tasks as the overall warehouse "data discipline" and it is critical that the people running the warehouse have a clear set of procedures for how and by whom

Acquisition	Storage	Access
		Solution Development
		Data Identification
Data Sourcing		Data Sourcing
Data Integrity Validation		Data Integrity Validation
Data Synchronization	Data Synchronization	
Back Flush Development		
	Storage Topology Mapping	Storage Topology Mapping
Data Transformation Mapping	Data Transformation Mapping	Data Transformation Mapping
Data Metrics Gathering	Data Metrics Gathering	Data Metrics Gathering
	Data Modeling	
	Database Design	

Figure 5-9. Data disciplines

these disciplines are to be performed before you can actually begin doing any real warehousing activities.

RECONCILING THE APPLICATIONS WITH MODELING AND DATA ADMINISTRATION

At this point, we can anticipate a loud hue and cry from those corporate organizations which advocate a data driven approach to systems development. Our adherence to an application driven method might appear to be in direct opposition to corporate initiatives aimed at the management of data as a corporate resource.

On the contrary, it is our claim that this approach can fit quite nicely with these corporate initiatives. The only difference is that the integration with these systems must occur after the business-determined demands of the warehouse itself have been met.

It is our intention with this approach to minimize data redundancy and to increase the manageability of data just as much, if not more, than the "purist" data administration advocates espouse. The only difference is that we will create this environment of shared data resources by adding applications in a serial fashion, making sure as each application is added, that any data that has been pulled under the warehouse umbrella is utilized by as many different applications as possible. The details of how we propose to accomplish this data administration vision of data utilization is illustrated below.

We begin this process by considering from this perspective (in a little more detail) what we mean by a warehouse application.

An Overview of an Application

Before looking at a few more of our rules for deciding what should or should not be included as an application for our warehouse, let's see what this application looks like.

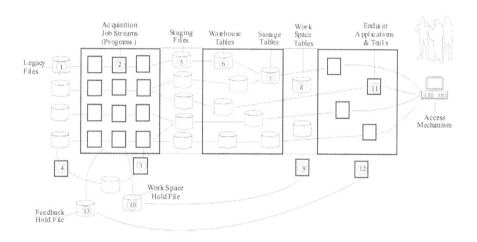

Figure 5-10. The components of an "application"

Remember, up until this point, our warehouse has held no data. All we have done is assemble the hardware and software necessary to run it, figured out how it would work, determined the rules for the treatment of management, monitoring and data discipline, pre-defined our feedback mechanisms and educated our staff in how to run the warehouse. Now it is time to see what it really looks like.

Notice that we have finally begun to include real Legacy systems, real programs, real data stores, real access programs and tools and real users in our conceptualization. We begin with the identification of all those Legacy systems, and the underlying Legacy system data files that hold information critical to the warehouse. (1)

Data from these systems is extracted, and passed through a series of acquisitions programs. (These programs perform our keying, hygiene, validation, cross referencing, formatting and storage functions.) (2)

At this time any back flush programs that will be required to feed clean data back to the Legacy systems are also developed (3). This includes those programs which will apply the clean data to those Legacy files. (4).

Eventually, we are left with a collection of staged data, ready to load into the warehouse. (5)

This staged data is then loaded into the actual storage area (usually relational database tables). (6) And any summary, cross reference storage tables are generated as well. (7)

In some cases, workspace tables will also be automatically created and loaded, (8) though this can also be postponed until the user specifically requests it.

A critical aspect of the workspace area of the warehouse is the inclusion of the workspace feedback mechanism, which periodically updates the acquisitions portion of the warehouse with the real-time information changes that the workspace contains. (9) Basically, the contents of the workspace need to be sent to an acquisitions component staging file, (10) where those changes can be included in the next reload/refresh of the main warehouse itself.

Finally, different end user applications and tools (11) can access those subsets of data that they require. These facilities may also include a feedback mechanism (12) similar to the one supporting the workspace area. In this case, each specific change made to the base warehouse tables is also recorded in a file (13), which is eventually fed back into the warehouse load process.

Data Warehouse Applications and Scope Control

Given this more complete picture of how the application will be put together, we can now turn to a more formal definition of what makes up each of the applications that will eventually make use of the warehouse.

Remember, the reason we are taking this approach is because experience has shown that complexity and the lack of focus is what has led to the demise of most warehousing systems. Therefore, it is

> A data warehouse "application" is a contiguous assembly of Acquisition, Storage and Access components which, when taken in their entirety, provide the end user with a functional set of usable data.

Figure 5-11. What is an "application?"

critical that we establish a set of rules for the definition of each of the applications so that these problems can be avoided. Remember also that we said our warehouse would be designed as an environment within which a great many applications could be added and that it was not to be considered as one application.

RULE NUMBER ONE - CONTIGUITY

A warehouse application is a contiguous assembly of acquisition, storage and access components which, when taken in their entirety provide an end user with a functional set of data, delivered in a form that is usable.

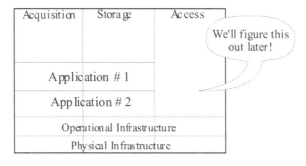

Figure 5-12. Don't do this:

It is important at this point to notice what we have, and have not, included in our definition of a warehouse application. First of all, we said that an application is a contiguous assembly of components, meaning, each warehouse application must include a data acquisition, a data storage and a data access component, each of which is dependent on the others. In other words, you cannot create a warehouse application which consists only of acquisition and storage components.

Unfortunately, many people believe that this is exactly what a data warehousing project is about. The thinking goes something like this: "We'll identify the data, extract it and load it into the warehouse. The users can figure out later what they are going to do with it."

This approach is destined for challenges, cost overruns and eventual failure for two reasons:

- First, it ignores the complexity of data access tools and their specific requirements.
- Second, it ignores the problems of data acquisition, valida-tion and storage.

In general, it greatly oversimplifies everyone's understanding of the process. The fact of the matter is that you cannot acquire and store warehouse data that is usable unless you know what people are going to do with it. Therefore, we will never advocate the building of an application that does not include an access component.

There is another way that some will try to attack warehouse construction in a piece meal fashion.

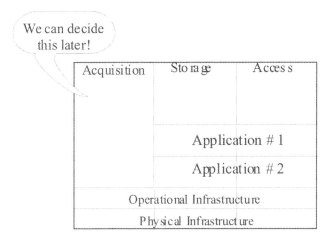

Figure 5-13. And don't do this:

In these cases users, and the advocates of specific data mining and data analysis solutions, develop a set of requirements and a whole lot of expectations about how a data access component is going to work. These individuals say, "We will figure out exactly what we want to do with the information first, and then build the warehouse to back it up."

This approach will fail just as quickly as the first approach. The designers will spend an inordinate amount of time figuring out how the data access portion is supposed to work only to find that the information they need is either not available or too expensive.

For example, we worked on one customer information system where, after nine months of design work, the builders of the system found that the only way to get the data they required loaded into the system was for a team of business people to input the five million rows of data by hand. This was not a feasible solution and the system had to be abandoned.

So our first criteria for selection of applications is that they be contiguous across all components. This guarantees that all the parts of the warehouse are going to be synchronized when it is time to use the system.

RULE NUMBER TWO - DECOMPOSITION OF BUSINESS CASES

Our second rule is applied to help make our definition of the application even more specific in scope. While saying that each application must be contiguous provides us with a guideline for what not to do when determining the scope of a project, it does little to provide us with the means to limit the scope. The application of the second rule will provide us with this limitation. Rule number two states that every application must be based upon a single, business sponsored, value proposition. In order to understand this rule, we will obviously need to develop an understanding of what a value proposition is.

Complexity in Systems Today

Every business computer system is designed to meet some kind of business need or collection of needs. In the early days, the name of the system often provided a good understanding of what it was designed to do. For instance, the Payroll system is designed to manage the process of recording people's time and issuing them paychecks. The Accounts Payable system was built to keep track of the corporation's debts and the payment of its bills. In each case, there is an implied business function which the system has been built to support.

As systems became more complex, it became more difficult to name them and have those names correspond to specific functions. Before too long we began naming systems with acronyms. The GENESIS system might be the General Engineering and Sales Integration System, PRMS identifies the Purchasing and Receiving Management System, etc.

Clearly, as systems have become more complex and multi-dimensional in nature, their purpose and focus has become less and less discernible. You may recall that in chapter two we spent a considerable amount of time discussing this aspect of business computer systems today. Systems have and will continue to become more and more complex, solving problems that involve the coordination of efforts of hundreds of different people and systems.

In today's development environment, it is not uncommon to find large numbers of people working on systems with no clear idea as to what the real reason for building the system is. To understand what the system is supposed to do requires that you read through pages and pages of descriptions. Many times, the core reason for the system is so obfuscated that you cannot figure it out unless you ask someone.

If we are going to build our warehouse in the incremental manner that we have described, we are going to have to figure out some way to break down these extremely complex business problems and solutions into small, well-focused parts. The only way to accomplish this is to decompose the business problems themselves into smaller, more manageable pieces.

Understanding Business Problems

Since we assume that:

1. Most of those applications which will be considered as candidates for the warehouse will be extremely large and complex in nature.
2. It is neither an obvious nor trivial process to break these extremely complex candidates into a collection of smaller parts.

We are going to need to develop an approach which allows us to perform this decomposition process as quickly as possible.

The Business Environment
and Systems Projects

To help us develop just such an approach, we will begin by examining the typical business environment today as it relates to business systems and especially to data warehouse development.

To start with, we must recognize that business people could care less about data warehouses. A data warehouse is a systems development concept, not a business concept. Business people live and focus in a world of business problems. While we have referred repeatedly to the confusing and contradictory nature of the systems development environment, we have yet to discuss just exactly how confusing and contradictory the business environment itself has become.

In the early days of the large corporate environment, businesses were organized around clear, hierarchical lines. The business could be viewed as collections of departments, each performing specific tasks, and each of those tasks contributing to some greater business good. These days, however, with the advent of matrix management, unstructured team approaches, steering committee mania and the flat, manager-less organizational structure, we find that business people are in just as constant a state of flux, as the computer systems people are. In an environment of this type, it is very difficult to define clear, well organized plans. Therefore, it is also difficult to develop requirements for a warehouse that are clear and well organized.

In most business environments, people are wearing a variety of different hats. The lines between sales, marketing, accounting, production control, etc. are becoming ever more blurred. As a consequence, the ideas about how to make use of a data warehouse will tend to be equally fuzzy and undefined.

In a typical environment, there will be a large number of users and managers from a diverse set of business areas, each of whom sees a completely different, but equally believable, way in which the warehouse can solve their problems. Each of them will advocate a different assortment of propositions of how the warehouse should be used to meet their needs.

If we were to take this collection of propositions at face value, however, we would become immediately embroiled in all sorts of business and technical problems. Unless we apply some kind of discipline and rigor to the prioritization and treatment of these propositions, we will end up trying to please everyone, and ultimately please no one.

The Decomposition of Business Propositions

Our assumption, therefore, will be that as soon as business people begin to understand what a data warehouse is and how it can help them, they will immediately come up with dozens of propositions describing ways that the warehouse can be of use.

Our job will be to help them to diagnose what those propositions really entail and to come up with some kind of a scheme for placing a value on each proposition, and a priority for which should be done in what order.

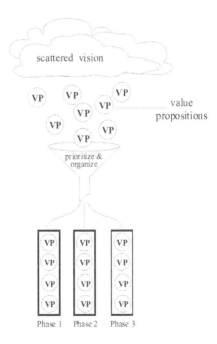

Figure 5-14. Value proposition development

Value Proposition Prioritization

We refer to each of the proposals made by a business person to make use of the warehouse to solve a business problem as a value proposition. The first step in determining which applications to place into our warehouse, therefore, will be to gather up these propositions, determine the merit of each, determine the relative cost of each, assign relative values to them, and then rank them according to their priority of importance.

Figure 5-14 shows a diagram of how this process works.

In some cases the process of identifying, analyzing and ranking value propositions will be managed as a formal project, or as part of a feasibility study. In other cases, the systems development people will simply, on an informal basis, gather up the candidate proposals and select those with the most value. Ultimately, the process of soliciting, analyzing and ranking value propositions needs to become part of the ongoing service that the administrators of the data warehouse provide. Remember, we said that the data warehouse is to be considered an ongoing service to the corporation. The identification and development of value propositions is the first and most important part of that process.

We also said that, if we were going to attempt to assess the value of the warehouse, then it should be based, not on how much information it holds, but on how often or how appropriately the information moves through the warehouse. The identification and implementation of more and more value propositions is the purpose of the warehouse.

The Scope of a Value Proposition

Of course, simply identifying a collection of value propositions does not in and of itself guarantee us any kind of good scope management. We must apply some rigor to those definitions. Among the rules about value propositions that we will apply are the following:

1) Each value proposition must be a specific business problem. A value proposition cannot be a collection or "laundry list" of unrelated problems, strung into the same sentence. For example, the proposition that the warehouse application, (a) will make it possible to keep track of customer inquiries, (b) develop geo-economic segmentations of the market and, (c) provide for the consolidation

of customer data from 25 different source systems is not one value proposition, but three. One regards customer inquiries, another market segmentation, and the third the integration of disparate information.

2) Each value proposition must have a single, responsible sponsoring business organization. Consider, for instance, the following: "The data warehousing application will make it possible for customer service personnel to respond more quickly when customers call in with questions, while at the same time making it possible for the marketing department to keep track of which customers have received what promotional item." This is not one value proposition, but two: one for customer service and one for marketing.

3) Each value proposition must define a specific, tangible benefit that the application will provide. (It is preferred that they be financial in nature, but benefits can be less tangible as well, i.e. market share, efficiency, etc).

The following value proposition, for example, is incomplete. "The data warehousing application will make it possible for customer service personnel to provide customers with immediate information about the status of their account." To complete it we would need to add the following: "We estimate that this additional level of service will make it possible for us to prevent the loss due to customer dissatisfaction by approximately 2% of our market per year." Now this proposition would be complete.

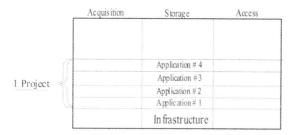

Figure 5-15. The build-all-at-once approach

RULE NUMBER THREE - SEQUENCING

The first two rules for the definition of an application tell us what an application should and should not be. They say nothing, however, about the order in which these applications are to be added.

In the worst case, people might define a collection of value propositions, turn them into application plans, and then attempt to build them all at once.

This one-shot-approach to warehouse development defeats the purpose of identifying distinct value propositions in the first place. By forcing the sponsors of each warehouse application to specify exactly what it is they want an application to accomplish, we have greatly reduced the complexity. If we were to try to develop them all at once, the majority of that complexity would then return.

Therefore, rule number three states:

"Applications that are dependent upon each other must be added to the warehouse serially."

In other words, if we have defined two applications, and they share any common acquisition, storage or data access components, then they must be added to the warehouse one at a time. The first must be finished before the second is begun, etc.

Why demand serial development?

This is one of the places where a lot of systems developers are going to have trouble with our approach. There are basically two reasons why people do not want to make this development serial. First, it forces the warehouse project to take longer. Instead of jumping on everything at once, we are telling people that they must get one part working before they begin the second. Second, many people believe that there are wonderful "economies of scale" to be gained by piggybacking one of these projects on another, especially if there is a lot of overlap between the corresponding acquisition, storage and access components.

While the arguments behind these cases may be vehement, it is our staunchest belief that, except in the most trivial of cases, to allow developers to attack interdependent applications using any approach other than a serial one, greatly increases the chances for failure.

We have discussed these reasons several times, but it basically boils down to the problems of increased complexity and inter-system inter-dependency. By attacking these applications one at a time, we make it possible for developers to stabilize the first set before taking on the second.

This is not to say that when you build the second application you cannot make use of the components developed for the earlier applications. Absolutely not. In fact, if you were not going to try to leverage the code generated, data stored and access mechanisms developed, then it would be foolish to build a warehouse in the first place. No, all we are saying is that the first one needs to be working and stable before you begin messing with the second. That way, all

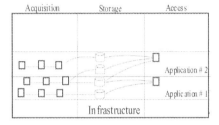

Figure 5-16. Serial development. Second application making use of components developed by the first.

of what you learned during the first project will make you that much smarter when it comes to doing the second.

It is in this area where we can get into many arguments about the "economies of scale" in systems design and the waste of people's time and efforts in apparently doing the "same job" twice, while forcing the delay of the ultimate system.

There are many ways that subsequent applications can leverage work done in earlier efforts.

Most obviously, data formatted and stored for the use of one application can be included for use by others, many times with little or no effect on the first system. Also, it is possible to make use of previously developed data formatting, cleansing and validation programs from the acquisition component, as well as programs, interfaces and tools utilized in the data access component. In other words, the efficiency and ability to leverage warehouse resources are not curtailed by our serial development rule. However, they are delayed and forced within our structure for the sake of risk minimization and complexity containment.

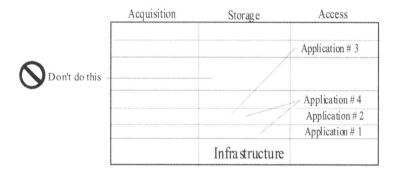

Figure 5-17. Simultaneous, autonomous development

RULE NUMBER FOUR - DEVELOPING MULTIPLE APPLICATIONS

Of course, in some situations, because of time constraints or other imperatives, people will insist that more than one application be developed at a time. We will allow this to take place, but only under a certain set of conditions.

This leads us to our next rule about warehouse layer construction . Rule number four states:

You can develop applications simultaneously, as long as they are completely autonomous."

In other words, if you are going to build two or more systems simultaneously, then do so without leveraging the work of the others still in process. Obviously, there is nothing wrong with developing those applications to leverage work which has been done on applications that are already completed, just stay away from the other development teams.

The reason for this rule should be obvious. Two teams trying to meet their own system requirements while constantly shifting their solutions in order to respond to another team's similar fluctuations is a guaranteed formula for failure.

"But what about the wasted effort?", skeptics will say, "If these applications are using the same data source, then aren't we doing double work?" The answer is a sympathetic but firm, "Yes." Unfortunately, there is no way around this dilemma. As soon as you allow for the crossing of these boundary lines, you court disaster.

Subsequent Integration

But what do we do if it is imperative that these two applications share the same data? What if part of the value is in their use of a common storage area? The only solution to this is to plan for a data integration project which eliminates the redundancy after the two systems are developed.

WASTED EFFORT AND EXTRA EXPENSE

At this point there is a good chance that a lot of readers have already slammed the book shut and said, "Ridiculous! This approach is too slow, too wasteful and too conservative. Surely, there must be a better way!"

Our only response is that, despite 25 years of research and investigation into every methodology, every CASE tool, every Systems Development Life Cycle and every "new, latest, greatest" technology under the sun, no one has been able to come up with a way to make anything that's incredibly complex and interdependent simple and easy to build. The author is anxious to hear about any approaches to these problems that have really worked in a production environment which did not involve a lot of extra integration expense and without a lot of time delays due to the failure to estimate the true nature of this complexity.

The real advantage of this approach is that the risk, the cost and the delays are predictable and manageable. The biggest shortcoming of all the other approaches are that they do nothing to protect you against that risk.

Certainly, you can get lucky, or you may be blessed with an extremely competent staff, an extremely simple and straightforward problem set, or an incredibly motivated and competent user community. Any combination of these might allow you to ignore our application layering rules. However, for the typical corporation, facing the typical set of business challenges, this is the only way that offers any chance of success. If nothing else, with our approach you can minimize your risk.

Flipping the Problem Domain

Another way to look at these issues, is to turn the tables on the advocates of big scope systems.

To the developers we say: "Why should we believe that you can handle the construction of an extremely large and complex data warehousing application if you are unable to develop a small, tightly defined one?" If the advocates of the "big scope" solutions are so sure of their approach, then let them do two things: First, explain how you will avoid the impending complexity gridlock that is going to occur. Second, develop a small one and prove that you can manage that first. Then come back to talk about bigger ones.

To the business sponsors of these big solutions we say in a similar vein: "Why should we believe that this big, multi-dimensional business solution is going to accomplish all of what you have stated? If the solution is sound, then surely there must be a way to implement a part of it, in order to prove that the assumptions are sound. Prove the small concepts and the big concepts will fall into place."

In other words, in both cases, the maxim we would apply is this: If the concept is sound, then it should be provable on a small scale.

Disclaimers

At this point, let's be clear about some assumptions behind this current train of thought.

Remember that we are talking specifically about data warehouses, not about computer systems in general. Clearly, there are hundreds of types of applications where you must deal with a high degree of complexity and establish a critical mass in order to show any value. For example, would any airline reservation system be useful if it only recorded flights but didn't record seating, flight schedules etc. Of course not. But that system is an operational system, not a data warehouse.

We can afford to be more stringent with our warehouse construction rules for several reasons: First, it is a passive information access system and the synergy it provides is, therefore, of a different nature than operational systems. Second, it has a limited set of specific business problems that it can address. A data warehouse is not the answer to all of your data processing needs, it is simply an option. Therefore, only in the rarest of situations will it make sense to violate the rules we have laid out.

Summary of Approaches to Application Layering

Given this understanding of what a value proposition, and our rules about how to define each of the applications which can be placed within the warehouse, we are ready to figure out how the warehouse is going to be built. Tis process of laying one application on top of the other we will call "warehouse application layering."

We have already considered two of our approaches:

1) Autonomous Layering, where each application layer is added independent of the others, and

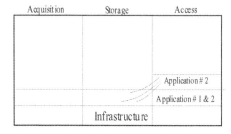

Figure 5-18. Access-only applications

2) Serial Layering, where we add each application layer in a pre-defined sequential order.

There are, of course, other ways that we can add applications as well.

3) Access-Only Applications

Another type of application that can be added to the warehouse is

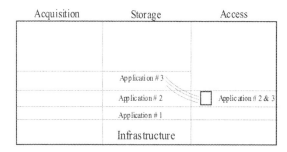

Figure 5-19. Data-only applications

one which provides the user with an entirely new access mechanism, but which makes use of data already collected and stored by a previously completed application.

At first glance, the reader might suspect that the access-only application is a violation of our first rule about applications, where we said that each had to be contiguous. In fact, the access-only application does not violate this rule, because it consists of an access, storage and acquisition component, just like any other application. Just because it is making use of previously developed components does not make it incongruous.

4) Data-Only Applications

In the same way that we can develop a new application by leveraging

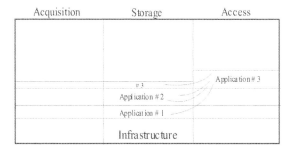

Figure 5-20. A hybrid application

previously developed storage components, so can we leverage previously developed access components. There is no reason that we could not add the functionality of a new value proposition to an existing system by simply creating some new sets of stored data and allowing previously developed access mechanisms to use it.

As in the previous example, our contiguity rule is satisfied since our application is complete.

5) Hybrid Approaches

What is most likely to happen, especially after the warehouse has had a chance to get started, is that hybrid combinations of these approaches will begin to make a lot of sense. For example, Figure 5-20 shows a new application that makes use of a lot of previously collected data, a little bit of new data, and uses an entirely new access mechanism.

CHAPTER 6

APPLICATION DEVELOPMENT AND THE DATA DISCIPLINES

No matter how you look at it, a data warehouse is first, foremost and always only as good as the data that it holds. It should come as no surprise then, that the development of an effective data warehouse depends on the existence of an extensive and well thought out discipline for approaching how that warehouse should be laid out.

As we have cited previously, the systems development life cycle has failed to meet the needs of modern systems developers in the vast majority of cases. In its place, we propose the following data warehouse development life cycle.

Before we actually begin to unveil this approach, let us begin by explaining that it is not our intention to propose the following discipline as the solution to the problems of systems development in all situations. Far from it. Different kinds of systems require different approaches. Indeed, it is the failure to recognize this which dooms the "one size fits all" systems development life cycle to failure. No, our approach is a very specific one and should be utilized only in those situations where our assumptions and our specified preconditions have been met. It would be disastrous to try to make use of this approach to assist in the design of OLTP, object oriented or client/server applications.

THE APPROACH

The process we specify for development takes into account the idiosyncrasies and diverse requirements that each of the three components (acquisition, storage and access) of the warehouse demand. Each of these components involves a different set of variables, different kinds of objectives and require a different kind of approach. Our development approach also recognizes that the key to the development of a successful warehouse is the integration of the data across these three components. The process therefore involves that we traverse these three domains many times.

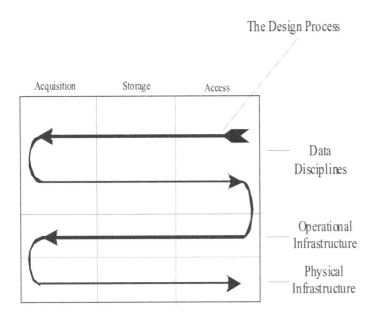

Figure 6-1. Design traverses and coordinates the activities of all three components.

At the same time, it is critical that whatever solution we develop be integrated across the different layers of the system (data disciplines and infrastructure); therefore, the approach also demands that we start at the top layer (data identification) and drive downward through the data discipline, operational infrastructure and physical infrastructure process at the same time.

AN ITERATIVE PROCESS

While it would be possible to develop a complete data warehouse system by going through this series of steps only one time, the realities of business environments demand that we actually go through them at least twice. The first time will be during the development of the overall warehouse strategy and plan. During the execution of these phases it will be critical that we gather fundamental information from each of the data disciplines, operational infrastructure and physical infrastructure layers. During this pass through the methodology it will be our objective to identify key requirements, validate key assumptions and develop preliminary estimates regarding the size, capacity, capabilities and viability of the systems being proposed. The end product of this first pass will be estimates for the cost and development time for each of the value propositions and a validation of the feasibility of the solution proposed.

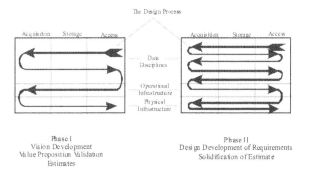

Figure 6-2. The data warehouse development process

After the solidification and approval of these value propositions, the warehouse development team will use the intelligence and documentation created by the project development team, and use that as the starting point for a second, more detailed pass through the same process.

APPLICATION DEVELOPMENT AND THE DATA DISCIPLINES

Given this basic understanding of how the data disciplines fit into the overall framework of systems development, we are ready to begin a more formal definition of each of the steps. We have identified the process of application development as consisting of the following steps:

1. Solution Development, a more detailed version of the vision development process
2. Validation and Estimation of the Solution
3. Development of a plan of execution
4. Actual system development

In order to perform these steps effectively, we will need to make use of the following series of data disciplines. These include:

1. Solution Development
2. Data Identification - Identification of the data that the solution will require
3. Data Sourcing - Identification of the Legacy or external sources of data that will meet the requirements specified
4. Data Integrity Validation - Validation of the sources of data, guaranteeing that the sources will actually be able to provide the information required and that the data is in a usable form
5. Data Synchronization - Determination of how the different sources of data will be synchronized with each other
6. Back Flush Development - Determination of how corrected and cleansed data is going to be fed back into the Legacy systems
7. Data Storage Architecture Development - Determination of the nature and identity of each of the transitory data stores that will hold the data as it moves from acquisition area to the user terminal.
8. Data Transformation Mapping - Determination of the specific transformations the data will go through as it moves from Legacy system to user terminal

9. Data Metrics Gathering - Collection of quantitative information about the data and its transformation, its access and any timing issues involved.

10. Data Modeling - Development of a formal data model for the data

11. Data Base Design - Development of a physical design for the database

As we proceed through the definitions of each, it will be important for the reader to keep in mind several things

First, that each phase of the process must be executed in the order proscribed if the process is to be managed efficiently, and the complexity and potential for design chaos is to be reduced. This technique has been developed based on feedback received from hundreds of data analysts and data warehouse developers who have found that as difficult as it may be sometimes, this sequence makes the most sense.

Second, that judgment must be exercised in the application of these phases. In some cases it will be possible to "shortcut" a phase because the information required is easily accessible and trivial. However, there are certain key deliverables each phase describes and these deliverables must be at hand if the rest of the process is to work.

The imposition of this kind of discipline in this order may cause the experienced practitioner to be concerned or even perplexed. On the one hand, the logical order dictated seems to make perfect sense from a logical perspective.

On the other hand, the traditional approach to data modeling and design would seem to dictate that this approach is somehow out of synch. Our response to this is that all of the components of successful data modeling and data base design effort, as they are traditionally described, are included within our definition of a data discipline. The difference is in the order in which steps are carried out, and the emphasis upon which we place our energies.

The traditional modeling and design approach emphasizes logical data modeling and the development of good, third normal form, entity-relationship based databases, which meet a set of theoretical criteria for soundness. The emphasis of our approach is upon the tactical delivery of the information that is needed. In reality, as any

DBA or Data Analyst will tell you, the developers of every system end up having to make these kinds of compromises during the late stages of systems development anyway. No matter how hard the data modeler and DBA try, the reality of system performance requirements will demand that this tactical, impending delivery directive will take precedence over theoretical considerations at some point. All we have done with our approach is recognize the reality of the situation and build it into our approach.

ROLES AND RESPONSIBILITIES

Another source of confusion during the execution of any kind of vision development or analysis and design process is the lack of understanding on people's parts about who should be responsible for what part of the process. During our chapter about the immutable laws of data processing, we stated that there were two things which contributed the most to the breakdown of the SDLC and the failure of projects.

The first was complexity overload, attempts made by people to try to take on more complexity than they could possible work through. Our solution to that problem was to break the system down into a collection of discrete value propositions and to form our approach around the minimization of scope based upon those propositions.

The second was the problem of responsibility ambiguity, one that arises when no one is exactly sure of who is responsible for what. In the previous chapter on value proposition development we outlined the different areas of decision-making that would be required to develop and deliver those visions, and we considered the appropriate allocation of responsibility to the management, operational and systems areas. At this point we will undertake to provide the same kind of allocation of responsibilities for the data disciplines. The only significant difference between the participation profiles of the three groups in the vision development phase, versus their participation in the execution of the data disciplines and infrastructure development, is that the role of management is greatly reduced. By the time we get to these phases, the vision and direction set by management should be clear and the operational and systems people should be able to carry the process out.

Although we have yet to provide a lot of detail about each of these steps, we will begin by identifying the level that each participating area will play in the process. We will specify three types of participants in the data discipline development process: Operational personnel (the user of the system), Legacy systems support personnel (the technical and business people responsible for the maintenance and execution of Legacy and external data sources) and the systems development personnel (the people driving the warehouse development process).

APPLICABILITY TO THE COMPONENTS OF THE WAREHOUSE

Step	Description	Legacy Support	Operational	Developers
1	Solution development		Heavy	Medium
2	Data identification		Medium	Heavy
3	Data sourcing	Heavy	Light	Medium
4	Data integrity validation	Light	Medium	Heavy
5	Data synchronization	Light		Heavy
6	Backflush development	Heavy		Heavy
7	Data storage architecture development			Heavy
8	Data transformation mapping			Heavy
9	Data metrics gathering	Light	Light	Heavy
10	Data modeling		Light	Heavy
11	Database design			Heavy

Table 6-1

Another perspective that can help us understand what the objectives of each of these phases will be, is to have a clear understanding of how each step applies to each of the components of the warehouse. Table 6-2 provides us with this perspective.

Step	Description	Acquisition	Storage	Access
1	Solution development			Heavy
2	Data identification			Heavy
3	Data sourcing	Heavy		Light
4	Data integrity validation	Heavy		Light
5	Data synchronization	Heavy	Light	
6	Backflush development	Heavy		
7	Data storage architecture development		Heavy	Medium
8	Data transformation mapping	Heavy	Heavy	Heavy
9	Data metrics gathering	Heavy	Heavy	Heavy
10	Data modeling		Heavy	
11	Database design		Heavy	

Table 6-2

SKILLS AND EXPERIENCE LEVELS

Of course, the levels of commitment considered in Table 6-1 assume a certain caliber of person or people involved throughout the process. Our assumptions regarding the type of person providing support in each area are as follows:

Operational Personnel - Familiar with the day-to-day operations in the business area for which the value proposition is being developed. This includes the related procedures, work flows, existing computer systems and interfaces with other operational areas.

Legacy and External Data Source Support Personnel - Familiarity with the targeted source systems. Specific knowledge about the systems themselves, their operational business area interfaces and computer system characteristics. Personnel familiar with both the business functionality and the inner workings of the computer systems. Access to the database and file layout information and the ability to quickly extract data from those systems, analyze it and explain it.

Systems Development Personnel - The skills required to fill those role are very diverse. It is not uncommon to have a team of specialists work within this area. Specialized skill requirements include:

Data Analysis

Business Analysis

Data Modeling

Data Base Design

Computer Systems Analysis and Modeling

It will be our assumption that the people assigned to work on this project will have the previously defined skill sets with a concomitant level of experience to make their assignment reasonable.

THE FIRST PASS THROUGH THE PHASES

We said that the process of bringing the design of a specific warehousing to completion was going to require that we go through these phases at least twice. The first pass will be very cursory in nature and will occur during the vision development process. During this pass the objective will be to identify all the critical success factors and resolve all of the critical unknowns. The deliverables from this pass

will include cost estimates, time estimates, resource estimates for the infrastructure, preliminary hardware and software selections, and high level metrics about the performance characteristics of the system.

The second time through the process occurs after the project has been approved. We go through the phases this time in order to conduct what has traditionally been described as the Analysis and Design Phases. During this pass our objective will be to generate a complete set of specifications for the construction of the warehouse application.

We will carry the reader through a set of the fundamental steps and issues involved for each pass.

The Solution Development Phase

The first time we go through the solution development phase, all we have is a general idea about what it is people think the system can accomplish. It will be our role at that time to turn this soft concept into some kind of tangible solution. After identifying what the business people would like to accomplish, it will be our job to make this vision a little more tangible. The steps to follow during the first pass through this phase are:

1. Define how the system will work in business terms

2. Define what the system will actually do

3. Define how this system is going to change/improve the way things are done today

The participation of experts in whatever business area the analyst happens to be working in can be extremely helpful during this phase of the process. It is at this time that people need to seriously consider exactly what it is they want to accomplish and how things can be done better and more intelligently.

The solution development process is a very creative, very spontaneous endeavor. It is often helpful during this phase to consider how other companies are solving these same kinds of problems. It can also be helpful to get an idea of the capabilities that different kinds of data mining products can provide. When completed, the team should have a pretty good idea about what they would like the system to deliver and how.

After this has been accomplished, we can then begin to develop the more specific systems aspects. The second time we go through the solution development phase, we develop a high level model of what the system will do. This is usually documented in the form of a series of screen layouts. At this point, we need to decide whether the system is going to be developed based on a "custom application" where a series of code is written specifically for the application, or if a package or software product can get the job done.

4. Turn the solution to the problem into a series of screens.

5. Determine if there are any existing applications or tools which can ease the delivery of this solution.

6. If such a tool exists, use it as your template.

After making the create vs. buy decision, you are ready to begin the process of data identification.

The Data Identification Process

The starting point for the definition of any kind of data warehousing initiative must be with the identification of the data the users want to see. No other approach makes any sense. Only when you know what people want to see at the end of the process, can you hope to be sure that the rest of the system is going to meet those demands. If you were to try to identify the source of a great amount of the confusion and chaos that typifies the failure of the vast majority of data warehousing initiatives today, you would find that disregard for this basic premise is at the source.

Provided that we have a good basic understanding of the screens that the system should have and the functions they are to perform, we can begin to identify the data that will drive the process. The steps we will follow include:

1. Define what each of the screens (or reports) is supposed to accomplish.
2. Define each of the critical data elements these screens must have.
3. Generate a list of data elements by screen and provide a brief definition of what each of these elements should contain.
4. Generate a list of candidate sources for each of these data elements.

The process of gathering this information can be formal or informal depending upon the size, scope and nature of the project being developed.

The first time through we will concentrate on simply establishing the correct number and types of screens, and identifying all of the critical data elements required.

Data Sourcing

During the first two phases of this process we worked extensively with the operational users of the system. At this point, we are ready to approach the Legacy and external data sources and begin the process of finding the data required.

During the data sourcing step we will take the list of proposed sources for the data required and validate that it can, in fact, be found where we think it might.

This process is usually more difficult than it seems. The key phrase for a person participating in this process is the motto for the state of Missouri: "Show Me." No matter how adamant people are about whether the data you are looking for can be found or not, the analyst must insist that samples of it be extracted from the Legacy systems where they should be located. These extractions need not be dumps of the entire data base or file, but they must include some kind of random sampling.

The Sourcing process therefore has the following steps:

1. Identify the candidate source of data (from previous step).
2. Validate with the Legacy/external data source expert that the candidate source is both, (a) likely to hold the information, and (b) the best potential source of it.

Verifying this second criteria is actually more difficult than the first. When we begin looking for the sources of data for our system it is possible that the one identified is not the original source of the information, but is, in fact, a copy from someplace else. Wherever possible, we want to load our warehouse with sources of information, not copies.

In those situations where better and more accurate sources of the information can be found in other systems, the analyst must play detective and backtrack the data to its original source.

Luckily, many systems have developed "Master Files" which contain the "real" values you are looking for.

After the source has been validated as the best one, the analyst then asks to see two things:

3. Copies of the data layouts for the targeted source files
4. Sample extractions of data from each of the files

It then falls to the analyst to verify that the data specified by the users is actually the data that is found in the file.

Data Integrity Validation

After the data has been properly sourced, the analyst must begin the process of validating its integrity. There are several kinds of integrity we must be concerned with. They fall under the general categories of identity integrity and population integrity .

The steps involved in the process are:

1. Identify the sources of identity integrity violation.
2. Identify the sources of population integrity violation.
3. Develop the approach to be used to rectify these violations.
4. Identify the programs and storage files necessary to execute.

Identity Integrity

We use the term identity integrity to describe whether or not the data that has been sourced actually describes the information the user wants. While in most cases everyone will concur with the gross meaning of a term, the more subtle meaning of the term may cause it to be something other than what the user intended.

For example, during the development of a large data warehouse for a manufacturing concern, we became embroiled in what I will call "The Great Sales Volume Debate." It seems that the marketing group had asked for a field called "Sales Volume" to appear on their reports. We traced the field back to the Legacy which was supposed to hold the "Sales Volume" number and found, much to the chagrin of the users, that the sales volume being reported was the real volume of sales for each product, but was adjusted for returns and was stated in terms of retail prices, not in terms of the discounted dollars actually collected from high volume customers. This caused the number "Sales Volume" to be greatly skewed and made their statistical analysis program useless. They needed unadjusted, fully discounted volume numbers, not the adjusted numbers they were getting.

We were eventually able to develop the means to get the users the numbers they needed, but it was a painful and time intensive process and one that no one had included in the project plan.

There are, in fact, many ways that the identity of the data in the source systems can turn out to be inaccurate or inappropriate for the users of the system. It is the job of the analyst, during the integrity validation phase, to identify those problems and rectify them.

Population Integrity

The second kind of problem occurs, not because the data is inappropriate to the user's needs, but because the way it is stored is not always up to standards. Oftentimes, only a small percentage of the data stored in a Legacy system is accurate or stored correctly. As Legacy systems get larger and more complex, they begin to play more and more tricks with the stored data. Problems with the population of the source file can take many forms. The two biggest are format problems and incomplete sets.

Data Format Problems

In the most blatant cases of polluted data, the information in the source file is not stored in the kind of field the system can read. In the perfect world, every field of a file or database will be defined as having a certain data type (character, numeric, binary etc.) and a certain size (two bytes, ten bytes etc.). Each of these storage areas is like a pre-defined "bucket" into which that data element can be stored. Unfortunately, ingenious programmers have often found ways to put the wrong kinds of data into the wrong places. So, lo and behold, when you dump out your customer file and look at the phone numbers, you may find that your list of numeric phone number values may be peppered with little areas of text (messages like "no phone number," or "XXXXX," or even a long list of little smiley faces that you cannot read).

Purge Processing and Data Reformatting Programs

There are only two things you can do when the data file identified as a source of information has data elements that are unusable. You can either fix the errant fields or eliminate the records from your population.

The first solution, the repair of the data, will require that special data reformatting programs be written to identify the bad records and take whatever corrective action is required. These corrective actions might include looking up the accurate values in another file, substituting a default value or deriving the correct value based upon other values that are available.

The second solution, that of eliminating the errant data, requires the creation of what are known as purge programs. Purge programs scan through the available data file and simply delete those records which do not meet the standards established.

Incomplete Sets of Data

The other big problem you can have with a given population of data, is that it may not hold the entire set of information for which you are looking. For example, you may have identified a Customer Master File which holds 1 million records. You would, therefore, assume that your company has about one million customers.

When you dump out the file, however, you find that only 500,000 of the records are actually complete. The other 500,000 records hold old, outdated, incomplete sets of information. As in the other cases, it is the job of the analyst to discover these data population deficiencies and develop a means for reconciling them with the needs of the new system.

Merge Programs

Incomplete sets of data present an entirely different kind of problem. Usually, the solution to these problems is to create Merge programs. Merge programs identify several different source files, each of which holds a different part of the entire population that you want to include in the warehouse file. The merge programs read in the records from all of these sources and merge them into one cohesive, complete file.

During integrity validation, it is the job of the analyst to identify exactly how bad or good the real data is, and develop a plan for reconciling the problems that are found.

Data Synchronization

After we have developed solutions to any integrity or population anomaly problems within the source file, our next challenge will be to examine the problems associated with synchronization.

Not only must the data in each file be accurate and have the integrity we require, but we also need to be concerned with synchronizing that information with the other disparate sources of information that it will need to work with. There are two major categories of synchronization issues, referential integrity issues and timing issues.

The steps involved in the data synchronization process include:

1. Identify sources of referential integrity violation.
2. Identify the sources of timing issues.
3. Develop an approach to rectify the violations and issues.
4. Identify the programs and storage files required to execute the solution.

Referential Integrity

The term Referential Integrity is used to describe the integrity of a given data element in its relationship to other data elements. There are three types of referential integrity with which we will be concerned: Utilization integrity, population standardization and inter-file integrity.

Utilization Integrity

A lack of utilization integrity occurs when the data being provided to the user is not in a form they can use. For example, the user may need to have all numeric values shown in the standard dollars and sense two decimal places format, but the data provided may be stored rounded off to the nearest dollar. In this case, some kind of conversion or re-computation of values will need to take place to make the numbers usable.

Population Standardization

The second condition that may occur might be that the values stored in a given field may be accurate, but they may be stored in several different forms. This is what is known as the classical "code table problem." For example, the field definition for the "State" where a customer is located may be stored in many forms. The state of New York, for example, might be stored as NY , N.Y., New York and New Yrk. To be usable, we need to standardize this field so that New York always appears the same way all the time.

Referential Integrity - Inter-File Standardization

After we have resolved the utility and population referential integrity issues, we must then check that the standardization applied to the information in one file, is applied equivalently to the corresponding fields found in other files that this file will be related to.

For instance, we may have standardized the State field in our customer file, but how is State stored in the Sales History file with which we are going to need to relate at a later point. The scope of our referential integrity concerns reaches across the entire collection of data sources that we intend to include.

Solutions to Referential Integrity Problems

Unfortunately, the process of resolving referential integrity problems is a painstaking one. In each case we will need to employ a combination of data reformatting programs and merge/purge programs before we can be sure that all of the data is going to be usable.

Synchronization Issues

Not only must we address the referential integrity of the source data, we must also be concerned about all of the other ways that the data being brought into the warehouse is going to synchronize with all of the other data. We have isolated the three key areas of synchronization to be involved with as Key, Timing and Historical Synchronization.

Key Synchronization

Whenever we deal with the merging of multiple files from different sources of data, we will inadvertently run into problems with keys. Keys are the technique that computer systems use to uniquely identify the individuals within a population of data, and it is the keys that drive these systems.

For example, a customer information system will inadvertently have a key called Customer_Id or Customer_Number, which uniquely identifies each customer. For each major population of data within a system (customers, products, distributors, employees etc.) you will find at least one key, if not a vast assortment of conflicting ones, to identify them.

There are actually three kinds of problems you will run into with keys: redundant-identification, hierarchy, and cross-system alignment.

Redundant Identification

The first kind of problem occurs when the users of a system abuse the key structure and use that key to identify the same thing over and over again. For example, a customer system may have two, three, or a dozens keys, each pointing to the exact same company.

This problem occurs when different people are allowed to make use of the system and create company records at different times. In these situations, different groups of users will think that different company records are the only ones applicable to the company in question. When we are asked to make copies of these records and pull them into our warehouse, we are going to have to figure out a way to re-combine all of these company records into one that is consolidated, and then provide it with one key to identify it.

Hierarchy

The second kind of problem occurs when systems need to keep track of hierarchies of things. Hierarchies occur in just about every kind of system. You can have hierarchies of customers (Parent Corporation, Subsidiaries, Branch Offices etc.), hierarchies of products (Groceries, Produce, Meat, Dairy) or hierarchies of people (Corporation, Division, Department etc.).

The problem with hierarchies is that it is very difficult to develop a scheme for keying them that works well in many situations. Usually, the Legacy systems involved will have a less than adequate structure in place, with a resulting amount of confusion about how exactly the data should be identified. These contradictory and confusing key structures usually occur because different people would like to see the data identified according to different criteria at different times.

For example, a hierarchy of corporations will have to be changed at least quarterly, if it is going to reflect the changes in corporate structures prevalent in today's business environment. In the same manner, human resource hierarchies, which reflect the almost daily shifting of the corporation's internal structure, are a common source of concern. Inevitably, wherever you have a hierarchy, you have the problems associated with the constant need to shift that hierarchy around, and it is the key structure that usually defines this arrangement.

Cross-system Alignment

The final, and biggest challenge to the person attempting to develop a warehouse and synchronize the data will be to reconcile those situations where different systems make use of different keying schemes.

One system may identify customers with a seven digit number. Another may utilize a code with eight characters and two numbers. Somehow, we must figure out how to get all the information going into the system to hold the same keys, while at the same time making it possible to refer back to the sources of data when required.

Solving Key Synchronization Problems

The development of key synchronization solutions usually requires that some pretty extensive work be done, and the solutions are never eloquent. There are two principle approaches we can take. We can drive the system off of one of the sets of keys provided and superimposing that key upon the others, or create an entirely new key structure unique to the warehouse.

Declaring a System to be the Owner of the Keys

One way we can force the resolution of incompatible keys is to figure out which of the existing systems has the best key structure for what we are trying to do, and impose it on the other systems. This approach only works well when the base system is clearly the biggest and most appropriate. In these situations we can then use it as the core of a series of merge/purge/data reformatting steps which transpose the new key over the old, while turning the existing key into an ancillary, informational field.

The Start Over Approach

An even uglier solution is developed when it is clear that none of the Legacy systems key structures is appropriate. In those cases, we create a brand new key structure and impose it on all of the Legacy systems data.

Reference-able Conversion

Whereas the cleaning up of data fields with inappropriate or inaccurate information does not require that we allow for the ability of users to get back to what the original value of the field was, we do not have that same luxury where keys are concerned. It is critical that, whenever we re-key data, we provide the means for users to go back to the Legacy systems and see where the tagged values originated. Somehow, the converted data must be made reference-able. This is usually accomplished using one of two techniques:

One approach is to store the old key and a tag indicating which source system the data came from on the record that goes into the warehouse. That way the user knows what kind of data he or she is looking at. The other thing that can be done is to create cross reference tables which point new warehouse keys back to the old source systems keys to which they refer. Depending on the requirements of the system, one or both of these techniques may be employed.

Timing and History Issues

The final type of synchronization we must worry about has to do with the timeliness of the data being transferred. We must keep in mind that the data within the warehouse is coming from many different sources, and each of those sources his its own timing characteristics. In fact there are several types of timing issues of which we must be aware.

The series of steps that we will go through in order to analyze and resolve time issues will be the following:

1. Determine the collection rate of each source system.
2. Identify any processing lags that may effect the timeliness of the information.
3. Determine the warehouse refresh rate and technique that will meet the needs of the users while recognizing the realities of the data sources.
4. Identify the programs and storage files necessary to execute the synchronization.

Collection Rate - Core Transactions

The first thing we need to understand about the data being fed into the warehouse, is the rate at which the information is collected. Many Legacy systems collect information on a real time basis. In other words, as soon as something happens, the system is changed to reflect it. This kind of collection rate is the most common in core Legacy systems like the Sales, Accounting and Warehouse Control.

Unfortunately, even the best system in the world cannot capture every event exactly as it happens. For example, systems that keep track of sales by mail will usually only update the sales information once a day after all of the incoming mail for the day has had a chance to accumulate.

Other times, the core Legacy systems that track transactions will be dependent on other systems for the information, and these systems may make use of a regularly scheduled upload program to update the core system on a periodic basis. For example, at one company where we were working, the phone sales system kept track of all of the phone sales for a given day, but that information was only uploaded to the main systems on a nightly refresh cycle.

In other cases, the information required may come from an external source, like mailing lists, Dun and Bradstreet financial reports, etc.

In these cases, the data available could be days, weeks or even months old before it can be accessed.

Processing and Derived Data

Another whole class of data timing problems can be found when we start trying to make use of data that is derived or calculated on a periodic basis. The classical case for this kind of data is the typical production control system and the generation of WIP (Work In Progress) files.

In a typical manufacturing process there are hundreds or even thousands of different variables that must be taken into account in order to keep track of the process and make sure that everything is running efficiently. The amount of computing that must occur to develop these evaluations requires an incredible amount of computer power, and also requires that everything in the plant be synchronized to a particular point in time.

The vast majority of manufacturing organizations today simply cannot afford to synch up and re-calculate all of these variables on a real time basis. Instead, they develop a WIP file which notes where everything was at the last synch point. This is usually done on a weekly basis, but some organizations have gotten it down to a daily cycle. If the users of the warehouse require any of this kind of WIP information, then they will to have to deal with this time lag.

Warehouse Refresh Rate

After we have developed an understanding of the timing characteristics of each of the data sources, the next challenge will be to figure out at what rate and by what method the warehouse will be refreshed.

Warehouse Refresh Techniques

There are actually three fundamental ways that the warehouse can be refreshed, but in practice, a hybrid combination of these are often used.

The Periodic Complete Refresh

The easiest and most common way to refresh warehouse data is to simply get rid of the copy of the data that currently resides in the warehouse, and completely replace it with a new copy. This technique greatly simplifies the workings of the warehouse and allows everyone to have an immediate and good understanding of exactly what they are looking at.

In order to figure out how timely the information in a particular table is, the user need only find out the last time it was refreshed from the source.

Problems with Complete Refresh

The complete refresh solution may be easy, but it is anything but inexpensive. The fact of the matter is that it takes a lot of time, and a lot of computing power to dump and reload database files and few systems can afford the luxury of waiting that long, or using all of that computer power just because the approach is easy.

Very, very large data warehouses can include tables which hold hundreds of millions or even billions of records, and it can take a very long time to load all of that data up. Typical load times for very large databases are measured in days and weeks, not hours. Few organizations can afford the expense or the time delay that these approaches entail.

The Store andForward / Update in Place Technique

To help ameliorate some of the problems imposed by the complete refresh approach, many warehouses are built to make use of the store and forward/ update in place approach.

To utilize this approach, the warehouse developers devise some kind of technique which will allow them to keep track of the changes that occur to the Legacy system and store information about those changes in a hold file. After these changes have been accumulated for a specified amount of time (hourly, daily, weekly etc.), the file is then used to drive an update in place program, which goes through the warehouse and brings the records back up to date.

There are two techniques that can be used to create these store and forward files. The first technique involves making changes to the Legacy system that updates the data in question. All programs making changes to the desired data are identified, and each of them is modified so that whenever they make changes to the Legacy system they send a copy of those changes to the store and forward hold file.

The second technique for the creation of store and forward files is for the managers of the acquisition process to keep a copy of the Legacy system data after it has been loaded the first time. When it comes time to create the new store and forward file, a new copy of the Legacy system data is made. The copy of the new Legacy file is run through a program which compares it, record by record with the old Legacy file. Any changed records are then copied to the store and forward file for processing.

The store and forward approach allows the users of the warehouse to have the best of both worlds, large volumes of data available on demand, with a periodic update to that data to keep it timely.

Real Time

In some situations even the store and forward approach to warehousing is not good enough. Sometimes people require that the warehouse be immediately updated to reflect changes in the core systems. In these cases, real time, update in place programs are used to coordinate source and warehouse files.

The Value of Time

Timing issues are critical to the success of any data warehousing endeavor. But it is almost critical that the designers of the warehouse and that the users of the system understand that the timeliness of data comes with a cost. In general, the more up to date you need the warehouse to be, the more expensive it will be to build and maintain. When going through the process of understanding each of the value propositions which drive our warehouse development process, it will be critical that the cost of the timeliness of the data be included in our value assumptions and cost estimates.

Back Flush Development

After we have figured out all of the different ways that the data is going to have to be transformed, modified, merged, purged and retrofitted in order to be placed into a form that is suitable for the warehouse to use, we are ready to take a step back and figure out what kinds of backflush mechanisms might be required. The steps in the process are straightforward:

1. Identify Back Flush Requirements.
2. Gather Requirements from Legacy systems managers.
3. Develop Back Flush Mechanisms.
4. Identify programs and data storage files necessary to execute the back flush.

Identifying Back Flush Requirements

The only way to identify whether or not back flush capabilities are going to be required is to ask the people in charge of the Legacy systems whether they want it or not. If they do not, then there is no problem. If they do, then it will be the responsibility of those areas to specify exactly what kind of data they want fed back into the Legacy systems and to specify the method in which this will be accomplished.

Developing Back Flush Mechanisms

In the vast majority of cases, the back flush requirement specification will simply be for the data acquisition process to export an additional, specially formatted file which the Legacy system can then read in to upgrade its current information.

When determining how this mechanism will work, the designer must be sensitive to all the same issues that were important when considering data for warehouse loading. Timing, synchronization, sanitation, keys... all of these issues will be as important to the Legacy system as they are to the warehouse.

Data Storage Architecture Development

After we have been provided with all this information, we are ready to begin the process of figuring out how the warehouse storage area will look, and how the data will move from the acquisitions component up to the user's terminal.

Up until now we have been referring to the data storage component of our warehouse as a big, open area into which a lot of different data tables are to be placed. At this point, we will get a little more explicit about what kinds of tables the storage area will hold.

Types of Storage Area Tables

In general, our storage area is going to hold several different types of tables. These include:

1. Core (Entity) Tables
2. Legacy System Reflection Tables
3. Code Tables
4. Bridge / Cross Reference Tables
5. Merge Tables
6. Subset Tables
7. Summarization Tables
8. History Tables

We will begin our discussion about the storage area by considering the purpose and nature of each of these table types.

Core (Entity) Tables

Core or entity tables are the foundation of any kind of database system. These are the tables which are developed based upon the execution of sound data modeling principles like normalization and entity-relationship modeling. A core table is usually defined as holding all of the information that pertains to an object of interest within our population of data. A core table in our warehouse environment will often be based upon a Master File in a Legacy system, or an Entity Object within our Entity-Relationship diagram.

A list of core tables that a system might hold would include:

- Customer Tables - having one record for each customer
- Parts Table - one record for each part number
- Vendor Table - one record for each company which provides the company with goods and services
- Employee Table - one record for each employee of the company, etc.

Role: Core tables are the heart and soul of the data warehouse. Most data warehouse processing will be totally dependent on the existence of a core table in order to help drive the processing.

Characteristics: Core tables are usually the source of the vast majority of the keying and hierarchy problems that systems developers face. They are also usually extremely large in nature, but users tend to rely upon them heavily for a lot of uses. This means that access must be easy to use and provide fast, sub-second response. This combination of characteristics make Core Tables the most difficult to design.

Location: Core tables are only found in the main storage area of the warehouse, never in a workspace area.

Legacy System Reflection Tables

Reflection tables are tables which hold copies of Legacy systems or externally provided source data. Their structure and layout usually mirror the structure and layout of the place the data came from.

Role: Reflection tables are often used to hold detail or history information for analytical or investigative purposes.

When used for investigative and reference purposes, it is important to the users that the data be stored and displayed in the same way that the Legacy systems display it. By providing the information in this way , it will be possible for users to investigate anomalies that are found in the system. This is often helpful in the resolution of problems with customers, in the investigation of problems and in the verification of findings.

When used to support analytical processing, the user requires that the data be in its original state so that the analytical tools that are being applied against it will have the best chance possible of working with the real values.

Characteristics: Reflection Tables tend to be extremely large, in fact they are usually larger than the corresponding core tables. Luckily, the nature of the processing against the tables is, for the most part, in terms of one record at a time. Therefore performance tends not to be a problem.

Location: Reflection tables are typically found in the main storage area of the warehouse.

Code Tables

A Code Table is a table which holds information about each of the codified values used within the system.

Role: Code Tables are provided to users in order to give them the ability to look up information about the different codes that may be found in other tables. For example, a State_Code_Table will hold all of the abbreviations for states (Il, NY, CA etc.) with translations into full state names (Illinois, New York, California etc.) along with any other important information about those states.

Characteristics: Code Tables tend to be small and easy to use. They typically present no processing or design challenges.

Location: Because of their importance, Code Tables are always found in the main storage area.

Bridge/Cross Reference Tables

Bridge and cross reference tables are tables which hold values which are used to relate two other tables to each other.

For example, our customer table has information about who the customer is and our product table will hold information about the different products that they may purchase. In order to relate these two we need a bridge table. In this case, a likely candidate for the bridge might be the sales table. The sales table will relate customers to the products they purchase.

Another good example of a bridge table occurs when building a system to educational environments. In this case we will have a core table for teachers and another for students. To see which teachers are associated with which students we need a Class table.

Role: To make it possible to relate two tables (especially core tables) to each other when they cannot do so on their own.

Characteristics: In general, bridge tables tend to be at least as large as the core tables they relate.

All of the performance concerns associated with core tables apply to the bridge tables as well.

Location: Bridge tables are usually found in the main storage area, but could also be located in the workspace areas under certain conditions.

Merge Tables

Sometimes, for the sake of efficiency or ease of access, we will combine collections of tables into merged supersets of the data that they hold.

Role: To make it easier for users to access combined collections of data from disparate tables.

Characteristics: Merge tables can be very large, or small, depending upon the reason they are developed.

Location: Merge tables are most frequently found in the workspace area.

Subset Tables

In order to work effectively or efficiently, a great many of the data mining tools require that the system cut down the amount of data that it needs to deal with. In these cases, copies of the subset of data that they need is copied down into a smaller table, specifically tailored to meet the demands of the product. Subsets are usually mode core tables, reflection tables and merge tables, but the other types can be subsetted as well.

Role: To greatly reduce the amount of data that the user or the data mining tools needs to deal with, making the process of investigation or analysis easier to do, or for performance reasons.

Characteristics: Subset Tables tend to be significantly smaller than most other types of tables on the system

Location: They are usually found in the workspace area, though main storage area subset tables might be developed.

Summarization (roll up) Tables

A final type of table for us to consider is the summarization or "roll up" table. These tables hold summarized or condensed versions of the data found within the other tables on the system. The design and construction of roll up tables could be the subject of a book in and of itself. What is critical to the development of these types of tables is a good understanding of the different keys and codes that will drive the user's access to the table, and the volumes of data that must be managed.

Role: Summarization tables allow users of the system to pre-summarize large volumes of information up into more usable, more informative forms. The technique is extremely common when making use of many kinds of analytical or holistic types of solutions.

Characteristics: These tables are dramatically smaller then the main tables from which they are derived, and they are much more rigidly defined.

Location: Summarization Tables are equally likely to appear in the main storage and the work areas.

Managing the Synchronization and Timing of Tables in Storage

While the synchronization and timing of data in the acquisition component of the warehouse is the most complex, there are just as many problems and concerns to consider when developing plans for managing the data within the storage component as well.

The problem is simplified by the more rigidly defined database environment, and the fact that a lot of these issues will already have been resolved before the data ever enters the warehouse, but we must still be concerned about the timing involved, especially in the utilization of summarization and subset types of tables.

History Tables

The last type of table to consider within our system is the History Table. History tables hold snapshots of how things looked in the past. There are actually several types of History Tables to be considered including:

1. Cumulative History
2. Snapshot Histories

and several ways that they can be developed:

1. Direct conversion from Legacy systems
2. Accumulation from the warehouse
3. Update from the warehouse

Cumulative history tables hold a record of all the different changes that have been made to each of the records of a given table. For the most part, our main storage area tables will contain the latest view of things being monitored and our cumulative history table will contain a collection of all the changes. In this kind of environment there will be sets of tables, the main, real table in the warehouse and a single history table which holds the changes.

Snapshot History tables freeze a table, or collection of tables as of a given point in time, and then make a copy of that table over to a completely new table where changes will no longer be made. With this approach, you will end up with many tables. The main, real table, and a collection of snapshot tables, each reflecting the status of the table at a different point in time. Snapshot tables are often developed on a yearly, monthly or sometimes weekly basis.

Role: History tables are created in order to provide users with the ability to do historical analysis of different characteristics of the business environment, or to allow for historical investigative work.

Characteristics: Historical tables, by their very nature are extremely large and infrequently accessed. The cumulative tables are often more difficult for users to work with, but the snapshot types of tables tend to take up vast amounts of disk storage.

Location: Historical tables are always found in the main storage area.

Steps in the Storage Architecture Development Process

The process that we go through in order to develop our architecture proceeds as follows:

1.   Identify all the different types and forms of data that users will require in order to meet the needs of their solution.

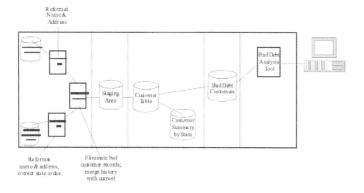

Figure 6-3. A simple transformation diagram

2.   Identify all the different sources of data and the staged files that will be available for loading into the warehouse.

3.   Identify each of the Core, Reflection, Code, Bridge and History tables that will be required to meet the user's requirements.

4.   Examine each of the types of access that they will make, and when performance or ease of access appears to be a constraining factor, intercede with the insertion of Summary, Subset and Merge tables.

The objective should be to try to do everything without the need of these intermediary types of tables.

5.   Identify and describe each of the programs or processes that will be required to load all of the tables and make these transformations.

Data Transformation Mapping

After we have figured out the basic layout for the storage area of the warehouse, we will be ready to take a step back and put together a diagram of how the entire data transformation process (the process of transforming external and Legacy data into usable warehouse data) will flow. The process of diagramming these transformations will be critical, because until we attempt to put it all together, there will be no way for us to know if we have taken everything into account. Data Transformation Mapping is as much a diagramming exercise as it is an analytical exercise.

A Data Transformation Map is made up of the following components:

1.   A list of all of the screens and data elements identified during the data identification phase

2.   A list of each of the Legacy and external source systems that have been identified as the legitimate sources of that data

3.   A list of each of the transitioning and sanitation steps that each Legacy system file will have to be put through

4.   A list of each of the transformation programs (reformat, merge, purge etc.) that the data will be subjected to. Included with this definition will be the specifications for each of the programs

5.   A list of each of the tables that the storage area will contain (including their names, types etc.)

6.   A diagram which illustrates this transformation process

Figure 6-3 shows a simple transformation diagram for a single source file.

Obviously, the actual collection of transformation diagrams will get to be a lot more complicated than this simple example, but it will be critical that we somehow capture this process in a graphical form so that everyone involved in the process will be able to understand exactly how their data fits into the big picture.

Data Metrics Gathering

Only after we have assembled our complete set of data transformation information and validated its accuracy will we be ready to seriously approach the process of gathering data metrics. Data metrics consists of all the information necessary for us to make decisions about the sizing and capacity requirements of the system itself. We are actually going to need to have three types of metrics in order to develop good and meaningful estimates.

1. User Metrics
2. Data Volumes
3. Access Rate and Processing Estimates

User Metrics

Included in our definition of user metrics is all that information about the users of the system that will be needed so we can make reasonable estimates about the performance requirements of the system.

The steps involved in the collection of user metrics include the following:

1. Identification of the Complete Population of Users (Number, Categories, Locations)
2. Identification of the Types of Access that Each Category of users will need (Simple, Complex, Work Area (Read// Write)
3. Identification of the data stores each category of user will be pursuing
4. Identification of the Rate at which each type of access against each data store will be executed

The process of collecting this information is probably most easily done at the same time the data identification process is going on.

Throughout the process it will be critical that the analyst assist the users in the development of this information. At each stage of the process, it is going to be necessary for users and analysts to estimate and project what they think the answer to many of the questions will be. Obviously, there is no way to know exactly what will happen until the system is completed. However, our intention in gathering this information is not to come up with a one hundred percent accurate answer, but only to provide us with some kind of rough estimate as to what the performance characteristics of the system.

Identification of the Complete Population of Users

It is amazing how many people will go through the process of computer systems development without even asking questions about how many users the system will ultimately have. Frequently, the answer will be "Who knows," or "It depends." Unfortunately, there is no way that we can come up with a good estimate of the effort and resources that will be required without some kind of best guess estimate of this most rudimentary form of information.

Clearly, it will not be enough for us to simply know how many people will be using the system. In addition to the raw number of user information, we will need to come up with an approach that allows us to categorize this population of users according to several variables.

At a minimum, we need to identify system users in terms of:

- How many different types of users there will be (The nature of this categorization depends upon the system, but it usually turns out to be a segregation by the user's job description (Marketing , Management, Clerical) or by the function (order taking, troubleshooting etc.)
- What the principle types of access will be, and how frequently the users of each type make use of that access.

Access can be typified by the product users will utilize to gain access to information (spreadsheets, query managers, multi-dimensional databases etc.) or by the type of query they will perform (simple, complex, read, write, update, delete).

Activity rates are usually measured in execution per minute, hour, day, week or month, depending upon the nature of the activity. For example, an extremely active system might be used every other minute, while a sophisticated trend analysis system might be utilized once a month.

Not only do we need to know the rate and nature of these transactions, but we would also like to have some idea about which tables in the warehouse these queries will be pursuing.

Where each of the users are going to be physically located. All in the same building? Different floors? Different states? Different countries?

The analyst responsible for collecting this information will usually find that the screen layouts developed during data identification will provide the best means of driving and clarifying the entire process.

Data Volume Estimates

After we have completed the collection of user metrics, we can turn to the development of estimates for the volumes of data that will be included in the system. This is usually a relatively straightforward and trivial exercise in mathematics.

Obtain Legacy System Metrics

We begin by gathering the volume statistics that are available about each of the Legacy system and externally obtained data sources that will feed into the data acquisition process.

We can then use this information to derive the volumes that we should experience with the rest of the tables in the systems.

Compute Acquisition Area Files Sizes

By combining the volume information available about each of the Legacy system files, and tracing it through the data transformation diagrams that we developed, it should be possible to derive the volume estimates for the rest of the data within the system.

As each Legacy system file proceeds through each of the cleansing, merging and purging steps, we can make assumptions about what percentages of data will be included or excluded from the final calculations. By the time we have traced these files through, we should have developed relatively accurate size estimates for every file and table within the system.

It is important in the development of these estimates that the analyst take the following into account.

1. The volume estimates for Legacy system data and all of the transitory files up to the staging area can estimated in a simple, straightforward manner, since it is our assumption that these will be flat files.

In other words the volume requirement for a file which is made up of 100 records where each record is 25 bytes long, would be 2500 bytes for the entire file (25 x 100 = 2500).

2. We should not include the volumes of Legacy system files in our final disk estimates since this disk area is not part of the warehouse system.

3. We must be sure to include the space required for all staging file areas. This includes the disk required to stage data that has been removed from the Legacy system before it enters the acquisition process, and the data staged, ready for loading into the warehouse itself.

4. Transitory disk space need not be estimated as the sum total of all the files in each data loading sequence. In most cases, these files will be short-lived (some may exist for only a few minutes.) However, it is critical that we estimate enough space to allow for problems to occur during the loading process. Usually , we choose a reasonable pad to be a percentage of the total disk space that could be required (fifty percent?)

5. Data base table volume estimates must be based on a number much higher than that required to house flat file data. We usually apply a multiplier to develop these estimates as well. This is because relational database tables us a lot more room to store data than flat files do. Relational database space estimates must include an adjustment for record overhead (each record needs room to store information about the data it holds), dead space (relational databases leave unused areas in-between records for performance and management reasons, indexes and overall system over-

head. Multipliers in the range from 2.5 to 10 have been used to effectively estimate this space. (i.e. take the amount of space that would be required to store the data in a flat file and multiply by multiplier to get the real volume estimate).

6. Do not forget to develop estimates for the work area data (calculate these the same way that you calculated normal database table volumes.

Usually, the volume estimates for the system are summarized in a table having the following column headings:

*   Table or File Name
*   Number of records
*   Size of an average record
*   Computed Volume Estimate

Estimating Computer Processing Requirements

Once we have collected the user and volume metrics information, we will be in a position to develop some rudimentary processing requirements.

Unfortunately, of all the estimation techniques that we will employ, this will be the least accurate and least scientific. The reason is that there is really no way to really derive the processing requirements that a group of users is going to put on the system without some pretty specific information about the kinds of queries they are going to be executing. In the world of relational databases, the most subtle changes in the SQL commands that you execute and the table designs that you settle upon, can result in drastic differences in the performance demands that will be put on the system. This fact leaves us with only two options for trying to develop these estimates, we can attempt to derive the system requirements based upon the performance of similar types of systems, or we can run benchmarks.

Benchmarking

Ultimately, when you are working with relational database technology, and you need to have a fairly accurate idea about what the performance is going to be like for a given collection of hardware, software, data and user requirements, the best thing to do is to build a benchmark system and test it.

A benchmark system is a database which simulates all the critical assumptions that you have about the environment (volumes of data, transaction types etc.) and allows you to establish for yourself what the real performance will be.

A benchmarking approach is expensive and time consuming, but if you have any serious concerns about the viability of the system you are putting together, it is a good idea to create one.

In a typical benchmarking situation , we identify the biggest and most complicated queries that the system will be expected to support. We then identify the source of data that will allow us to test those queries and load it into the database in its original form (we do not bother with the data preparation and sanitation steps).

After loading the high volumes of data required, we then run test queries against it. In the most severe cases, programs are written which simulate the execution of dozens or even hundreds of queries in succession in order to try to attain the same activity level as the one anticipated for the system.

When finished, the designers of the system will have a very good idea as to whether the proscribed hardware and software will get the job done or not.

Comparing Requirements Against other Systems

The other approach to developing these kinds of estimates is a lot less expensive but also less accurate. When taking this approach we identify the type of system load that the applications will put on the database and then try to find a similar system to compare it with. Sometimes the vendors of hardware or database software products can be of assistance in this exercise.

The fallback solution is to make use of published statistics like those provided by the TPC (Transaction Processing Council). This group sponsors well regulated, benchmark tests which are run against combinations of hardware and database software. The results of these tests are published in tables, which can then be used as references for people trying to derive the performance requirements of their own systems. The results of the TPC tests are available for a fee, are often given away by hardware or database software vendors, or can even be accessed via the Internet.

Unfortunately, the TPC has a severely limited set of tests that they run (TPC A, B, C and D) and are only run for the proscribed table layouts and volumes.

However, the reports can be very insightful and can help the designer zero in on clearly acceptable and unacceptable types of solutions.

See the appendix for more information on the TPC.

By the time we have finished collecting our metrics, we should be in a position to develop some reasonable estimates as to the types of hardware and software the system will require.

Data Modeling

After we have developed the rest of the detail about how the overall data warehouse is going to work, we are ready to begin the modeling step. The term data modeling has been used to refer to all kinds of different processes, but we will use the term to describe the process of mapping all of the data identified by the users and all the data provided by the Legacy systems, into one cohesive, comprehensive collection of data element groupings and definitions.

The data modeling process will go through the following steps:

1. Identify all the user defined data.
2. Identify all the Legacy system provided data.
3. Identify all the storage area tables that have been specified.
4. For each storage area table, identify and document each of the data elements that users will require and associate it with the appropriate table.
5. For each of user data elements, identify and document the source of information from among the acquisition area staged files.
6. Provide definitions for all elements

Data Modeling is an incredibly detailed process which usually involves many hours of research, reconciliation and documentation, but without it, the developers of the system leave themselves open to error, misunderstanding and without the most critical input necessary for the database design process.

At this point, many of the advocates of traditional data modeling may feel that our approach has slighted this critical aspect of systems design. We have certainly recommended that occur at a different point in time within the framework of overall systems development.

In response to them, all that can be said is that if you want to start off the process of data discipline with the development of logical data models, then go ahead. Their existence can only help everyone understand the entire process we have just laid out.

The other response to this concern is that it has been our intention from the outset to limit the scope of what people are looking at to those which are narrowly defined by a specific value proposition. It is our hope that the process of narrowing this scope has made it so that the need to get involved in sophisticated and complex data modeling exercises unnecessary.

The only problem with this super-imposition of traditional data modeling over our data warehouse development approach is that it may tend to de-focus people from the task at hand. It certainly has been known to frustrate, infuriate and confuse users who could care less about third normal forms and the correct placement of foreign keys.

Those types of discussion are best left to the technician's meeting rooms. The emphasis for the users, the warehouse developers and the Legacy systems experts needs to be focused on the task at hand, delivering important information to the users as quickly and efficiently as possible.

Database Design

The final step in the data discipline process is the design of the actual physical database itself. During this step, database administrators can be provided with all the information that has been collected up until this point and be asked to develop the actual physical layouts that each of the proposed tables will have, in addition to the development of indexing schemes, storage approaches, backup/ recovery procedures and the tuning of SQL access queries.

The process of database design will therefore involve the following steps:

1. Identification of all previously specified tables in the storage and work areas (see data modeling step).

2. Population of these tables with all data elements (see the data modeling step)

3. The development of a physical key structure for each table (Physical keys are not exactly the same thing as the logical keys we have been specifying up until now)

4. The development of an indexing structure for each table

5. The validation of these structures against the user access requirements

6. Development of physical database layouts (schemas or DDL)

7. Development of backup/recovery, history accumulation and other utility functions

When the process of database design is complete, the developers of the system will have everything they need to begin construction of the real data warehousing application.

SUMMARY AND OBSERVATIONS

To any person who has never been through the process of data warehouse development before, this chapter may seem a bit overwhelming. Indeed, the process of reconciling all of the issues involved with the data within the data warehouse is extremely complicated and detail oriented. To any person that has been through the process, these steps will undoubtedly seem familiar. No one has ever been through the process of developing a warehouse application without going through each and every one of these steps.

The biggest difference in the approach, as we have specified it here, is that we recognize these idiosyncrasies and complication from the outset and attempt to build our solution around them. This approach is in direct contradiction to the traditionally accepted beliefs about how the warehouse should be developed.

According to the traditional model, you begin by defining the data bases, then you try to apply those database designs to the user requirements, then you try to find all the data that was specified in a Legacy system source file.

In other words, the traditional approach takes a highly optimistic stand. It assumes, in general, that if you do a really good job on database design, then user requirements and Legacy system sources are going to simply fall into place. It also assumes that developers are going to be given enough time to do a good job.

Years and years of experience with hundreds of systems has proven otherwise.

Our approach is decidedly pessimistic. It assumes the worst. It assumes that users will be unclear about where data will come from. It assumes that the people in charge of the Legacy systems are not aware of what data their systems contain. It assumes that preliminary data models will be bad ones, not perfect ones. It also assumes that people are going to be in a hurry to develop these systems, and that everyone is going to be expected to put things together as quickly as possible, regardless of how well it is done, or how usable it will be in the future.

In other words, this approach assumes that you are going to have to develop a system with less than optimum resources, in less time than is reasonable in an environment that is far from stable or well understood. Our approach assumes an environment similar to most of the business environments we deal with today.

In the next chapter, we will continue with our diagnosis of the different layers of the warehouse application development process by proceeding to take the information we have gathered from the application of the data disciplines to the warehouse, and apply that information to help us solve the problems with the development of an operational and physical infrastructure.

CHAPTER 7

THE OPERATIONAL INFRASTRUCTURE

Now that we have a much better idea about how the warehouse is going to look and of the process that we will need to go through in order to put it together, we are now ready to explore, in the same level of detail, the infrastructure that will be required to support it.

The reader may recall that we said the infrastructure would be made up of two layers, an operational layer, which is concerned with the management and efficiency of the warehouses operation, and the physical infrastructure, which consists of all of the physical hardware and software components with which it will run.

THE OPERATIONAL INFRASTRUCTURE

In chapter five, we introduced the concept of the operational layer, and said that it included the feedback mechanisms, data disciplines, management software, procedures and support staff necessary to make the warehouse a viable entity.

In the previous chapter, we invested a significant amount of time developing an understanding of the data disciplines involved in warehouse construction and maintenance, and in the specification of feedback mechanisms.

We have yet to consider the other aspects of the operational infrastructure: staff, procedures and management software. We will delay our consideration of staffing until later.

Management Software

It should be quite clear from our discussion up until this point that a warehouse can be a very complicated thing. A typical warehouse can involve the coordination of the activities of dozens or even hundreds of people and hundreds or even thousands of source files. Experience has shown repeatedly, that if we do not approach the management of this extremely complex environment with the same kind of rigor and discipline that we have been applying to the rest of our process, all of our efforts will be wasted. It does no one any good to spend hundreds of hours and millions of dollars on the development of a data warehouse that is unmanageable, confusing and intransigent.

Management Challenges in the Warehouse Environment

When we approach the issue of managing the warehouse environment, we are faced with certain paradoxical challenges.

Stability vs. Flexibility

On the one hand, we want to make the environment easy to manage. Many times, after the initial burst of energy around the construction of the warehouse is through, the people responsible for managing it have found themselves left with a hodgepodge, disorganized, incredibly complex and highly unmanageable warehouse disaster area that they are then asked to contend with. If the warehouse it to be useful and cost effective, then it must be easy to control. On the other hand, one of the big benefits that the warehouse offers is the ability of the users and of application developers to change things quickly, and to develop new types of applications "on the fly."

Unfortunately, these objectives can be contradictory.

On the one hand, a stable management environment is most easily and most cost effectively attained by locking down the characteristics and functions that the warehouse can perform. By limiting the functionality and by limiting the flexibility you make management easier.

On the other hand, a flexible environment demands that we establish the ways and means to allow the hectic rate of business change to drive the rate at which the warehouse itself changes.

Ease of Use vs. Flexibility and Power

The second dichotomy that we need to be concerned about revolves around the user and the way in which the warehouse makes itself available.

On the one hand, the users of the system want the system to be easy to use. They want the complexities and idiosyncrasies of the warehouse to be transparent to them. All they want to do is "push a button" and let the warehouse do the rest.

On the other hand, users want the warehouse to be powerful and flexible. They do not want to have to make any commitments about what they might want the warehouse to be able to do at some future date. They want the ability to change the way that the warehouse works at any time, in order to get the new kinds of information that they want.

These objectives are also contradictory. You cannot make the system work at the push of a button, while at the same time making it possible to change what the button does on the spur of the moment. In both cases, some kind of compromises must be reached.

We therefore are faced with two related infrastructure management problems when we build a warehouse; issues about user interface, and issues about overall warehouse management.

User Interfaces and the Warehouse

Before we can address the issues about overall warehouse management, we must first decide upon what the interface with the users is going to look like.

The process of determining how complex or simple that interface will be depends upon a number of variables, including:

1. The nature of the users relationship with the data (the user's data utilization profile)

- the nature of the data mining tools that will be used
- the nature of any customized applications that will be used

2. The size and complexity of the overall environment
3. The availability and allocation of computer resources
4. The availability of support resources

The User's Data Utilization Profile

The first thing that we need to consider when exploring the nature of the user's relationship with the data is to establish a good idea of the user's data utilization profile. The data utilization profile gives us a good idea about exactly what kinds of things the user will be doing with the data. Armed with this information, we can begin to put together an idea of how best to meet that user's data access needs.

The Data Utilization Profile is a snapshot which provides us with all of the critical data access requirements that the user will have for the data that they are working with. This profile is made up of the following:

- Information about the different types of access that the user will perform
- Information about the timing requirements for that data

Types of User Access

In order to understand the different types of access that a user may need to have, we need to consider their activities from several perspectives:

- The type of activity performed
- The population of the data being accessed

Types of Access Activity

We can categorize the users type of access activity into the following:

- Simple Lookup
- Simple Search

- Relational Search
- CRUD
- Data Chains

Figure 7-1. Types of Access activity

In order to help us to illustrate each of these activity types, we will make use of a simple example. We will assume that the user has access to a population of customer information, information about sales, information about products and some demographic information about the areas in which those users reside.

The information in each of these tables can be related to the others through the relationships shown on the diagram (a line indicates a relationship). As illustrated by the diagram, demographics records are related to customers via their zip code, customers are related to sales via the customer number, and sales are related to products via the product number.

Simple Lookup

The easiest kind of access to manage in a relational database environment is the simple query. When executing a simple lookup query, the user simply asks for the information from one of the targeted tables making use of one of the keys to that table.

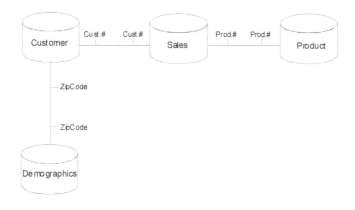

Figure 7-2. User activity types - Example tables

For example, we might want to look up a certain customer record, by name or by customer number. The relational data base will be able to do this in almost any situation without placing too much strain on the system or on the user.

Simple Look Up queries form the foundation of the vast majority of systems, especially of the holistic and operational varieties.

Simple Search

In a simple search operation, the user may not know the customer's name or number, but will know some subset of information about him or her. The search may ask to see all records for customers in the state of Texas, or it may ask to see all products that are the color "blue" and cost more than $25.

These access types also occur frequently within almost any warehouse environment and they can be used for simple information gathering (as in the case of the simple look up operations). The more important aspect of the simple search type operation however, is that it is often utilized as the first in a series or "chain" of operations that may be required for more complex processing.

Relational Search

The next example of access activity is the relational search. When doing a relational search, the user wants to know something about the relationship between things. For example, which customers have purchased more than $200.00 worth of products in the last three months, or what kinds of products (product table) to people (customer table) with large homes (information from the demographics table) purchase (sales table) most often.

In order to execute this kind of query, the keys of all four of these tables must be related to each other.

Relational searches can also be used to answer direct user questions and to serve as part of a processing chain.

CRUD

Our final type of simple access is the acronym CRUD. CRUD stands for Create, Read, Update and Delete and indicates that the user needs not only to find certain records, but to make changes to them as well.

CRUD access is the more difficult type of access for us to deal with because the imposition of Create, Update and Delete capabilities on our warehouse makes it extremely difficult to manage and maintain. We went through a lot of trouble to get the warehouse to be accurate, synchronized, sanitized and ready to use, but if we allow users to now make changes to the warehouse without the imposition of controls, then we will quickly breach the integrity of the warehouse and greatly curtail its usefulness.

We will have to impose an especially rigid set of constraints around this kind of access, and it should be limited whenever possible.

Data Chains

If we could simply categorize all of the different types of data access by the three previously mentioned approaches, our job of managing the data environment for users would be quite simple. Unfortunately, an increasingly large percentage of the operations that users require involve the development of what we call data chains.

Data chains are created when users need to perform a series of operations against a population of data in order to get it into a usable form. Data chains address a number of problems faced by the modern user of data.

In many situations, the user needs to perform so many different kinds of subset, search and relational operations against the data in order to get it into the form they want, that it would be impossible for them to perform all of those operations through the execution of one query.

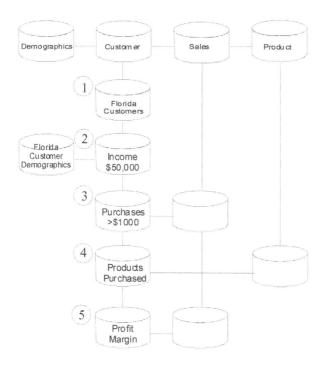

Figure 7-3. Data chains

For example, a user may want to:

1. Identify all customers in the state of Florida
2. Associate those records with the demographics for the state
3. Eliminate from the collection all customers who have already purchased over $1000 of product
4. Get a list of all of the products that the remaining customers have purchased
5. Take a look at the profit margin received on these purchases

While it might theoretically be possible to get this information through the execution of one large, complex query, it is unlikely that many users would be able to develop them, and more importantly, it is also unlikely that the system would be able to execute it in a reasonable amount of time.

By breaking down complicated problems like the one just presented, into more manageable steps, the user makes it possible to do highly sophisticated types of analysis in a relatively short amount of time.

Data Chains are the most common form of access in a typical warehouse environment, and they are often required in order to do a wide assortment of modern data analysis tasks. They are usually required for:

1. The pre-loading of data mining tools
2. The execution of complex analysis operations
3. The creation of subsets of data which the user can access for their own processing purposes or the preparation of reports

The Population of the Data Being Accessed

As if the amount of complexity that the different types of access present were not enough, there is another very important aspect of data accessing characteristics which must be taken into account. The thing to keep in mind at this point, is that the way we approach these different types of access is going to vary, depending upon the nature of the population of the data being accessed.

Volume vs. Performance Tradeoffs

One of the major characteristics of the data warehouse that we talked about in the first chapter of this book, was that data warehouses typically involve the housing and distribution of incredibly high volumes of data. In fact, it is the ability of modern data base technologies to work with these volumes that has contributed to the popularity and feasibility of data warehouse solutions. Unfortunately, the fact that a database can manage billions of records, does not mean that it is a good idea to do queries against such a large population.

As we move up our continuum of access types from simple lookup, to simple search to relational search to CRUD access, we also move down our continuum of database performance capabilities. In general, the bigger a database gets, the harder it is to get it to do the operations we have just discussed.

For example, if we were to create a data warehouse where the population of records was relatively low (populations of data in the hundreds, thousands or even hundreds of thousands of records), it would be possible to place a lot of the burden for processing on the database itself.

1) Any Lookup
2) Any Search
3) Any Relational Search
4) Any CRUD
5) Few Data Chains

Figure 7-4. Low volume population

In this kind of environment, we could design the system so that the vast majority of access requirements could be driven by good query writing. This would also eliminate the need for a lot of data chains; however, as the sizes of the populations of data increase, the flexibility of the system becomes curtailed. As the size increases we will need to cut back on the types of access that we allow directly against the database, and replace those accesses with a combination of data chains and accesses.

1) Restricted Lookup
2) Restricted Search
3) Restricted Relational Search
4) No CRUD
5) Heavy Use of Data Chains

Figure 7-5. High volume population

In effect, what we discover is that when the volumes of data get higher and as the complexity of the users' data manipulations tasks get greater, we end up using data chains in order to bring the volume of the population that the user is accessing down to a level where the system can manage the query activity and where the user can more easily understand what is going on. In effect, we break the access process down into a series of intermediary steps.

This realization comes as a mixed blessing. The good news is that as soon as you recognize this capability, and the fact that you can "trade" volume and complexity for data chains, you realize that:

1. There are really almost no physical restrictions on the size of your warehouse. The amount a database or a collection of databases can hold is the only limitation on how large your warehouse can become.

2. You have a built-in escape clause that you can use whenever performance or complexity begins to be a problem. When it begins to look like the volumes of data you are working on are going to place undue strain on your hardware or that the complexity of the processing is going to put a strain on the users, then you can simply back up and

re-approach the problem through the application of data chains.

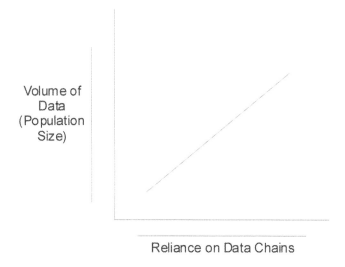

Reliance on Data Chains

Figure 7-6. The volume/data chain tradeoff

The bad news is that this built-in flexibility (the ability to switch from direct to data chain access) also makes the environment much less stable and less manageable and makes use of more disk storage and CPU resources.

It boils down to is that direct access requires very little operational infrastructure support while data chaining requires a lot.

Timing and Availability

The other thing that helps us understand the composition of each user's data utilization profile has to do with the timing and availability required of the data. There are actually three aspects of timing that we need be concerned with:

1. The timeliness of the data itself
2. The timing of the data preparation process
3. The timing of the actual delivery of data

The Timeliness of the Data

One of the most important things that users need to know about the data they are working with has to do with the timeliness of the data itself. In order to do a meaningful analysis of data, users need to know for what time period each piece of data is valid.

What we can easily forget when we begin looking at this process from the user's perspective, is that the data held within the warehouse is data that has been pulled from several sources and mixed together into a single, apparently homogenous collection. In reality, when we mix that data from a lot of different sources, we also tend to mix the time frames for which that data is valid.

For example, in a typical customer data warehouse, we could end up combining customer information from several source systems. In this case, the timeliness of the customer data could very well be different, depending upon where the customer data came from.

If our customer table holds information from a customer service system whose data is refreshed in the warehouse on a weekly basis, an accounts receivable system whose information is updated on a daily basis, and an externally provided credit rating source which is obtained and loaded on a monthly basis, we can end up with a pretty convoluted picture of that customer's status.

When a person gets a call from the customer complaining about something, and we check in the warehouse to figure out what the problem is, we could end up with three different pieces of information, each of which tells us something different about what is really going on.

The same kinds of timeliness issues are important for performing analytical work with the data. Statistical analysis, trending and forecasting are meaningful only when the people preparing the statistical models understand for which time frames the data applies. For example, a person performing trend analysis between bad debt over a three month period will get very poor results if they fail to realize that the most recent month's data failed to get loaded for some reason, and that they had in fact run this months analysis against last month's results.

Regularly Scheduled vs. on Demand

The second characteristic of data timing requirements has to do with how frequently or regularly users need to have access to data. In many cases, it can be worked out so that the warehouse managers can make the refresh or construction a regularly scheduled event. For example, we could promise to have the new sales and marketing data loaded by the fifth of every month.

Regularly scheduled data refresh and construction is easy to manage and easy for users to work with and schedule for.

Unfortunately, there are many situations where setting up regularly scheduled jobs is not good enough. Sometimes users need to have data preparation done on an as needed basis. These situations usually occur when the nature of the data that needs to be generated is so volatile from one time period to the next that there is no way for the managers of the warehouse to anticipate when it will need to be delivered.

Immediate vs. Delayed

The last aspect of timing has to do with how soon the users need the data after they request it. In the ideal world, the user could have anything they wanted as soon as it was available. Unfortunately, this is not always possible or even desirable. In many situations, the users can live with a situation where they request data at one point in time, and then wait for it for anywhere from several minutes to several days. By structuring their work in a way that allows them to wait for the data to be delivered, the managers of the warehouse can "batch" up the requests, and provide a more efficiently run warehouse.

Managing Timing and Access Issues

We therefore find ourselves in the position of needing to make decisions about a lot of variables before we are able to develop a data accessing profile which will meet the needs of the users and the warehouse managers.

The user's requirements for data are going to involve access to different sources of data, different types of access and different kinds of timing requirements. This combination of factors can lead to the development of terribly complex and confusing solutions.

Who is Responsible for What?

The first challenge that we face when we decide to implement a data access solution, is to figure out who should be responsible for doing what part of the process. There are only three alternatives: either the managers of the warehouse themselves will be responsible for the construction of all of the accessible data stores and the users will be limited to making queries against those stores, or the managers can provide a base set of tables and the users can develop their own chains and workspace data sets "on the fly," or some combination of the two approaches.

You may recall that our list of table types in the warehouse included:

1. Core (Entity) Tables
2. Legacy System Reflection Tables
3. Code Tables
4. Bridge / Cross Reference Tables
5. Merge Tables
6. Subset Tables
7. Summarization Tables
8. History Tables

Of these tables, the baseline functionality that must be guaranteed by the warehouse management team in any situation is that they provide support for all Core, Reflection, Code, Bridge and History Tables. The other types of table (Merge, Summarization and Subset) fall into the area of negotiated functionality. In some situations it will be the responsibility of the warehouse managers to generate them; in other cases, the users will build them themselves.

In general, we will refer to the basic set of tables (Core, Reflection, Code, Bridge and History) managed by the warehouse as the baseline tables, and we will refer to the rest as derived tables.

As far as construction is concerned, we can assume that the baseline tables are built from within the acquisition area of the warehouse, and the data that they contain is loaded directly from the staging area into the storage area. We will also assume that any of the derived tables will be built through the construction of data chains.

At the one extreme are those cases where the warehouse managers are going to build the data chains. In these cases the process for the end user is quite simple. The end users, or people responsible for the building of custom applications or the integration of data mining tools, simply provide the warehouse managers with the specifications for what the end product of the data chaining process should look like. It then falls to the warehouse managers to deliver what was requested.

For example, in order to develop data for preloading into a multidimensional database product, the specifications will be for a series of tables, each with an assortment of interconnecting key structures. The responsibility will then fall to the data warehouse management team to figure out how those tables should be derived.

In another case, the end users may require access to a particular subset of data in a list selection and scoring software package. In this case, the parameters for the pre-scored set of data is provided as a specification which the warehouse will then need to fulfill.

The advantage of this approach for the end users is that they never need worry about how the data gets formatted, developed or delivered. The process is transparent to them. They simply tell the warehouse team what they want, one time, and the rest is taken care of. When the user turns on the data mining tool, everything is preloaded exactly the way they need it.

This approach also provides the managers of the warehouse with many advantages. They only need worry about this process of data generation one time. They can write specific "data chaining" sequences of jobs or stored procedures and then turn them into regular jobs that run themselves on a periodic basis. This kind of solution will only work when we have:

1. A predetermined type of access
2. Against a pre-defined set of data ,and
3. The updating of the data stores can be scheduled

In other situations, this kind of arrangement will not work. In these cases we will need to develop a mechanism which makes it easy to the user to do some of this work themselves.

The User Workbench Environment

At some point, the complexity with which the end users are going to have to deal will demand that we provide some kind of management environment software to simplify the process of dealing with the warehouse. As soon as we decide that the managers of the warehouse are not going to have full and absolute responsibility for the delivery of everything to the doorstep of the users. As soon as we decide to provide for any kind of flexibility or on-demand delivery capabilities. As soon as we find that the end users are going to have to stay aware of the time subtleties of the data within the warehouse itself. Or as soon as we realize that the entire process of acquisition, staging, storing, chaining and delivering the data is not always going to happen without some kinds of delays or glitches in the process, we are going to realize that this kind of software will be critical.

Let's take a look at some environments where this kind of software was put into place.

Timing Notification Software

One organization that installed a warehouse with this kind of facility ran into problems with data timing. The warehouse that we built was for a major banking institution, and it was loaded up with data from over 25 different systems. Each of these accounting systems had a different "close date" which meant that at no time could the warehouse ever be completely in synch as far as timing went. We needed to provide end users with a screen that let them see how timely each set of data was and when the next refresh of that data was scheduled. The system could also be used to inform system users when problems occurred in the acquisition process. When source tapes failed to arrive at the data center, or when batch jobs failed to run, user were notified, so that they could anticipate when the right data would be available.

Organizations that have implemented data warehouses without this kind of facility have found that the warehouse support staff lands up spending a large amount of their time running around answer users question about timeliness and readiness.

Data Extraction Scheduling

Assuming that we will allow the users to develop their own data chains in some kind of ad hoc manner, we are faced with the challenge of how to make that process as painless as possible.

The easiest solution is to train users in the use of the SQL - DDL language, allowing them to run create, delete and update table commands, and giving them the ability to actually build and load the tables themselves. While this is certainly the easiest for the systems managers, it can get a bit hard on the users.

The compromise solution is to create or purchase a software package which makes the process of data extraction, table construction and table loading a menu driven process.

There are several products available in the marketplace today that provide the user with this kind of flexibility. It is also a capability that can be found built into many data mining products. The answer for many organizations has been to develop their own customized software to drive the process. In all cases, this provision allows system managers to ameliorate the risks of giving users carte blanche access to system resources, while at the same time making the whole process easier for users.

Many organizations which have found themselves needing to provide end users with the ability to create ad hoc requests for data extractions, or to develop their own on-demand data chains, have created software which allows the users to specify the extraction or data chain steps, and turns it into a batch job request that is run overnight (or when computer resources are available). This kind of facility gives the users the kind of flexibility they want while allowing systems managers to protect the resources of the system and balance work load demands.

By the time we are done examining the end user's data utilization profile, we should be in the position to specify exactly what kind of user workbench environment will be the most appropriate.

The Warehouse Manager's Workbench

It should come as no surprise that the managers of the warehouse are probably going to find this kind of environment useful in the execution of their jobs as well. As the size and complexity of the warehouse increases, it becomes exponentially more difficult to keep track of everything that is going on. A workbench application like this may be optional for end users but it is critical for the managers of the warehouse.

Relationship to the Storage and Work Space Areas

Before we can begin to consider the issues of workbench construction, there is one additional aspect of the management process which we should consider and that has to do with the locations at which each of the steps in a data chaining process will take place, and where each of the derived data sets will be stored.

It can safely be assumed that those tables which we have defined as the base population of tables within the warehouse are going to reside in the warehouse storage area. These tables are loaded, managed and controlled by the warehouse management team. When it comes to the derived tables however, we are going to find that we have several options for the storage of that data. In fact, derived warehouse data

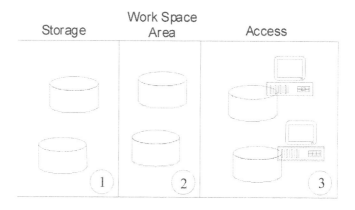

Figure 7-7. Storage of derived data

can be stored in three places. It can be stored in the:

1. Warehouse Storage Area - along with the base tables
2. Work Space Area - In-between the users and the storage area, or it can be stored in the
3. Users own computer disk storage area - on their PC or workstation hard disk or floppy

Our decision to place this data in one of these three locations is going to depend upon:

1. How much data there is
2. Who will be responsible for managing it
3. The types of access that will be used against it

In general, we store data within the warehouse storage area only when:

1. It is generated on a regularly scheduled basis
2. It is under the full control of the warehouse management team
3. It is to be shared by more than one user
4. No create, update or deletes of the data is going to occur (except for rare exceptions)

We will want to store data within the user's workstation disk space only when:

1. It is to be used exclusively by that user
2. It is of a low enough volume as to not strain the user's workstation resources
3. It does not require the utilization of feedback mechanisms except those of the most rudimentary nature

Any data whose definition falls between the two extremes of the previous two options will land up being stored within the workspace area. These include:

1. Data sets which require that feedback mechanisms be put in place to feed back changes into the warehouse itself
2. Volumes of data that are so great they cannot be managed on the user's own disk area
3. Data that must be updated and shared between users

The purpose of the workspace area is to serve as the intermediary no mans land where the definition of responsibility and management for the data is not as clearly defined as it is in the other two areas.

We will continue with a more in-depth examination of the issues of data placement and physical management in the next chapter on Physical Infrastructure.

Specifications for the Workbench Systems

The reality of a workbench system which end users and warehouse managers can use in order to make the data warehouse easier to work with, is going to depend in no small part, on the size, complexity and importance of the warehouse itself. If the applications being added to the warehouse are small and simple, and if the number of data sets being managed is minimal, there is no reason to invest heavily in sophisticated management software. On the other hand, as the system grows in complexity and size, the need for the software gets greater.

Warehouse management software falls into two major categories (scheduling and status reporting). A typical application might include one, some or all of these features to varying degrees. At this point, we will simply describe one way that products of this nature could be developed, drawing upon our experience with systems that have been developed in the past in order to meet the same needs. At the same time, we realize that new applications of this type

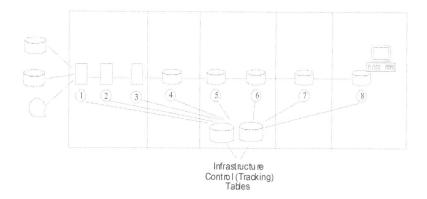

Infrastructure
Control (Tracking)
Tables

Figure 7-8. Infrastructure tracking tables

are being developed all the time, and there is a range of products available in the marketplace today that perform some, if not all of these functions.

Status Reporting Capabilities

Obviously, what will be needed for warehouse managers and users is some way of finding out the status of the data being loaded into the warehouse at any given point in time. In order to do these, we are going to need to build a special set of tables within our infrastructure.

These tables, which we shall call the Infrastructure Tracking Tables, will be physically located within the warehouse storage area. Their purpose, however, will be to hold status information about every

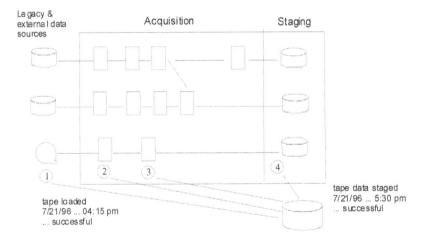

Figure 7-9. Tracking the Acquisition process

major event that has occurred within the warehouse environment. By storing all of this information in this table, it will become a trivial matter to develop a set of screens that allow users and warehouse managers to check on status at any time.

Tracking the acquisition process

The first thing we will want to keep track of is all the activities that occur within the acquisition area of the warehouse. You may recall that a typical data extraction and loading sequence can be made up of a long series of data cleansing, formatting, merge and purge processes. It is going to be critical that we put some kind of mechanism in place that keeps track of all these steps.

In a lot of cases, the users of the system will not need to have any kind of access or familiarity with any of the steps; however, for the managers of the warehouse, the availability of a centrally defined and controlled repository which holds a history and current status of these operations is going to make the job of managing the environment many times easier.

Tracking the Loading of Storage Tables

The next event that we are going to want to keep track of is the loading of the Core, Reflection, Code and Bridge and History

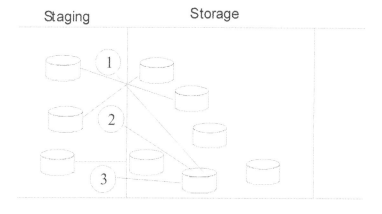

Figure 7-10. Tracking Storage Area activity

Tables. These tables, you may recall, make up the foundation of the overall warehouse environment and they are typically loaded on a periodic basis.

By using the same control and management tables to keep track of load activity, the warehouse will be able to inform the warehouse managers, and the end users, about when each of these tables was last successfully loaded.

Tracking the Propagation of Derived Tables

Of course, the most difficult type of data loading activity to track involves those tables which are derived for use by the end users. Up until this point, our system has simply been tracking whether regularly scheduled events have been successfully completed or not. In this case, we want to be able to keep track of not on the regularly scheduled derivation activities, but the ad hoc, on demand and other unscheduled data extraction activities as well.

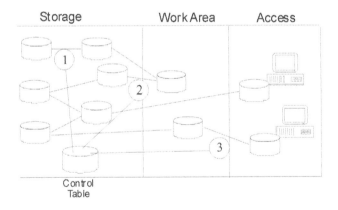

Figure 7-11. Tracking the propagation of derived data

In this case, the existence of a software product which manages the extraction and data chaining process itself will be key (see the next section on scheduling software). Without this kind of software to manage the users ad hoc activities, there would be know way to keep track of exactly what they were doing with the data, and how many computer resources they were actually using.

Tracking the History of Access to all Tables

You may recall from one of the earliest chapters in the book, that we said that the best way to measure how well the warehouse was functioning was in terms of the "turns" or levels of data activity that occurred within it. All of the warehousing activity in the world will be a waste of effort if nobody actually uses the data that is propagated.

From a management perspective we have an even more immediate need for this kind of "turning" information. If the manager of the warehouse is going to take his or her job seriously, then they are going to need to be constantly monitoring the activity level of users against the different data sets. If it turns out that a data set is accessed only infrequently, then that data set may be a candidate for removal from the warehouse and placement in some other kind of environment. The managers of the warehouse should constantly be looking for better ways to make optimum use of the disk space and CPU power that they are commissioned to manage.

The only way to do this kind of activity tracking is to have some kind of history of the different types of access that the users are using against the warehouse tables.

While in the worst case, the managers of the warehouse might need to figure out some way to capture and store this kind of information on their own, in most cases, the database software that you choose the run the warehouse will have this kind of end-user activity logging built right into the product.

All the managers of the warehouse need do is figure out how the user activity logging facilities work, engage it, and make use of the reports provided.

Scheduling

In addition to providing people with information about what has happened within the warehouse, it can also be advantageous to make use of the same mechanism to keep track of what is supposed to or going to happen. We will want to build this mechanism on top of the tracking mechanisms that we have already put into place, in order to get as much consistency and integration of the two types of system as possible.

The types of scheduling systems we may want to put into place will include systems which:

1. Keep track of when activities are supposed to occur
2. Provide facilities for the construction and execution of data manipulation events for scheduling or for immediate execution.

Activity Scheduling

Having information available about when different events within the warehouse have occurred provides us with valuable information. However, it will be even more valuable if we also know when these things were supposed to occur, or the next time it is going to occur.

In order to make this kind of information available we will need a complementary set of control and management tables to exist in parallel with the tracking tables we have just defined. Into these tables the managers of the warehouse and will place information about when each of the data transformation events is supposed to occur.

For each activity within the warehouse, from extraction to merge/ purge to staging to the loading of derived tables, we should be able to record the targeted dates and times when we anticipate each event to happen. By placing this scheduling information into the system, we can create a mechanism which allows us to predict warehouse activity, to anticipate problems and to get a better overall picture of whatever we happen to be looking at.

This scheduled activity information will especially be valuable to end users who depend upon certain events occurring in order to plan their business activities.

Building Data Chain Specifications

The last facility we want to build for our operational infrastructure will be the system that allows end users to develop their own data chains.

Customized data chain construction will allow end users to:

1. Build their own input data sets for loading into data mining tools

2. Develop complex sets of data for utilization with their query and analysis tools

3. Build source data sets for operational applications

4. Create personal, transient copies of data for their own processing needs

By providing end users with a pre-defined set of screens which make this kind of activity possible, the managers of the system help to bridge the gap between system manageability and flexibility and between system user friendliness and technical complexity. It allows the system managers to give the end users the flexibility that they want, while defining a structure within which they can operate, making system management and system use easier.

Specifications for the Tables

In a typical system designed to track and schedule warehouse activity, the following tables can serve as examples of a minimal set of data. The tables will include:

1. Data Identity Table - Holding information about each file, table and data set within the warehouse environment.

2. Data Transformation Table - Holding information about the process of converting data from one data set to the next.

The Data Identity Table

The data identity table holds one record for each data set and table within the warehouse environment. It holds information which includes:

1. The name of the data set of table

2. Its physical location

3. Its minimum, maximum and current size

4. Its current status (loaded, empty, corrupted, available etc.)

The Data Transformation Table

The data transformation table holds process information for moving data from one data set to the next. The information it holds includes:

1. The name of the source data set
2. The name of the target data set
3. The activity that is supposed to or has occurred (copy, merge, extract, etc.)
4. The name of the program or stored procedure which performs the activity
5. The outcome of the last execution
6. The next scheduled execution

Obviously, as the scope and complexity of the system varies, and as you try to use the system to do more and more work the nature and complexity of these tables will increase. However, even this bare minimum of data capture can be of immense value to systems managers and users.

Tying the Tables into the Warehouse

While the capabilities that we have just described will provide an incredible amount of "value added" to the overall warehouse environment; ironically, the cost to implement this kind of facility is minimal. All we need to do in order to build the foundation for this type of system is to create the tables to hold the data in the storage area. We then build a step into each data extraction, formatting and loading the job which makes an entry in the corresponding tracking table.

It is easy and straightforward to do this, as long as build it into your understanding of how the warehouse is going to be managed. If you try to ignore the building of this capability until after a large amount of the warehouse infrastructure is already in place, then the cost will be much greater.

Main Menu Screen Functionality

The main menu screen defines the principle areas of workbench functionality. It includes menu items which allow the user to look at the process of data transformation:

1. Data Extract and Preparation - The status of data as it moves from Legacy systems to the staging area
2. Data Loading - The loading of staged data into the warehouse

3. Data Chains - The movement of data from the base warehouse tables into their derived forms

The status of individual data sets and tables:

4. Data Set View - Allowing the user to check the status of a given data set or table
5. The ability to build data chains
6. Data Chain Construction and Scheduling

Individual screens underneath this menu can then be designed to carry the user through the different processes and views of the warehouse's activity.

CONCLUSIONS

In this chapter we have concentrated on the workings of the operational infrastructure of the warehouse. We found it consisted of the identification and placement of data sets, the provision of mechanisms to allow for different types of user access, and the development of mechanisms which can ease the tracking and management of the overall warehousing process.

In the next chapter, we will complete our view of the warehousing environment by examining the physical infrastructure of the warehouse.

CHAPTER 8

THE PHYSICAL INFRASTRUCTURE

At this point, there are a great number of readers who may be uttering a sigh of relief by the time they get to this chapter.

Finally!

The author is going to tell me what I really wanted to know about the warehouse. I don't want to know about business issues, management approaches, data disciplines and operational infrastructures. All I really want to know is, which computers should I buy in order to build the warehouse. Just tell me what to use, and I'll figure the rest out myself. Unfortunately, it just doesn't work that way. And the last thing we are going to do is tell you about the one right way to build a warehouse infrastructure.

We are not going to withhold this information out of some kind of perverted desire to torture the reader. On the contrary, we would like nothing better than to simply say "Buy two of these, one of these, and tie them together this way, and everything else will work itself out."Unfortunately, we cannot. The issues around physical infrastructure decision-making are the most complex in the warehousing world, and require us to take many variables into account.

It might seem to the reader, based upon the amount of time that we have spent on all the business, organizational, data discipline and operational characteristics of the warehouse, that the physical infrastructure is the least important aspect of the system. Nothing could be further from the truth. However, in order to have an intelligent discussion about that physical infrastructure, we needed to establish all these other warehouse characteristics in order to have a framework within which our discussions could be held.

A warehouse is a diverse and complex thing, and the physical infrastructure upon which it runs will be the most complex aspect of all.

As soon as we begin entertaining issues about what kinds of hardware, software and networking environments we should use to build the warehouse, we get into a quagmire of conflicting needs and demands. We will use the framework that we have presented up until this point to guide us through the process of making intelligent infrastructure decisions.

PROBLEMS WITH PHYSICAL INFRASTRUCTURES

The fact of the matter is that as soon as we begin talking upon physical infrastructures, we get into a whole range of issues and debates that in the past, have proven to greatly curtail, and even destroy some very well grounded warehouse development efforts. The problems fall under several categories:

1. Investment in existing infrastructure
2. Tool Drivers
3. Territorial imperatives
4. Religious Debates
5. Organizational history
6. Vendor promoted misconceptions about ease of use and low cost solutions
7. Integration, Management and Performance Problems

We will consider each of these issues before proceeding with our investigation.

Investment in Existing Infrastructure

The first problem that we run into when we begin discussing what the best physical infrastructure for the warehouse should be is the problem presented by current investment in different existing physical infrastructures.

This problem is best understood by referring back to our earlier discussions about the history of data processing within the business environment and the way in which different systems, and their correspondingly diverse physical infrastructures, may have propagated themselves across the enterprise.

In each business, we are likely to find several types of physical infrastructures, each vying for organizational supremacy in the environment. For different organizations, at different times, these battle zones may be different, but in general, "turf battles" of this nature are quite common.

In the olden days of data processing, the battle lines for physical infrastructure turf were pretty cleanly drawn. At the center was the infamous IBM mainframe environment. These computers were the unchallenged kings of the business data processing environment. Even today, the functioning of most major corporations is highly dependent upon IBM mainframe processing in order to survive and thrive.

Other players in the marketplace tended to specialize in niches for which the IBM mainframe was ill suited. Departmental level processing was handled by the Xerox, Wang, IBM-System 36, 38, AS/400 and DEC. Specialized large applications and government work were handled by Burroughs and Sperry. Specialized scientific and engineering were handled by Hewlett Packard and SUN. In general, these systems hardly ever competed with each other, since each met specific business needs.

Turf battles in these days, at least in the mainframe environment, centered on the propagation of database management system software. IBM's IMS, IDMS, Supra, Model 204 and a range of other major contenders all vied for ownership of the mainframe database marketplace.

As the computer evolved however, the battlefield changed significantly. Scientific workstations by Sun and Hewlett Packard began to challenge the supremacy of the mainframe. The personal computer become a standard fixture on every desktop in the world. Soon, the nicely drawn, well organized battle lines became blurred. With the corresponding improvements in network technology, the propagation of LANs and the designation of "client/server" technology as the approach of the future, the environment became a free for all. Suddenly every vendor became a potential provider of every kind of data processing needs.

People began considering PC's with LAN's or PC's working with UNIX based servers as potential replacement environments for the formerly dependable mainframe. All of a sudden, every decision about every computer system turned into an overwhelming debate about infrastructure, future directions and long term hardware/software planning.

The problem with the selection of any kind of a physical infrastructure decision is clear. Every time you invest in hardware, software or network architecture, you make a commitment not only as an immediate solution to an immediate problem. When you make these decisions you limit people's choices in the future. These decisions are limited because you cannot afford to tear out the old systems every time you bring in a new system and you cannot afford to re-train people every time a new, fancy solution comes along.

Unfortunately, as we have discussed earlier, there is simply no way to make the "right decision" about infrastructure and be assured that the decision will hold up as the technology continues to expand and evolve.

There have been dozens of documented cases of organizations stymied by precisely these kinds of issues.

Many organizations have tried over the past 10 years to eliminate their mainframe computers and replace them with UNIX servers or even distributed PC based LANs. In general these efforts have failed. No matter how hard they have tried, it has proved to be an almost insurmountable task to try to replace the efficiencies and incredible organizational and procedural investments that typical mainframe environments represent.

Others have tried to hold steadfastly to the mainframe only processing approach. These organizations, for the most part, have found themselves deluged in a flood of user based PC, LAN and Server based initiatives which have created havoc within the overall data processing environment.

The challenge therefore is to come up with some kind of approach that allows us to leverage the current investment that the organization has while at the same time making it possible to take advantage of the new potential benefits that new infrastructure approaches may present.

The investment that an organization will have in an existing infrastructure will not be trivial. Included in our understanding of this investment is:

1. Investment in the hardware and software itself
2. Investment in the development of roles, responsibilities and procedures for the management of this environment.
3. Investment in the skills and experience level of users and support personnel.

Any consideration of the construction of a new system must take these costs into account, either as a cost already paid which developers can capitalize on, or as a cost to be suffered if it is determined that the new physical infrastructure is going to require radical changes to the existing environment.

Tool Drivers

As if the straightforward questions about which hardware and software to use would not be complicated enough, we are reluctantly forced to take even more variables into account before continuing our discussion.

The second problem that we encounter when trying to determine an optimal physical infrastructure becomes evident when we start to look at the specialized data mining tools and warehouse infrastructure management tools that promise to ease some of the overall development effort required to construct the warehouse. Unfortunately, new tools and approaches usually run on new types of infrastructures. Therefore, we are going to have to take the needs of these solutions into account as part of our physical infrastructure decision making process. If we find that we need a data mining tool that only runs on a Silicon Graphics Workstation, then we are going to have to include these workstations, their cost, and their connectivity costs into our overall physical architecture plan.

If we decide we need a product like InfoPump, which makes it possible for us to pre-schedule and pre-manage the data acquisition process using a set of easy to use menus, then the physical requirements of that solution must be included. There is no way around it. New tools bring with them a set of environmental factors that need to be included in our plans.

Territorial Imperatives

Another more insidious form of physical infrastructure decision making occurs on the organizational level. For every specified physical infrastructure that is supported by an organization, there are groups of people who are heavily invested in that solution. Any attempt to choose infrastructure alternatives that differ from their chosen power base is going to create a great deal of dissension and controversy.

These territorial imperatives can take two forms, one on the systems support side and one on the business user side.

Systems Territories

The territory defined by different groups of systems support organizations is clear and straightforward. A typical corporation has mainframe support, UNIX support and PC/LAN support departments in some form or another. The decision to choose one of these environments to support the new warehouse is a decision to promise more work, a bigger budget, bigger staff and assured survival for who ever the "winning " environment happens to be. The tendency of individuals to promote their own infrastructure approach and to discount and undermine the approaches that others propose should be expected and anticipated during the physical infrastructure development process.

The fact of the matter is that all of the physical infrastructures could very well be appropriate choices to solve some, or all of the warehouses needs. The problem is that no project can afford to get hung up too long on the resolution of these issues. Our approach must minimize the chances of this kind of controversy occurring.

Business Area Territory

The users of systems which are based upon different types of platforms will have an almost equal vehemence in their attempts to defend whatever their infrastructure of choice might happen to be. Different groups of users within the organization are going to have experience with different assortments of tools and platforms. Some may work heavily with their own PC's and enjoy a great deal of autonomy from centralized data processing. Others may be comfortable using mainframe based applications which provide them with "push button" ease of use they have come to expect.

When you begin making physical infrastructure and software recommendations, there is a good chance that you are going to threaten their way of doing things. The designers of the infrastructure need to take these territorial issues into account just as much as the systems issues.

Religious Debates

Perhaps the most frustrating kind of issues to combat when trying to make sound infrastructure decision come from the area we call "Religious Debates." These debates are often, but not always, founded within the territorial imperatives of different groups of users, tend to promote blanket solutions as the only answer to any physical infrastructure issue. These "religions" fall under the heading of " Mainframe Good - Everything Else Bad" or "Client/ Server" or "Object Oriented" or the most devastating of all: "Just Leave Everything the way it is," or "Just change everything and start over."

Our response to these issues must fall back upon the basic premises upon which our whole approach is based. The developers of the warehouse are not out to solve the physical infrastructure problems of the universe, or even the corporation. The objective is to deliver usable applications in a cost effective manner. Period. If the solution proposed can do that great. If it can't, then it is immaterial.

Organizational History

Once we have cleared the territorial and religious issues around infrastructure development, we often run into problems that involve the performance history of the people being asked to participate in warehouse construction. Whether the platform we decide to use for the development of the warehouse is a mainframe, a UNIX server or a PC, if the users of existing systems within the organization have had a history of bad experiences with the people slated to build and manage the system, then the project will be in serious jeopardy before you even get started.

A typical situation occurs when a mainframe support group begins to advocate a mainframe based warehouse solution. Users may find that the value proposition holds considerable merit, and may even find that they need the new warehousing application in order to survive. Yet, if that same mainframe support group has failed at their last three attempts to deliver other types of applications, or if that same system is forcing users to wait weeks or even months in order to deliver badly needed enhancements to existing systems, then the users will be far from enthusiastic about the new initiative being built within that group's sphere of influence.

Many times, it is dissatisfaction not with the mainframe technology, but with the mainframe support organization which causes people to promote alternative platforms for new systems. On the other hand, within some organizations, the failure of previously attempted "client/server" initiatives might cause people to favor the "old stand by' mainframe approach.

MIS-Conceptions About Ease of Use and Low Cost Solutions

Another source of challenges when it comes to developing a physical infrastructure plan is the influence that the vendors of different sets of products bring into the equation. Unfortunately, the vendors of different types of products tend to present users, managers and systems personnel with pictures of how their products work that are in many ways too optimistic. The job of the vendor is to present their product in the best light possible. This, of course, includes telling you how easy it is to use, how inexpensive it will be to run and how transparent its operation will be to everyone. Unfortunately, in their exuberance to paint a rosy picture of their product, vendors tend to overlook the consequences and assumptions that go into these claims.

In some cases, our challenge will be to simply be aware of the realities involved and to separate those from the misconceptions. In other cases, these claims can undermine our efforts to develop a robust, sound and cost effective overall warehouse solution. This is especially true in those cases where data mining tools claim to be able to handle all of the warehouse management for us, and in those cases of warehouse management products which provide some, but not all of the functionality that we require.

The solution in these cases is to develop an understanding of the individual products as they fit within the warehouse template that we have been developing here. The process of checking the claimed functionality against our logical understanding of what the warehouse must be able to provide, can help the physical infrastructure developer from making mistakes in tool selection that can create problems down the road.

Integration, Performance and Management Problems

Finally, and of the biggest concern for the physical infrastructure developer, is to choose infrastructure components that are going to make the integration of the different parts of the warehouse, the performance of the warehouse overall and the management of the environment as efficient and friendly as possible.

A solution that involves the utilization of five operating systems, fifteen platforms and three networks might meet the needs of all the different political and financial groups within the organization, but it will certainly create a nightmare environment for the managers of the system.

On the other hand, an overly dictatorial and simplistic architecture might meet the minimum needs of the organization, and be incredibly easy to build and manage, but can leave the users short of the potential benefits that might be enjoyed with a more robust type of solution.

So as we can see, deciding upon the appropriate physical infrastructure is much more than the simple process of picking the best tool for the job. It involves, people, investments, history and expectations. It can never be a purely technical decision, but will always be influenced by politics and feelings in addition to the simple costs and capabilities that we would like it to include.

IMPERATIVES

The imperatives for our physical infrastructure development process must therefore be:

1. To keep the approach as modular as possible. We want to create an environment where we can plug and unplug different parts of the application so that different parts can respond to different kinds of efficiencies whenever possible.

2. To leverage as much of the existing physical infrastructure, both in terms of physical plant (the physical hardware, software etc.) and the people investment (skills, aptitudes and experience), as possible.

While at the same time --

3. Bringing as many appropriate and cost effective new solutions to bear on the problem as possible.

This is not an easy task.

PLATFORMS

The first and biggest discussion that we will have around physical infrastructures will therefore be that of choosing the physical platform(s) for the warehouse. Under the term platform, we include definitions for all of the hardware, database software, operating system and network software components that will make up the system.

The Single Platform Solution

We will begin our examination of the different kinds of physical infrastructures and their corresponding strengths and weaknesses by starting with the simplest case, the single platform architecture.

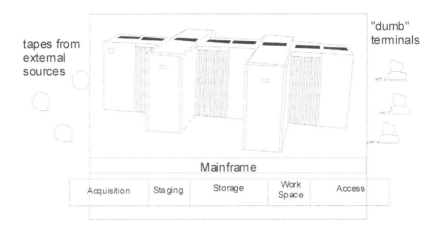

Figure 8-1. The single platform architecture

It may come as a shock to some readers, but a single platform infrastructure for a data warehouse is not only allowable and feasible, but it is often the best option available to system developers. Long before the vendors of UNIX based database products and PC based data mining tools came along, people were successfully building and deploying warehouses by making use of existing technologies.

A single platform solution can be built using existing corporation mainframe technologies, mini-computers or even UNIX based servers. The feasibility of the solution, however, depends upon several factors. In the single platform based warehouse, all operations in the Acquisition, Storage and Access components occur from within the framework of the same technology.

Obviously, if this kind of solution is going to work, then our first assumption will have to be that all of the Legacy systems that feed

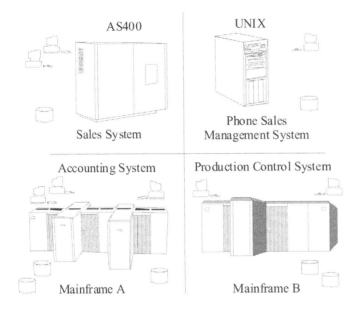

Figure 8-2. Disparate legacy system platforms

the warehouse already reside on the same warehouse. Our next assumption will be that the platform in question will be big enough and powerful enough to handle managing all the data that the storage component needs to deal with.

Our final assumption will be that the the this same environment can support the management of end user data mining and data access applications.

There are many situations where this solution will be both economically and organizationally the best solution possible.

A single platform solution greatly reduces the risk and expense of system construction, and makes the issues involved in system design and support a lot less cumbersome. In fact, one of the first approaches that we take when asked to evaluate platform alternatives is to see if there isn't some way to make a single platform approach work. Unfortunately, there are many factors at work which can serve to make this a less than optimal approach. For any number of reasons the single platform may prove to be inadequate or undesirable. Among the issues that will contra-indicate this kind of solution are:

1. Capacity

In may situations, the existing platform environment may not be in a condition suitable for the installation of a new major implementation. In a lot of cases, the existing Legacy environment may already be stretched to capacity, making it impossible to upgrade the hardware and software to the state required for warehouse support.

Even if the physical capacity exists (CPU and Disk Space), the environment itself may be so complex or the support staff so overworked that they cannot envision making the changes necessary to support this kind of effort.

2. Competence

Even if the existing Legacy system environment could be retrofitted to meet the demands of the warehouse, it may be that the support staff is ill - equipped to build and support it. Unfortunately, Legacy system environments tend to be based upon older and sometimes outdated technologies. Technologies which require specialized skills that are not readily available.

One organization was considering the development of an extremely large, super-data warehouse. The only hardware that seemed capable of meeting the processing needs was a Cray type super-computer. After considerable research into the possibilities however, the organization had to abandon the project. Even though the capacity was there, it was discovered that there would be no way to hire or train a staff large enough to develop the system.

A technological solution that cannot be implemented by making use of readily available and reasonably priced technical support is as infeasible solution as one where the technology itself cannot be attained

3. Availability of data mining tools

One of the biggest driving forces prompting people to consider warehousing solutions is the existence of high powered, low cost data mining applications. These tools make it possible for users to perform analysis and data manipulation tasks that were previously available only within the most rigidly defined academic environments. Unfortunately, hardly any of these tools runs on Legacy system environments. Oh, there is a smattering of UNIX, mainframe and mini computer based applications here and there, but in general, the vast majority of the products run on Windows, OS/2, MAC and X-Term type environments.

4. Disparate Legacy data sources

Another precondition which can make the single platform an untenable solution occurs in those environments where Legacy systems exist across a wide variety of platforms. A typical corporate environment can include many mainframe computers, a collection of specialized mini and UNIX computers and an assortment of PC based operations. With these many different sources to deal with, a single platform approach becomes untenable.

5. Strategic Platform Directions

Many organizations today have established strategic platform directions which dictate which platforms can or cannot be used for new systems development. Corporations that make these kinds of declarations have been accepting that diverse and incompatible platforms cannot be immediately eliminated. By choosing these directions, the corporate directors hope to encourage the atrophy of old systems and encourage the development of new ones. In these environments, the strategic direction chosen must bear influence on the platform decision making process.

Separating the Legacy Environments

So, probably the first thing that we will have to figure out for our physical infrastructure, is how to incorporate disparate Legacy system platforms into the environment.

When we to try to incorporate this data into our overall warehousing environment we are going to have to make some decisions. It is a given that the extraction of data from each of these Legacy systems will occur on the platforms where those systems exist. However, what about all the other steps of the acquisition process? Where will we develop and execute the data cleansing programs and the data synchronization routines? Will we attempt to do those on the existing Legacy platforms as well?

More importantly, how will we manage the merge/purge kinds of processing that need to occur, especially when the two files that need to be merged exist on different systems. How do we decide which one to run it on?

In many cases, we will realize that it is going to be necessary to establish an additional Legacy systems neutral location where the majority of the data preparation work will occur.

Platform Allocation for the Acquisition Component

When trying to decide which platforms to use to do the different parts of the acquisition process, several issues will help drive the decision making process.

First of all, we need to be aware of the capacity available on each of those Legacy systems. If a system is already strapped for capacity (disk and CPU), then there will be little hope of using it to do anything except provide us with the initial extract file.

Secondly, we have to make allocation decisions based upon the availability of resources that can work in each of the targeted environments. Many times, especially with smaller platforms, the organization will have limited or no in house staff capable of developing the programs required. In these cases the data will have to be moved to an environment where people who can work with the data are available.

On the other hand, some Legacy system environments may have ample capacity and ample resources. In some situations, these environments may also be equipped with software which makes the development of data cleansing and formatting programs easy and cost effective. In these cases it may make sense to port all data to that platform and allow it to function as the main acquisitions component platform.

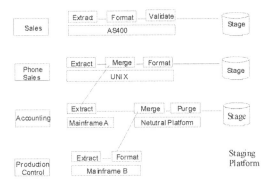

Figure 8-3. A multi-platform acquisition component

In some situations, warehouse developers have opted to create a new, neutral environment where extracted data can be ported and manipulated. This kind of solution has several advantages.

1. The environment can be optimized for data transformation operations. It can be equipped with tools that make data cleansing and formatting easy.

2. The environment can be staffed with people that specialize in the use of these types of tools.

3. It makes the overall process of managing data acquisition easier to do, easier to manage and easier to track.

In most cases, organizations end up developing a solution that involves a combination of these approaches.

In all cases it will be critical for the developers of the acquisition component facilities to keep several things in mind:

1. The need to make use of infrastructure control tables to track the process

The more complex the acquisition component gets on a physical infrastructure level, the more important it will be to be sure that the centrally defined infrastructure control and tracking tables are

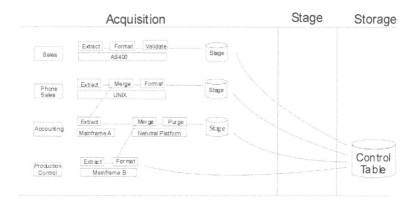

Figure 8-4. Keeping the control table updated

being utilized. This kind of centrally defined source of information about each step in the process will make it possible to manage an otherwise unmanageable environment.

2.   The need to reduce complexity

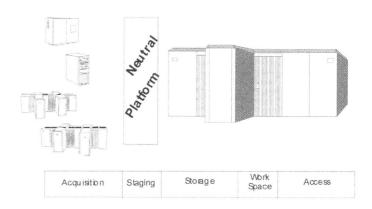

Figure 8-5. Physical infrastructure with multiple legacy platforms

Many an organization have found themselves swamped in incredible amounts of complexity and poor coordination when these kinds of multi-platform solutions develop. You can easily end up relying upon dozens of programmers in dozens of environments to each perform a part of the overall data conversion task. Yet since they are so scattered, and are working in such different environments, it can become an incredible task just to keep them coordinated and working in the same direction.

3. The need to guarantee the integrity of data transformations

One of the side effects of the increased complexity of the multi-platform type of solution for the acquisition component is that the integrity of the data as it goes through each of the transformation steps can become compromised. You distribute the task across so many different environments and involve so many different people that it becomes easy to lose the meaning of the data being manipulated.

In addition to the more subtle form of data integrity compromise, is the problem that occurs on the physical level when you cross so many different technological boundaries. Different platforms store data in different ways, and they are not always compatible with one another. We need to worry not only about the logical integrity of the data as it moves through the acquisition process, but also must assure its physical integrity as well. As we can see, our nice, simple physical infrastructure decision making process has now been made a lot more complicated.

What will be critical for the developers of the data warehouse at this point is to understand that while the development of the acquisition component many involve disparate platforms, and will most certainly involve getting support from a wide variety of organizational units, the overall responsibility for the integrity and efficiency of the acquisition operations, as an overall process, still rests on the shoulders of the warehouse developers.

DATA TRANSPORTATION
ISSUES (ACQUISITION)

Up until this point we have been talking about the movement of data between programs and between platforms as if it were a trivial process, and in some situations it is. In a single platform kind of environment there is very little overhead or expense associated with the movement of data from one process to the next.

However, as soon as we begin to talk about moving data (the data created by one program to be read by another program) or information (the tracking records for our infrastructure control table) from one platform to another, we create a whole new set of problems and concerns.

Moving Data from One Platform to Another

The fact of the matter is that depending upon the platform you are moving data from, the platform you are moving it to, and the network connectivity established between them, this process can be very easy, or extremely difficult.

There are in fact, four major categories of inter-platform connections that we will need to consider. It is important to note that these same

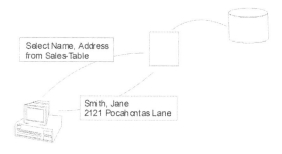

Figure 8-6. Real-time network connections

---

inter-platform connectivity issues will pertain to the access and work area component platforms as well as the acquisition platforms.

1. Real time network connections
2. Data ports
3. Shared Disk
4. Tape Transfer

Real Time Network Connections

The most intimate kind of connection we can establish between two platforms is where a process or program running on one of the platforms can make use of resources on the other. This is the type of functionality provided by many types of client/server or cross-platform manipulation products. Depending upon how the hardware has been set up, it can be made possible for programs on one of the platforms to read from and write to disk spaces on the other computers. In many cases these same connects can allow those programs to actually execute programs and schedule events on the

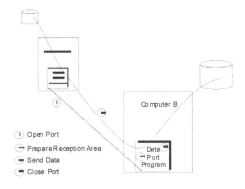

Figure 8-7. Data ports

other platform as well. This tight coupling of platforms is usually available between different platforms of the same type. For example, cross platform mainframe processes have long been feasible. However, the ability to do this kind of cross platform activity when the platforms are of different types is much rarer.

The recent popularity of client/server technology and the propagation of TCP/IP as an industry standard network protocol has made this kind of inter-platform work a lot easier to develop. Unfortunately, even when this capability is present, it may not be configured to operate at the volumes and rate that is required for our purposes. At a minimum, this kind of tight coupling will make it feasible for our data transformation processes to update a remotely defined Infrastructure Control Table.

Data Ports

A second kind of inter-platform connectivity is made possible via the creation of "data ports." Data ports are inter-system mechanisms which make it possible for utility programs on one system to send massive amounts of data to the other system, at a high rate of speed and of reasonable volume.

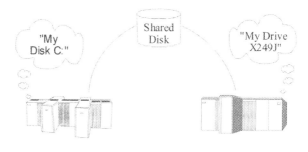

Figure 8-8. Shared disk

Data ports, like real time connections, require that each platform involved in the process be especially configured to handle the transfer, including the presence of special hardware, special software and sufficient network capacity to handle the loads anticipated.

Shared Disk

Another way that the transfer of data can be handled is through the use of shared disks. Under a shared disk configuration, a neutrally

Figure 8-9. Manual media to media transfer (tape)

defined disk storage area is set up so that each platform recognizes it as its own. By convincing both systems that the disk space is its own, it is possible for programmers on the first system to write data to this neutral area, which programmers on the second system can then read.

The biggest differences between the Shared Disk and Data Port solutions have to do with speed and ease of use. Access to a shared disk is typically very fast, as fast as any intra-platform read/write operation. On the other hand, data port transfer rates are usually much lower.

It is also much easier to make use of shared disk. In a shared disk environment, each programmer treats the data set as just another native dataset. No special jobs, procedures or machinations must be executed. Just read the data and write it again.

Data porting on the other hand requires the scheduling and execution of data porting software, and can get complicated.

Manual Media Transfer

Finally, when all else fails, we can always fall back on the way to move data between platforms that always works, manual media transfer.

Under this arrangement, the programmer on the first platform writes the data to an external media (like a tape or a floppy disk). After this, the media is transfered to the new platform where another programmer reads the data in.

	Cost	Timing
Real Time	High	Immediate
Data Port	Medium	Internal Speed
Shared Disk	Low	Program Bound
Manual Media	Low	Human Bound

Figure 8-10. Data transportation options

While manual media transfer is not pretty, it is reliable and inexpensive. In those situations where no other connectivity is available, it becomes the only alternative.

Using and Choosing Data Transportation Options

The development of a data transportation approach to tie the platforms within our Legacy system environment together is a critical one. The first step in making this determination, is to find out what capabilities are already in place, and verify that they can handle the anticipated volumes and rates.

The decision to make use of one approach vs. another will have several consequences:

- Platform cost - The more tightly we couple two platforms, the more expensive the networking solution.
- Timing - As we move down the scale from real time to manual data transportation, we increase the time delay. Part of our infrastructure decision will have to be based upon whether or not the proposed coupling technique will meet our timing requirements.
- Development cost - The more complicated the linkage between the systems, the more costly the development.

Probably the least expensive solution in the majority of cases is a shared disk approach. Data ports are cumbersome to work with, and real time connections are complex to execute and are also resource intensive.

Supporting Data Transportation

We really have two sets of concerns when it comes to figuring our how to configure our physical infrastructure from a data transportation perspective. The first and biggest set of issues revolves around how to transform data from its raw, extracted form into the staged

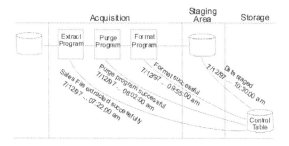

Figure 8-11. Direct update of control tables, using Direct SQL

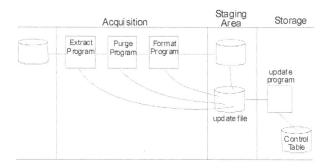

Figure 8-12. Indirect update of control tables by writing to a hold file.

form required for warehouse loading. For these cases the optimum solution is a shared disk, followed by data porting options. Real time and manual transfer are only feasible as last resorts. The first because it is so resource intensive, and the second because it can cause significant time delays and requires manual intervention to work.

SUPPORTING THE INFRASTRUCTURE CONTROL TABLES

On the other hand we have just about the opposite set of preferences when it comes to figuring out how to keep our infrastructure control tables up to date.

Ideally, each program that performs one of our data transformation steps could include within it an SQL "call" to the control tables located within the storage area. This way, the control table could be kept up to date, up to the minute.

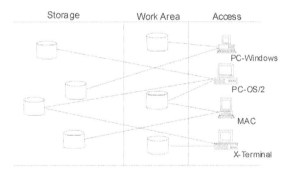

Figure 8-13. Diverse user platforms

If this is not possible, the only other option would be for these programs to write information about the successful completion of each step to a special file, which could then be transported to the storage area, and loaded up into the controllable via a special update program. In these cases the file would get moved via either shared disk, port or manual means.

ADDING USER WORKSTATIONS

Of course, not only do we need to worry about dealing with disparate platforms on the acquisitions side of the warehouse, but in most situations we are going to have to figure out how to deal with a vast assortment of user workstation platforms as well.

While it is possible to build a data warehouse making use of whatever "native" user terminal interface that the Legacy system may happen to provide, usually we will be faced with a wide variety of users, each of whom have their own preferences for separate user workstations.

By far the most common form of user workstation in the business environment today is the personal computer, running with Windows and DOS as the operating system environment. Also popular in different areas will be personal computers with OS/2, MAC computers and UNIX X-Terminals.

One of our challenges is going to be to get these diverse platforms to fit within our infrastructure as well.

Workstation Selection

It is in the area of workstation selection that we get into some of the biggest "turf battles" over infrastructure. The problem is that for a given population of users, you are going to find that there is an investment in technology and approach that is not easily abandoned. Different users are going to want to see different infrastructures put into place.

We have already reviewed many of the issues that are going to have an influence on what types of workstations we choose.

Issues involving the existing investment in:

1. Hardware
2. Software
3. Networking infrastructure
4. Management and support staff

Users Familiarity with Existing Technologies

In addition to the preference people have for the protection of their existing investments, the battle for a workstation environment can also become the means for groups to advocate their solutions over others. For example, in one manufacturing organization where we worked, there were two groups of people. The first group consisted of engineers. These people were familiar with UNIX and C and were very comfortable maintaining a "hands on" technically intimate relationship with their environment. They felt that fancy graphics and user friendly interfaces were a waste of good computing power. Their preference was for UNIX based scientific workstations as the access mechanism of choice. Another equally avid group was made up of the management and clerical staff. For them there was no question about what the user interface should be. They were comfortable with a Windows based personal computer environment. They had no desire to learn about the joys of FTP, grep-ing and other technical details. They wanted a transparent environment that allowed them to work on the computer with ease and comfort.

In the worst cases, advocacy for different kinds of workstation solutions can become not too clever ploys designed to gain the users the type of workstation environment they really want, regardless of the particular application under consideration.

For many organizations, the size, power and capabilities of the workstation at your desk serves as a corporate status symbol. The bigger your PC, the more memory it has and the more disk drive attached represents more power, prestige and worth in the corporate environment. In organizations like this you will find users "shopping for solutions" that get them the workstations they really want.

Getting Something for Nothing

Whenever we get into these complex situations where large numbers of people have disparate demands about what the workstation environment should look like, you can usually get down the issues about the real value of the alternatives being considered if you take a discerning look at the budgeting process.

Everybody would like to see a solution provided which gives them the most benefit for the least cost, and this pertains to workstation selection as much as anything else.

The problems come when it is unclear about who exactly is going to pay for the workstations as a part of the ultimate solution. Workstation expenditures are not always part of an overall systems development budget, especially if there is already some kind of infrastructure in place. In these cases, the question becomes:

"Do we modify our solution in order to make use of the existing infrastructure, or do we propose a solution that includes a large financial investment on the hardware/software/network side in order to get a more robust set of tools delivered into the user's hands." If we choose the former, and simply "make do" with what we have, does it undermine the overall objectives of the system? On the other hand, if we choose the latter, who is going to underwrite the additional expense?

Many times users will advocate and support powerful and sophisticated workstation alternatives, as long as they are going to get some new, and from their perspectives "free," new toys to play with. When the solutions become plainer and less friendly, they often lose interest.

Ultimately, the solution to choose one workstation alternative over another is going to boil down to the same issues that we have faced at every other step of our process. When making these decisions, we must weigh the benefits against the costs, and if a justification for the cost cannot be found, then the solution should be abandoned for a more economically sound approach.

There is never anything "free" in the systems development environment and workstation environments can be extremely expensive.

On the other hand, some organizations have already invested heavily in robust, well run workstation type infrastructures. In these cases the decision making process is much easier. Our objective in these cases is to simply figure out how to best leverage what is already in place.

Terminal Illness

Some organizations have not had such an easy time of developing workstation infrastructure approaches. Within these types of organizations, it is not uncommon to find end users with two, three or more terminals at their desks, each tying into a different system. In these cases it will be imperative that we try, if at all possible, to simplify the environment and either leverage what is there, or somehow replace it.

Diversion from Objectives

Unfortunately, as soon as we begin to get into this area, it becomes very easy to get diverted from our main objective, which is to develop and deliver low cost data warehouse applications. Issues regarding whether to user Personal Computers, Dumb Terminals or UNIX Workstations represents our first level of controversy. After that is resolved, the next issues will revolve around operating systems (Windows Vs Windows NT Vs OS/2), (SUN Vs HP Vs SCO UNIX). Then we will need to argue about windowing environments (Windows, OS/2 , Motif, OpenLook etc.). Then we will need to argue about network protocols (NOVELL, TCP/IP, MS-NET).

There is no easy way to resolve these issues, and the developer of a data warehouse solution is going to have to get involved in the controversy if they are going to be able to deliver the data to the user. Our only recommendation is that the project team working on the warehouse concentrate only on those issues having to do with the delivery of the applications at hand.

The Study!

One of the biggest sabotages of warehouse projects in this department happens when the issues about infrastructure are raised and suddenly, someone says, " These decisions are too all encompassing and too important to be made in hurried manner." A committee will be assigned to study the problems and make recommendations at a later date.

Unfortunately, as well meaning as this solution may be, the decision to wait for a study before proceeding with warehouse development is a decision to postpone the warehouse indefinitely. Committees take, at best, several weeks or months to make their decisions, and even if the organization was ready to act on those recommendations immediately it could take months or years to implement the recommendations. Ultimately, the warehouse project will never get started.

Taking a Pro-Active, Profit Driven Approach

The only way to function in an environment like this is to concentrate on the value propositions at hand, and figure out how to deliver them as well as possible given the current environment. If the value propositions you are dealing with are financially sound and of strategic importance to the business, then the case can, and should be made for the development of immediate compromises that allow the project to move forward.

At no time, however, should the developers of the warehouse allow the workstation decision making process to be put on hold while the rest of system developments continue. The mistaken belief in this case is that the workstation decision is a trivial and / or secondary one and that after everything else has been finished, the workstation can simply be tacked on the end.

Taking this approach is a good way to guarantee the failure of your project. Just as we must constantly synchronize all of the data discipline activities across all components of the warehouse, so too must we coordinate physical infrastructure activities. Failure to do so can seriously jeopardize the entire process.

Work Station Decision Making

Given that the environment that we are working in may, or may not force us to contend with a collection of non-technical issues, we nonetheless do have some specific things that we can base physical access component decision making on.

Tool and Product Availability

In most cases, the single biggest driver towards preference for one type of workstation platform over another is type of platform required to support the data mining tools selected. Almost every data mining tool and programming language works only in specific platform environments. The limits of the tool set selected are going to define the limits of the platform options that are available.

In addition to the availability of specific tools for a given platform is the availability of different programming languages, Graphical User Interfaces and Windowing environments. The customized portions of the workstation environment will have to be written using some kind of language or product and these too have platform limitations.

Workstation Disk Storage Area (Storage vs. Work Area vs. Personal Disk Tradeoffs)

Less clear is the requirement that we develop for disk space on the workstation. Should our solution involve the extraction of small amounts of data onto the users workstation, we will have to be sure that those workstations have the disk space available.

Disk space availability is no where near the problem it used to be. In the past, personal computers were severely limited in the amount of disk they could handle, but nowadays, it is possible to attach several Gigabytes of storage for a very lost cost. It is also much easier to upgrade this disk space than it used to be.

When deciding about what kind of disk storage capacity we will want the workstation to have, it will be important to remember that we always have other options. We can always think in terms of trying to figure out how to leverage work area disk space or even storage area disk space in order to supplement the workstation's own capabilities.

Workstation Processing Power (Central vs. Own Processing Power)

Another capacity to consider is the computer processing power that the workstation will need to have. Just as with disk space, there is a way that we can trade-off workstation power with the power that the work area and storage area platforms can provide.

For example, if the user needs to create a data chain, which requires that a number of data reading, manipulating and writing processes occur, that functionality can be built into the workstation itself, or can be offloaded onto the bigger work area and storage platforms through the use of stored procedures and remote applications.

Workstation Network and Data Transport Capabilities (Availability and Capacity)

The thorniest set of issues around workstations can be found in the area of connectivity. How will the workstation be connected to the warehouse? In the perfect world, the workstations will have connections that allow for real time, shared disk and data porting capabilities. In the real world, we may be forced to settle for less. At a minimum, each workstation must at least provide for real time access via remote SQL capabilities.

The simple establishment of a connection between the workstation and the warehouse is not enough to guarantee success. We must also be concerned about the capacity that this linkage will support. A real time connection between the warehouse and the workstation that provides for a 10 minute response time is not going to be very functional in most cases. Our workstation networking decisions must therefore include a robustness that will support the anticipated loads.

Remote Access to the Warehouse

It is becoming increasingly popular for developers to come up with data warehousing solutions that provide for remote access to the warehouse. This remote access usually takes the form of a dial in capability which allows sales people, customer support personnel and managers to make use of phone lines, radio linkages or cellular networks to allow the user to get at the warehouse from anywhere at any time.

The capacity and network capability issues that we have considered up until this point take on an added importance when this is the type of environment being envisioned.

Homogenous Solutions

One of our principle drivers in any data warehousing construction exercise is to try, at all costs to minimize the complexity of the solution being developed. This is especially true in the area of workstations and connectivity. The more different types of user environments we need to support, the more complex the corresponding physical infrastructure, operational infrastructure and application characteristics become. The conflicting drives, one force driving us to simplify the architecture at all costs, one demanding that we minimize the expense and another dictating that we maximize the flexibility and diversity of the solution for the users, leaves us with very difficult decisions to make.

Decision Making

Our process of determining the best workstation (data access) physical infrastructure, therefore, consists of the following decision points:

1.   Determine requirements

At this stage we will want to identify each of the data mining tools that are required in the environment and the workstation capacity that will be required. (This will include requirements for disk space, CPU power and connectivity.)

2.   Evaluate current environment

Based upon these requirements, we will then want to turn to the environment itself and develop an inventory of exactly what kind of existing infrastructure is available.

3.   Develop compromises

Finally comes the hard part, where we compare the lists and develop a "gap analysis" which analyzes where the existing infrastructure falls short and specifies the cost/benefits involved in the upgrading/ modifying of those situations.

Separating the Storage Area

So far we have considered the issues involved in the utilization of multiple platforms for the support of the acquisitions component of the warehouse and for the access component. in some situations this level of platform dispersion will be enough.

In some cases however, we will also need to consider the possibility that the Storage Area, and the corresponding staging and work areas might also be placed on multiple platforms.

While there are lot of reasons for us to prefer that the storage area of the warehouse be a single platform solution, there can be extenuating circumstances that make this impossible or undesirable. There reasons for choosing a multiple storage area configuration can have to do either with:

1. The Leveraging of Existing Platforms
2. The Establishment of Scaleability

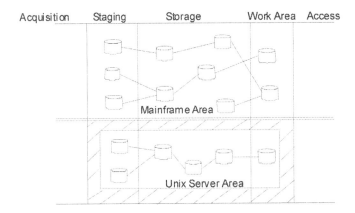

Figure 8-14. Example of a multi-platform storage area

Leveraging Existing Platforms

By far the most common situation that people find themselves in is that there is an existing platform infrastructure already in place that can be used to easily meet some of the needs for the warehouse, but for many reasons that same platform may not have enough excess capacity available in order to use it for the delivery of the complete storage solution.

For example, an organization may have an existing mainframe environment within which some of the warehouse storage can be managed, but constraints within that environment make it impossible to use it for the complete solution. These constraints may come from disk space limitations, the financial inability to cost justify CPU upgrades or the technical inability to upgrade the existing platform any higher. In these situations it will be possible to complement the existing platform with another one, which can then be utilized to support the rest of the warehouse's storage needs.

Homogenous vs. Heterogeneous Solutions

When the decision is made to "split" the storage area across platforms, we introduce another set of complexity and management issues. Where will the Control Tables reside ? How will the organization manage to coordinate the activities on each of the platforms? How will the organization provide technical support for both environments equally well?

These problems are not trivial and their solutions are very expensive. The decision to support different types of platforms at the heart of the warehouse is a decision to double the technical support staff and to more than double the complexity of the technical solution and corresponding management software.

Regardless of these problems, the multi-platform warehouse storage area is not only feasible it can be incredibly cost effective as well. If the people involved in the process of designing and managing the solution are aware of the complexities, costs and risks involved and are able to address them effectively, then the solution is a viable one.

Partitioning Warehouse Storage

When you begin looking at ways to keep different sections of the warehouse's storage on different platforms, you must address the issue of storage area partitioning. Partitioning is the term used to describe the process of breaking a database up into logical blocks. There are several partitioning approaches that will make sense.

Subject Area Platforms

The first and most logical approach to separating different populations of data onto different platforms is to partition the data based on subject area. The term subject area is used to describe a logical grouping of data tables into logical / functional clusters.

For example, a typical data warehouse might have subject areas called, Customer_Information, Product_Information and Sales_ History Information. In this case we might decide to keep the Customer and Sales History information on one platform and place the Product Information on another.

User Access Partitioning

Another good way to partition data is by who will use it. If it is possible to separate different collections of data that different groups of users will need access to, then you can identify a "natural" breaking point for the partitioning decision.

History Platforms

In many situations, it makes a lot of sense to store historical information on a different platform than the main warehouse storage. History data is usually accessed a lot less frequently than storage tables, and it usually involves extremely high volumes of data as well. Separating history data out to a separate platfrom might be done even if the existing platform could handle it because by separating it out, you make it possible to optimize each environment for the type of processing it will require.

Associating Data from Disparate Platforms

While at first glance the decision to partition data across multiple platforms might seem like a very good idea, there are several reasons why it should be avoided. Along with the already considered complexity and management overhead, we must also determine how to allow users to associate data when part of it is on one platform and the other part is on a different platform.

Multi-DB Joins

The principle means that users have to associate data from different tables will be via the SQL - JOIN command. When an SQL command identifies data from two different tables, the database system takes care of finding it and associating it for the user.

Unfortunately, when we store data on multiple platforms we make it difficult or even impossible for the system to provide that functionality depending upon the hardware platforms involved, the database software that each one will be running, and the network capabilities present.

In the best case, the decision to split the storage area across multiple CPUs will involve storing each of these partitions of data on a similar hardware platform running a similar database product. In these cases, there is a good chance that the database product selected will be able to take care of the cross-platform joining of data automatically.

For example, in the IBM mainframe environment, multiple mainframe based DB2 databases can be forced to function as one logical database from the users perspective through the use of the built in distributed database capabilities. This facility ties each DB2 database on each mainframe to all of the other databases on the other mainframes. When the system is presented with an SQL command, it figures out where the data is and takes care of the cross platform activities transparently.

In the same way, the major vendors of UNIX based database products (Sybase, Informix and Oracle) also have built in cross-platform capabilities.

In those situations where the two platforms and databases involved are not totally synchronized, there are still some ways to make it usable. These techniques include:

1.   The use of middleware

Middleware is the name given to 3rd party software (software not provided by the hardware vendor or database vendor) which makes it possible to tie disparate systems together so that they function as one system from the user's perspective. Middleware can make two different hardware/database platforms look like one to the user.

2. The construction of data chains

Another approach that users can take in this kind of environment is to construct data chains which extract the required data from each of the hardware environments and place the resulting sets into the Work Area. The user can then do their cross-table manipulation from that area. The execution of this type of approach assumes that data extraction and transportation linkages exist between the user workstation, the work area and all storage area platforms.

3. The Replication of Data

Probably the least popular of the solutions to this problem is for the managers of the warehouse to actually make copies of key data and store them on both platforms of the warehouse. In this case, the complexity and waste of disk resources can be quite limiting. But in some situations it provides the most viable solution.

When the multiple-platform replication approach is taken it will be critical for developers to :

1. Ascertain that no other approaches are viable

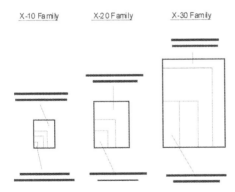

Figure 8-15. Upgradability and computer lines

2. Determine if the database products include any replication facilities that can make the job easier

3. Determine that the data being replicated is the minimum required to get the job done

Upward Scaleability

The other reason we had for advocating a multiple platform solution for the warehouse storage area was the need to establish Scaleability. Scaleability is the built in ability of the system to grow bigger or smaller as the demands for system resources change. In order to understand how the selection of a multiple platform solution can provide us with a foundation for scaleable types of solutions, we must take a moment to understand something about the ways in which computers can be upgraded.

Families of Computers

When you first buy a computer system, you buy it with certain operational assumptions in mind. Based upon those assumptions you will specify a certain amount of memory, a certain amount of processing power and a certain amount of disk space. As your needs change however, you are going to want to upgrade these decisions.

In the olden days of data processing, this upgrade process was a pretty expensive and complicated process. Nowadays, for the most part, however, upgrading is accomplished through the simple replacement of chips or cards in the machine. Our first level of upgrade-ability therefore, is the ability to bump up the capacity of the given platform to whatever maximum it can handle.

Once you have maxed out the upgradeability of a given machine, your next option will be to go back to the manufacturer and see what "family" or "line" of computers your machine belongs to. Most manufacturers provide an upgrade migration path which makes it easy to switch from a lower capacity machine to a higher one within the same family line.

This is therefore our second level of upgrade ability. Moving up the family line.

Why Upgrade Along the Family Line?

The next question that someone may have is "Why upgrade along the family line at all ?" Why not simply upgrade by changing to a different line of computers, or by buying a bigger computer made by a different manufacturer?"

The answer to this question is simple. Every time you change the platform on which your databases and applications run, you must undergo the time and expense involved in converting it to the new environment. Despite the claims of "open systems" and "industry wide compatibility" the fact of the matter is that any attempt to change platforms outside of the vendor provided migration path is going to cost you big in the conversion department.

Our problem , therefore, when it comes to choosing platforms for the warehouse is, "How do I choose a platform that will be big enough, or upgradeable enough to anticipate all of my future needs?" The answer to this question is that you cannot.

Making platform decisions today is going to have consequences tomorrow, and the architects of the warehousing solution need to make these decisions based upon some expectations about how big the system might ultimately get.

Distributed Architectures

An alternative approach to the direct upgrade of the warehouse storage platform, is to assume from the outset that the warehouse is going to be made up of multiple platforms. By choosing the architect and the warehouse around a multiple platform solution, you guarantee that it can be scaled up to however big you might happen to need it. Under this plan you upgrade the system by adding more platforms.

Required Characteristics for a Multiple Platform Warehouse

If we are going to choose to go with a multiple platform architecture from the outset, then we are going to need to understand and make decisions about all of the problems that we considered earlier. How will the user effect multi-platform joins. How will we keep complexity to a minimum?

At this time, there are several vendors of hardware/database software solutions which make it possible to tie the systems together so that they function as one system from the user's perspective. While these products are still relatively new, their presence makes it feasible to consider basing a long term architecture on this kind of multi-platform approach.

Separating the Staging Area

Our decisions about whether or not we want to partition the storage area notwithstanding, there also may be reasons to separate out the staging area from the main storage platform. The staging area, after all, is mostly an area used to simply hold data before it is loaded into the storage area. While it is certainly the most convenient to stage data on whatever storage platform it happens to be loading, it is also feasible to make use of the Legacy platforms or acquisition platforms to hold the data.

What will be critical when deciding whether to stage data on the storage platform or not will be to be sure that whatever alternative we consider, it will be easy and fast for the storage area to access and copy the data over.

The ideal situation is one where the staging area is made up of shared disk space that both the acquisition and storage platforms share. When this is not possible, it will be imperative that some kind of high capacity data porting capabilities exist.

Scenario 1

	Storage	Work Area	Access
Data Storage:	80%	0%	20%
CPU	90%	0%	10%

Scenario 2

	Storage	Work Area	Access
Data Storage:	50%	40%	10%
CPU	60%	30%	10%

Scenario 3

	Storage	Work Area	Access
Data Storage:	40%	60%	0%
CPU	60%	35%	5%

Figure 8-16. Leveraging the Storage, Work Area and Access Area platforms

Separating the Workspace Area

The only area of the warehouse that we have yet to consider for its own platforms is the workspace area. Here too, we may find good reasons to give this area its own platform to work from. The decision of whether or not to place the work area of the warehouse on a platform separate from the storage area is going to depend upon several things:

Our first consideration will be for disk capacity. If the storage area is constrained for space, then the use of a separate platform for the work area will certainly be called for.

Of more pressing need, however, will be for us to consider exactly how much processing power is going to be associated with this area. If the environment we are building is going to require that a large amount of processing be done, creating data chains, executing those chains, performing other kinds of re-formatting or re-arranging of data, then the CPU requirements of the storage area might well exceed those for the warehouse itself.

In general, the entire suite of issues revolving around the storage and transition of data from the storage area to the user can be viewed as having several alternative approaches, each of which makes use of the idiosyncrasies and capacities built into the storage, work area and access areas.

Any non-baseline data (all of the derived tables and data chains) can be constructed and stored within the storage area, the work area, on the users own workstation, or making use of some combination of the three.

In some situations, the user's need for customized data chains, and the storage of massive amounts of personal or limited share data, makes the need for dedicated work area platforms a necessity.

In other situations, the user's needs can be met without the existence of any kind of work area at all.

The creative utilization of the work area can greatly enhance the functionality and flexibility of the overall warehouse environment.

Tying in the Work Area

Of course, as soon as we decide to make the work area a separate platform, we once again greatly increase our complexity. A separate work area platform must provide compatibility with the storage area, and be able to function as an extension of that area, and it must also have all of the tie ins to the access area workstations.

Platform Selection

Having completed our review of the different components of the warehouse and their relationships to platforms, we cannot begin to consider the issues involved in selecting those platforms.

Before we begin to make the mistake that so many theorists make in this area, let's begin by considering what people are actually doing today and planning to do in the future.

Sources of Data

Recently, an independent survey was taken of a sampling of large corporate organizations regarding the issue of data warehousing and future plans. That survey yielded some interesting results. The first question asked was, "What technologies (platforms) house the Legacy system data that you anticipate loading into your warehouse?"

Their response:

- Twenty-five percent of the data will come from mainframe DB2 systems
- Twenty-one percent will come from mainframe VSAM files
- Thirty-three percent will come from other mainframe sources
- Twenty-one percent will come from other sources

In other words, the vast majority of Legacy system environments will be mainframe based

Target Platforms

In the same survey, individuals were asked which platforms they intended to use for the storage component of the warehouse.

Their response:

- Over fifty percent plan on using UNIX based client/server databases like ORACLE, INFORMIX and Sybase.
- Over twenty-five percent plan on using DB2
- The rest will make use of other technologies

While these statistics do little to answer specific questions about what one should do in a given situation, it does provide us with some direction in terms of which way the industry seems to be going.

First of all, if you are planning on designing the acquisition component of your warehouse, then you will almost inevitably need to base that portion of the system in a mainframe environment. Since most of the data will be coming from mainframes, it will make sense to build your acquisitions component with that technology.

Second of all, when it comes to the platform for the storage component, you are probably going to have to make some tough decisions about:

1. Whether to build it in an mainframe DB2 environment, or
2. If you are going to build it in the UNIX environment, deciding upon which UNIX database to go with

Both of these decisions are difficult, but are critical to the success of the warehouse.

As far as helping the reader to make those individual decisions, all we can say is that we have spent this chapter clearly examining each of the issues and considerations that should be taken into account when making platform and infrastructure decisions. There is no way to make the process of weighing these issues any easier than to assure the reader that everyone must go through the process, and to say that there is never only one right answer to any of the questions and that compromises are going to have to be made.

CONCLUSIONS

This marks the end of our process of examining each of the different layers and components that make up the data warehouse. We have defined them, analyzed them and considered the tradeoffs involved in making decisions in each of these areas.

Armed with this more intimate knowledge about the warehouse's make up and structure, we are now ready to return to the issues of management, construction approaches and cost estimating techniques.

CHAPTER 9

A MODEL FOR OVERALL WAREHOUSE PLANNING

Equipped with a more detailed understanding of exactly what is going to be involved in the construction and running of the warehouse, we are now ready to return to the issue of how we are going to manage the overall warehouse construction process.

So far we have identified that our process will consist of two major phases, the first has to do with developing a common understanding of what the warehouse will be, and a set of requirements for how it will be built. We call this the Overall Warehouse Development Project. The second phase, consists of the construction of a series of autonomous, value based applications, each to be placed within the subsequent warehouse environment.

Figure 9-1. The two major phases of warehouse development

THE OVERALL WAREHOUSE DEVELOPMENT PROJECT

We then proceeded to define some of the individual steps within the warehouse development process. These included:

1. Vision Development
2. Validation and Estimation
3. Warehouse Planning
4. Infrastructure Development

Figure 9-2. Steps in the overall warehouse development

Each of these steps in the process plays a critical role in the development of the overall warehouse solution, and none of the steps can be skipped or taken out of order. Later, we will consider some of the ways in which variations to our proposed approach can be worked into the plan, but for now we will continue to describe the process as it would be executed in the ideal environment.

Let's begin by developing some understanding of what should happen within each of these steps, and what the outputs from each should be.

Vision Development

The objective of the vision development step is to assist the organization in developing a consistent, realistic and meaningful consensus about what the warehouse will be. The process we will go through in order to develop that consensus will vary with the situation and environment, but the end result must be a vision statement, describing the warehouses scope, intent and characteristics, and most importantly a collection of specific value propositions, each of which defines an autonomous, value added function that the warehouse can deliver.

The output of the process is therefore:

1. A meaningful definition of the warehouse
2. Consensus
3. A collection of well defined and well documented value propositions, each of which can be used as the starting point for the execution of a warehouse application development project.

Validation and Estimation

Using these value propositions as input, and armed with the advocacy of all management, operational and systems personnel that the solutions are desirable and valuable, our next step is to validate and

Figure 9-3. Output of the vision development process

estimate their costs.

At this stage, each of our value propositions will be little more than rough outlines of how people think things could work. During the validation step we apply some rigor to them and ascertain whether they are financially, organizationally and technically feasible. Most importantly, we will need to determine whether the proposed solutions will actually be financially feasible or not. When we say financially feasible, we mean that we must validate that a) the organization can afford to build them and b) that the value that they will deliver will be greater than or at least equal to the cost.

Of course, when we attempt to validate these assumptions we may encounter situations where there is no way to know whether they are feasible or not, unless we develop some good estimates as to the effort it will take to develop them, and as to the technical resources that will be required to deliver them. We therefore will need to conduct the validation and estimation processes in tandem, each one feeding information to the other.

The output of the validation and estimation process will assure we have ascertained with a high degree of confidence that both the overall warehouse proposed, and the individual applications therein can be delivered on time, on budget and with the subsequent delivery of value to the organization. The physical deliverable is both a set of greatly enhanced value propositions, which now include a set of requirements for the applications to be built, and a set of specifications for the infrastructure of the warehouse itself.

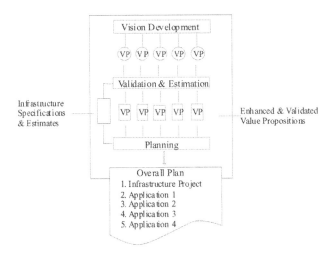

Figure 9-4. Validation, estimation, and planning

Planning

Once the feasibility of the overall warehouse, and of the individual value propositions has been determined, we can then turn to the development of a plan to deliver the overall solution to the organization.

The end product of the planning process will be several things:

1. An overall plan for the construction of the warehouse
2. Budget , timing and delivery deadlines for each application
3. A plan and budget for the construction of a physical and operational infrastructure.

Infrastructure Development

Once the plan has been proposed and accepted, we will want to develop the actual physical infrastructure that will support it.

Figure 9-5. Execution of the warehouse plan

VARIATIONS

While it would certainly be our objective to see all warehousing projects proceed according to the structure in a nice, organized, serial series of steps to be executed, the reality is that for a lot of different reasons, we are going to have to get creative in the way we approach these projects in the real world.

The steps, phases and processes that we have been describing are each critical components of a successful warehouse implementation, but the realities of business, finance, technology, corporate environment and finance are going to force us to vary our plans to meet the needs of the situation.

When you look at this progression of steps and develop an understanding for exactly what is supposed to happen during each phase, it is clear that this is the order in which things should be done.

Variations Under Vision Development

Obviously, you need to begin with a good vision of exactly what it is you are trying to build. During the process of vision development we assemble that picture and enlist the aide and participation of all the parties that will benefit from the endeavor. Only through a rigorous and formally defined process of vision development can the builders of the warehouse hope to prevent all the organizational misunderstandings and infighting that sabotages projects after development has begun. We have also established that the objective of the vision development process should be the definition of tactically applicable value propositions. By basing our overall project plan on specific, attainable and immediately beneficial pieces, we guarantee that the entire warehousing project will yield maximum benefit to the organization.

Unfortunately, sometimes, the environment that you are working in will not support this kind of overall vision development initiative. Sometimes, upper management opts not to participate in the process, feeling that these are technical or operational issues and not worthy of their attention.

Other times, the environment is so laced with animosity and negativity based upon the history of relationships within the organization, that you will be forced to function without the benefit of participation from people that would seem to be key to your success.

The question that we must answer, when trying to work within situations like this is "What is the definition of a minimally acceptable vision development process?" Assuming that we cannot enlist the participation of everyone needed to do a good job, where do we draw the line and say that we have involved enough people?

The answer to this question is really pretty straightforward. The success of our warehousing project, and of our vision development efforts must be viewed in terms of its scope and breadth.

If the warehouse we are developing is being proposed as a major corporate undertaking. If it is being put forward as a major strategic direction for the entire computer systems development area... If it is being proposed to involve the collection and dissemination across all organizational units of the corporation, then the vision development phase must involve all the key upper management executives, and the key management staff from each of the operational areas. There is simply no way around it. The budget requirements for a project of this size, and the participation required from the people at all levels of management will be so high, that if you fail to get their participation during vision development, then there is no way that you can expect them to "buy in" to the project at the later, more painful and more expensive phases.

In a sense, the vision development project is a thermometer, which allows the sponsors of the project to test the water...to see if the project will gain acceptance or not.

Many times, data warehousing initiatives are sponsored by the data processing organization. In these cases, the ability or inability of the group to present the concept of the warehouse in the kinds of business terms that operational and upper management personnel will respond to will be a good acid test of the overall approach. If your warehouse initiative is one based upon technical sophistication and upon the simplification of the operational data processing environment, then who will care other than data processing people. If on the other hand, the warehouse is presented and perceived as the means to quickly deliver valuable capabilities into the hands of operational and managerial personnel, then the reception will be much warmer.

Limiting Scope

Of course, within many organizations, it will not make sense to approach warehousing projects in such a grandiose manner. If the receptivity on the part of upper management or certain operational areas is not there, then the proponents of the approach will need to lower their sights a little bit, and come at the problem from a much humbler perspective.

In these cases, the developers of the warehouse will need to identify specific operational areas within the organization which a) have needs that the data warehouse can meet and b) have the predisposition to get involved in the process. By limiting the initial scope of the vision development process to include only those areas who will immediately benefit from the effort, the project advocates greatly increase their chances of success.

The long term strategy may be to roll out a limited scope project, in order to prove to people what the warehousing concept can accomplish, and then to approach the more grandiose overall corporate direction.

The Single Application Warehouse

At the low end of the scope spectrum are those situations where it is decided to build only one specific, discrete application, making use of the warehousing approach, in the hopes that the results will gain the interest and trust of a bigger group of users.

In all cases, what is critical is that we define the scope of the project (in terms of the operational groups to be supported and the functional areas to be addressed) and then assure that the vision development process is executed for that group.

Vision Development is not an optional step.

Variations in Application Development

The second area where we have already developed a well defined set of steps to follow is in the area of application development. Our chapter on the data disciplines lays out the progression of steps that you will need to go through in order to deliver an application in the most efficient way possible.

Of course, the data discipline process described does not correspond too well with the accepted industry practice of using data driven design and data modeling as the core of systems development. It probably most closely aligns with a general understanding of the RAD approach (Rapid Application Development). RAD, like our data disciplines, advocates the streamlined, minimalist focusing of your efforts on the delivery of small, tactical relevant applications in the shortest time possible.

The fact that the "old school" data driven approaches were conceived over 20 years ago, and were developed to support specifically, the development of data based, on-line transaction processing systems is immaterial. The fact is that it is simply "the way things are done" for many organizations.

Recognizing this fact, we allow for the variation of our data discipline approach. We will do this for two reasons.

First, we do it in order to take advantage of whatever work organizations may have already done that may make the process of application development easier. Existing enterprise models, data models and data analysis certainly cannot hurt the effort, in fact they can contribute greatly, as long as they accept the shift in focus that we require, namely, the shift towards the more practical, tactical and immediate needs of the users of the warehouse vs. the more general overall needs of the organization as a whole.

Second, we will incorporate the data driven approaches in order to help increase the comfort level of the people involved in the development process and to leverage existing skills as much as possible.

DATA DRIVEN DATA DICIPLINES

Our proposal for the blending of the traditional data driven and our newly proposed data discipline approach, will involve our starting , of course with the data models. Under this variation we will add several data modeling steps to the front end of the procedure. After this data analysis has been completed, we can then proceed with the previously described steps.

1. Identify the data required to support each value proposition

2. Develop subject area models to support each value proposition

3. Develop an inventory of principle entities for each subject area

4. Develop an integrated key structure for each

5. Consolidate subject area models into a overall warehouse model

6. Instigate the previously detailed data discipline process

There are actually some advantages to this kind of approach, and in some cases we may decide to append this process to our project plan whether the people involved require it or not. By doing this kind of data modeling work up front, we will certainly make the rest of the application development process easier. The development of these subject area and entity models can only serve to help people understand the business areas they are working with and the early attack of key issues will certainly prevent problems in the future. We will also identify and additional place where this kind of preliminary research and set up work can be helpful when we consider the validation and estimation processes.

While the developers of a warehouse application do not absolutely require this kind of preliminary data modeling effort, it can certainly be helpful, and if data modeling work that pertains to the application has already been done, it should be leveraged wherever possible.

We emphasize at this point, however, that the level of data modeling activity we propose at the front end of this process is very rudimentary and shallow in nature. Under no circumstances should any warehouse development resources be spent in the development of detailed entity attribution processes. There is no way that the appropriate identification of specific data elements for the warehouse can occur without a great deal of information about the data mining tools being utilized and the needs of the users taken into account.

It is here, in the area of when, where and how detailed data attribution should occur where we vehemently resist the premature application of data modeling efforts. Experience with hundreds of data modeling projects has proven one thing beyond a shadow of a doubt. People that go off and develop attribution information without knowledge of the applications that will use it, end up going through the process twice. Once on their own, and than again when the needs of the application become known. While there is certainly some small amount of benefit that can be gained from the research and development effort done ahead of time, the amount of information that can be carried forward is usually minimal.

This is not usually due to the abilities of the people doing the modeling, it is simply a function of the very specific needs for data that most applications have and the realities of where data is actually going to come from. The development of a theoretically sound database schema that doesn't hold the information in the form that users want it is useless. So is a schema that identifies data that cannot be located.

Other than the subject we have just considered, there are really no other places in the data discipline process where we can get away with much variation. Any attempt to shortcut or skip these steps is going to result in a major disconnect in the ultimate delivery of the application.

The Blending of Steps

So far we have considered variation in the vision development and the application development processes, but we have said nothing about making changes to the validation & planning or the infrastructure development steps. That is because it is in these areas that the most drastic and often fatal kinds of variations occur. It is also because we have yet to actually describe the validation and planning steps in any kind of detail.

We have postponed our discussions of these processes for several reasons, but the biggest is that until we described the rest of the environment within which we would be working, it would be too difficult to explain how it fits in. The other reason is that the variations that can be and often are utilized can make the whole discussion very confusing.

The biggest temptation in the development of any large, expensive complicated system like this, is to look for shortcuts and to look for ways to leverage the efforts of one stage to make the next easier. We will address each of these reasons.

Other Variations Within Application Development

Of course, our consideration of ways in which the application development process can be varied does little to address the vast majority of variations that people traditionally apply to the process. The assumptions that we make when we talk about application development are that:

1. The organization has gone through the vision development process and the application has been defined as being tied to a specific, narrowly defined value proposition.

2. The system has been carried through the corresponding validation and estimation steps.

3. The physical and operational infrastructures are already in place.

4. The application developers can concentrate on the task of building this one focused application.

The real variation in the process that we need to worry about are those cases where people fail to carry their project through these steps, in this order. What is more typical of the application development process is that people try to accomplish vision development, validation, estimation and infrastructure development at the same time they are doing the development of the application itself. These attempts to cut corners lead, invariably, to complexity, confusion, waste and in some cases utter failure.

We live in a real world however, and there are good reasons for trying to blend these steps together. In the next chapter on estimation and planning, we will consider some of these situations and see how we can include this kind of variability into our planning process without allowing it to get out of hand.

Shortcuts

Unfortunately, there is absolutely no such thing as a shortcut when it comes to warehouse development. There are certainly a large number of people claiming to know about how to do shortcuts. There are even vendors of products that claim to be able to sell you shortcuts. But the reality has been proven again and again, that shortcuts have only three potential outcomes:

1. They cause you to underestimate or skip key steps in the process

2. They cause you to underestimate the cost and level of effort necessary to complete the project

3. They build "traps" into your project which can and will be "sprung" by someone, somewhere along the line

Types of Shortcuts

Shortcuts in Validation

There all kinds of ways that people delude themselves into thinking that there is a way to get around the work that must be done in order to do a good job of warehouse development. In the area of validation, people often try to minimize or dismiss problems found in the business area :

1. Developing an understanding of the business issues

Many times people assume that if the business solution sounds like it makes sense, everyone will simply agree and go along with it. It is critical that all operational areas involved have the opportunity to truly understand what the solution proposes and validate that it can be done. Many times organizational issues, budgeting constraints, time factors or business procedures can invalidate otherwise sound business plans.

2. Developing strong advocacy and support from operational and management areas

The second area where developers get themselves into trouble is to minimize the need to have advocacy from the operational and management areas. The solution is so good, they think, that surely everyone will go along with us. We'll just get started and they'll see the light. This is the kind of thinking that gets projects in trouble.

3. Validating the existence of the data required

A critical business assumption that must be addressed is the assumption that all of the data that is needed can be found somewhere. Somehow, these assumptions must be validated.

4. Validating the effectiveness of a data mining tool

Another situation where business users can set themselves up occurs when people become enamored with data mining tools before finding out the details about how they work, what it will take to make them work and what it will take for the users to make use of them.

And in the technical area:

5. Validating that the technical solution proposed will actually work

It is appalling how many computer systems projects get proposed and budgeted, where the technical staff has no way of knowing whether the proposed solution can actually work or not. Assumptions about the volumes of data to be handled, the capacity of the hardware, the nature of the network environment and the validity of vendor claims have created a great many situations where projects were undertaken only to be abandoned late in the process because somebody's assumptions were incorrect.

6. Validating the technical solution proposed can be delivered on time or on budget

The other place where technical assumptions are usually far out of touch with reality comes in the area of the estimation of the person effort required to bring a system to completion. The data processing industry is notorious for the underestimation of timing and the overestimation of the abilities of staff to work with complex new technological approaches.

All in all, the validation process we will be defining shortly, must be followed vigorously if the rest of the planning and execution process is going to be valid.

Shortcuts in Estimation

Right in line with the use of shortcut assumptions in order to skip timely validation steps, is the slip shod manner in which most organization perform the estimation process. This process involves developing estimates for hardware, software, systems development , user participation and overall budget dollars as well as timing.

We will also spend a significant amount of time analyzing the estimation process in greater detail in the next chapter.

Shortcuts in Planning

It is actually quite amazing the process that many people go through when planning systems development projects. Some spend no more than fifteen minutes discussing what to do next and then tell everyone to get started! Others spend days and weeks in the creation of Gantt charts and project plans which ultimately turn into nothing more than footnotes to the real systems development process.

Somehow, we need to define a project planning mechanism that prevents people from skipping this step, while avoiding becoming a career unto itself.

By providing everyone with a physical and organizational framework for the development of a warehouse, we have already taken some big steps in this direction. In this and the next chapter, we will complete the picture and provide a more comprehensive approach to the process.

Shortcuts in Data Disciplines

We have already spent a considerable amount of time documenting and explaining the many ways that people try to get around having to do the tedious process of data identification, sourcing, mapping and synchronization. As with the other phases of the development process, any attempts to avoid these steps simply lead to problems in the future.

Shortcuts in Infrastructure Development

Of all the areas of short-cutting, the tales and woes of organizations that have underestimated the complexity and expense of infrastructure development are the most legion of all. In case after case people have dismissed infrastructure development as a trivial or automatic process, and paid the price.

Major Variations

Given that we accept the premise that there are a lot of bad reasons for trying to shortcut the warehouse development process, and given that by allowing shortcuts and variations to occur that we can oftentimes get into trouble, we must nonetheless accept that reality does not always correspond with our wishes. We must therefore establish some criteria for determining what kinds of variations should be permissible and under what conditions they should be allowed.

The variances that we have been considering up until now are relatively minor in nature, and will not change our overall plan to any great degree. The overall sequence of events that we have laid out as the perfect execution plan would be as follows.

Overall warehouse development:

1. Vision development
2. Validation and estimation of the warehouse
3. Planning for the overall warehouse
4. Development of the infrastructure

Project approval:

5. Project approval and budgeting

Figure 9-6. "Normal" sequence of events

System development:

6. Construction of the infrastructure
7. Construction of individual applications

There are three major areas of variance in this proposed approach which we are going to have to deal with head on. While it is clear that there are certain steps that simply cannot be skipped if you are going to succeed, in the following areas, there is a strong likelihood that if you cannot come up with some kind of alternative solution, you are going to condemn the project to budgetary obscurity before you even get started. These variances include:

1. Attempts to minimize the planning costs and time: variance in the overall warehouse development project

Many of the examples cited above were examples of ways in which people attempt to shortcut critical planning and estimating steps in order to move the project forward. While we cannot condone the skipping of these steps or any attempts to execute them in a different order, what we do realize is that there may be times when the formal execution of these steps would be redundant. Many times you will find that different people have already accomplished a lot of the objectives of the planning and estimation steps.

For example, in some organizations, there may already have been a great deal of thought and planning put into the development of a warehouse vision. Or you may find that certain value propositions are so simple, easy to do and so clear cut, that very little work needs to be done to accumulate and document them.

In other cases, validation and estimation may be trivial processes because the solutions proposed are so easy to deliver, and involve no exceptional volumes of data, system complexities or problems with source data identification. For example, a system which is designed to pull data from a purchased list and provide ad hoc access to it will be relatively easy to turn into a proposition, and the requirements determination process will be practically completed before you start.

Basically, our criteria for the minimization of any of the steps in the process will be simple. You can skip the work involved, but you cannot skip the deliverables. Each step in the process has a set of documented deliverables which communicates things about the system to the readers and developers of the system. Failure to spend a lot of time analyzing is not a problem. Failure to thoroughly document assumptions and gain consensus among all of the parties involved is a sure road to ruin.

2. The need to ameliorate the up front infrastructure costs: variance in infrastructure development (incremental infrastructure building).

The second area where there will be a lot of resistance to the approach proposed is our insistence that the infrastructure, both physical and operational be put into place before the development of actual applications begins. The accepted way of building systems is to develop the infrastructure while you develop the application.

Actually this is the perceived truth, not the reality. The reality is that when the systems development life cycle methodologies and procedures were being developed, there were no major infrastructure issues to deal with. Applications were built on platforms that were stable and known parameters for capacity, management and development. The problem is that the builders of applications these days try to minimize the tremendous amount of work involved in the establishment of these new infrastructure environments.

Assuming that we are unable to get the funding for infrastructure development up front, then our only other option is to proceed with a scaleable infrastructure architecture and attempt to build it up over time.

This approach can actually be not as bad as it might first seem if it is handled correctly.

- Scaling up the storage component -- by making use of scaleable database / platform architectures such as distributed database mechanisms and middleware.

- Scaling up the access component -- by rolling out the physical terminal and network components only to users that need them at each stage.

- Scaling up the acquisitions component -- by continuing to upgrade the acquisitions platforms and capability as the size of the component grows.

In all three cases, it is essential that we determine how to scale the infrastructures development so that applications gaining the enhancement are paying only for what they need.

We can greatly enhance our chances of making use of a scalability approach to infrastructure development, if we determine the following at the outset:

- The current, intermediate, and ultimate makeup of the acquisition, storage and access components.

- Wherever possible dictate hardware, software, standards and procedures compatibility at the outset.

- Keep long range objectives in mind while building each layer of the system.

The long term efficiency of the effort may be reduced by this approach, and the complexity will certainly be increased, but adherence to goals, objectives and decisions made at the beginning of the process will greatly enhance the chance for final success.

1. The need to resolve validation or estimation problems. (Proof of concept projects, prototypes and benchmarks).

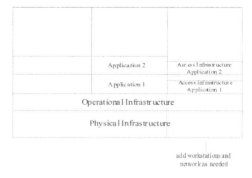

Figure 9-7. Scaleable infrastructure (access component)

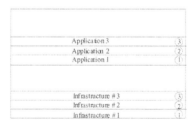

Figure 9-8. Scaleable overall infrastructure

By far the most challenging situation, requiring us to vary our approach, is when we are unable to validate or estimate the overall construction effort due to insufficient information. There are several ways this occurs:

a) We may be unsure about how the end users need the final application to function.

b) We may be unsure that proposed hardware or software can handle the volumes, access rates, or complexity of processing.

c) We may be unsure about what the development effort for a proposed application will actually be. This is prevalent when many untested technology or business assumptions are in play.

d) We may be unsure that the proposed solution can actually work.

e) We may unsure that the desired data can be located.

When these kinds of situations occur, we have only two choices: 1) Make up some numbers and blindly proceed with the rest of our development steps, hoping that somehow our guesses are good. 2) Create non-conventional development techniques to help resolve these problems for the good of the overall project.

While all the techniques we are about to consider can provide great value to the overall warehouse development effort, it is important to establish several ground rules for their use at the outset. The problem is that these solutions tend to become real projects in the minds of the people who sponsor them. When this happens and we attempt to skip all intermediate steps, and just start construction, we usually end up with trouble. Because the utilization of these techniques is expensive and time consuming, and because they yield no real value in and of themselves, there is a strong tendency to pretend that they are more than they really are, just to get them approved.

It is also critical that we minimize fantasies about leveraging the work we can count on from the execution of these kinds of alternative approaches. We should not be deluded into thinking that a heavy investment in benchmarks, prototypes, or proof of concept projects will drastically reduce the cost of real systems development. The way that these projects are often sold is -- that the development work can be reused in the ultimate system. This kind of double-think causes nothing but inaccuracy and disappointment. If you knew what was going to happen when you instigated a benchmark, prototype, pilot or proof of concept project, then you would not start them in the first place, you would simply begin with normal construction. You sponsor projects of this type when you need to discover things about the system that you do not already know. These projects are not simple assumption validations They are experiments and fact-finding missions that provide us with the information to successfully estimate and build the real system.

When these kinds of projects are worked into our project plan, they need to be identified as separate projects in our overall project plan. We should not replace any real projects (infrastructure or application) with these alternatives, and we should not drastically reduce our estimates of the effort that subsequent projects will take.

Even more importantly, if the point of the project is to determine the ultimate development effort, then we need to make it clear that no estimates of overall effort will be forthcoming until after they are completed.

For each of the alternative approaches we will consider:

- What they are
- What they should be used for
- What their deliverables should be

Benchmarks

A benchmark project is designed to ascertain whether a targeted combination of hardware and software can meet the anticipated workload created by a warehouse system. Benchmarks are narrow in scope and are utilized to test assumptions about the ability of a proposed system to perform well under anticipated conditions. They are usually associated with the storage component of the warehouse.

We should make use of a benchmark whenever we are unsure of the capabilities of the hardware or software that we propose. They are most often used to validate:

1. The ability of the database storage area to support the volumes and loads anticipated
2. The ability of the access component networking structure to handle anticipated traffic

The deliverable from the process should be an identification of suitable hardware and software for the subsequent project and accurate cost estimates for each.

Prototypes

Prototypes are usually proposed to resolve questions about whether analysts are unsure about the assumptions that have been made regarding how the system should work or behave. A prototype is a scaled- down working model of the real thing. Therefore prototypes usually consist of mockups of the screens that the ultimate system will utilize, loaded in small samples of the types of data that it will manage. These are usually associated with the Access component of the warehouse.

A prototype, therefore, has an entirely different objective than a benchmark. While a benchmark answers questions about technical capacity of the overall warehouse environment, prototypes answer questions about functional and operational feasibility of a specific application. Because a prototype is a mockup and not a real system, it can be instrumental in helping people visualize solutions.

Under no circumstances should people assume that the screens and functionalities of a prototype are investments in the ultimate application. The shortcut methods used to develop these components quickly make them usable only as guidelines for the real thing.

When an artist makes a miniature prototype of a sculpture, or when an engineer makes a prototype of a bridge, he does not try to use those prototypes as part of the real objects. He simply uses them as examples of how the real objects should look and behave.

In summary, the output of a prototype process is a collection of screens with a minimal functionality.

Proof of Concept Projects

Proof of concept projects are defined to help substantiate a collection of assumptions that have been made about systems development that cannot be validated without more hard proof. Proof of concept projects are usually much larger than benchmark or prototype efforts, and actually begin to work with at least some of the components of the real warehouse environment.

A proof of concept project will often be a combination benchmark and prototyping effort, but it can also be developed to test even larger feasibility issues. For example, you cannot ascertain how difficult it will be to identify data in source systems and transport it through cleansing , formatting, staging, loading and access with either a benchmark or a prototype. In fact the biggest difference between them is that the other two test singular components of functionalities of the warehouse, while a proof of concept tests end-to-end functionalities.

When we begin talking about proof of concept projects we enter an area where it can become exceedingly difficult to avoid the "and then we can leverage it all to minimize construction costs" trap. Proof of concept projects are stripped down versions of real applications, developed in a manner that allows developers to test critical assumptions awaiting validation. For example, we might develop a proof of concept project to validate whether the keys for the data required by a data mining application can be identified and exported to the access area.

We might also develop a proof of concept project to validate our ability to interconnect a collection of legacy, warehouse and access components. In all cases the output of a proof of concept project is a set of loosely-defined working code that performs some key functions required of the warehouse, but without all the detail to make it truly usable.

Figure 9-9. Adding benchmarks to the plan

Adding Alternative Projects to our Planning Process

As we can see, based upon the objectives for each of these types of projects, they need to be included at a different point in our project execution process.

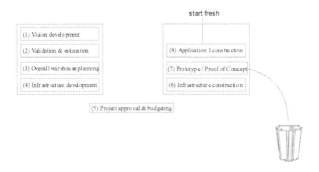

Figure 9-10. Adding prototype or proof of concept projects to the plan

The Benchmark tests, since they are executed to test the overall ability of the warehouse to perform, need to be executed as a part of the validation and estimation process for the overall warehouse project.

Pilot and proof of concept projects, however, have to do with the validation of assumptions about specific applications. They should be executed only after the overall warehouse plan has been approved and after the infrastructure has been developed. Then they can developed, and we can learn from them, before discarding them.

Pilot Projects

A pilot project is designed to deliver a fully functional part of an overall application. As such it will be treated and developed as any other application would, except that its scope has been drastically reduced. The deliverable from a pilot project is a fully functional part of an application.

Unlike the other types of projects considered, the pilot project is not discarded. A pilot project is nothing more than a scaled down component of an overall application. Therefore, when planning for its utilization, we include it as part of the cost of developing the application it "pilots" for.

Rapid Application Development

Figure 9-11. Adding pilot project to the plan

The last type of variance to application development that we will consider is a relatively new approach to development called RAD or Rapid Application Development. Under RAD, developers approach application development as an iterative process, where they move quickly between prototyping, construction, delivery and back again. The cycle is repeated until the application is complete. RAD has strength to it, and approaches some of the problems we have been addressing in the same manner.

Experience has shown that the RAD approach will work well -- if and only if -- the infrastructure environment is stable and the objectives of the development effort are clearly defined.

There should be no disharmony between the approach we propose and a RAD approach, as long as all aspects of the data disciplines we have identified are considered in the process.

CONCLUSIONS

Throughout this chapter, we have concentrated on presenting the reader with an overview of some of the challenges involved in the planning of the overall warehouse, and some of the ways that variations can and will occur.

In subsequent chapters we will be zeroing in on the vision development, validation and estimation steps in more detail. We will then be able to return to a more in-depth discussion of the planning, management, staffing and budgeting processes.

CHAPTER 10

VISION, VALUE AND FOCUS

THE VISION
DEVELOPMENT PHASE

VISION DEVELOPMENT

We are ready to start formally defining the first of our phases, vision development.

In an earlier chapter we presented a diagram which provides us with a picture of what the vision development process should look like and we began the process of fleshing out the details of how the process would work. We are now ready to complete this picture and come to a full understanding of how this process can work.

The Vision Development Process -- An Overview

We can break down the vision development process into the following two stages:

1. We start with the collection of the different ideas and visions that each of the individuals involved in the warehouse development process might hold.

2. We then analyze this collection and distill from it a collection of specific, well defined value propositions.

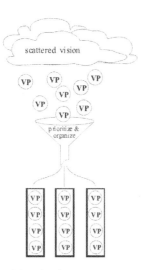

Figure 10-1. The vision development process

After this is completed, we can proceed with the validation, estimation and planning steps, which will allow us to assemble and organize these value propositions into a strategy for warehouse deployment.

This approach starts at the earliest phases of a proposed warehouse's life cycle. Our assumption is that for any given organization that is in the process of considering a warehouse; the people involved in all areas of the business, management, operations and systems, perceive the warehouse in a different way. And that each will approach the project making a different set of assumptions about what the warehouse is supposed to do, and how it will be cost justified.

Getting a Clearer Picture of the Warehouse

Our first job is to talk to the people involved in all areas of the business, who are interested in using the warehouse, to help them determine what they would like to see the warehouse provide and how they view its potential value. The process of collecting and analyzing these proposals can be very informative.

Our experience, based on conducting hundreds of interviews of this type, enables us to identify certain thought patterns that most people apply to the warehousing issue.

SpecificPhases of the Vision Development and the Validation and Planning Processes

We will call this process of gathering up everyone's visions, and developing a common vision of the warehouse, the vision development process. We will call the process of validating the practicality of these approaches, the development of estimates for delivery and the development of plans, the validation and planning process. These processes can be conducted by an internal computer systems group, an operational area, or by an outside consulting firm specializing in this kind of activity. No matter who does it, the process involves interviewing all the people who might be involved in the warehouse development process. The following steps are required.

Vision Development

1. Collecting the visions

Our first task is to interview everyone who has expressed an interest in the warehouse (or anyone we suspect might benefit from the warehouse), and determine their vision of how the warehouse could help them.

2. Evaluating the visions

Our next step is to evaluate each of these visions for their scope, focus and hardness or softness. During this phase we will begin to understand what each vision is really about and what the underlying objectives might be.

3. Decomposing the visions

After evaluating each vision, we begin the process of decomposition. During this phase we will attempt to break the larger, less focused and broader scoped visions into a collection of smaller, more tangible ones. Any large vision should be able to be decomposed into a collection of smaller ones.

4. Verify the decomposition

After decomposing the visions, we can return to the people who originally provided them to ensure that the decompositions and valuations make sense, and that the solutions defined are practical and desirable.

5.   Recruiting of sponsors

After the verification stage, we are left with a collection of well-defined, narrowly-scoped candidate applications. We can take each of these candidate applications and identify the business areas that would be willing to sponsor them. In the vast majority of cases the identification of sponsors is easy. However, the willingness of the sponsors to lay claim to them may be more difficult. Once a sponsor has been identified, the candidate application becomes a proposition for systems development.

6.   Determination of hard benefits

The first thing that the sponsor of the application will be asked to do is verify and assign hard benefits to the effort. In other words, the sponsor is asked to state that -- should this application be delivered, the following benefits would accrue.

Validation and Planning

After we have determined the benefits associated with these propositions, we are ready to begin validating them and developing a plan. This includes:

7.   Determination of reasonableness and cost estimates

After the assignment of hard benefits, the evaluation team needs to develop rough estimates of the cost of delivering the solution for each proposition.

8.   Development of formal value proposition statements

By combining our hard benefits estimate with cost estimates, we can define value propositions. A value proposition proposes that a certain type of system should be developed. It further details the cost of delivery and what the benefits of the effort will be.

9.   Consolidation of value propositions

After the solidification of each of our value propositions, we can look at all the value propositions that have been developed and determine the overlap, consolidation, integration or sequencing requirements we may have. Remember, warehouse applications must be developed either autonomously, or serially.

10.   Development of deployment strategy

Finally, an overall strategy for warehouse development is assembled.

ROLES AND RESPONSIBILITIES

If the previously described process is going to be successful, we have to make assumptions about the various roles of the different participants in the process, along with a corresponding set of expectations about the level of their commitment. In order to successfully implement this process, we are going to need the participation of individuals from three groups:

- Management,
- The operational area being considered, and
- Systems

The first question that anyone would ask when getting ready to set up a team to tackle this process will naturally be, "Who is responsible for driving this process'? As we have previously noted, one of the biggest sources of problems in the development of requirements for systems is that no one seems sure of their role.

We will therefore propose an allocation of resources that seems most logical. If the situation at hand forces some variance of this proposal, it certainly does not mean that the project will fail. This allocation simply makes the most sense for the majority of cases.

Since it makes the most sense that the computer systems area (or specialized consultants) will drive the process, then it will fall upon them to be responsible for ensuring that everyone else is aware of what is expected of them.

Vision Development				
Step	Description	Management	Operational	Systems
1	Collecting the Visions	Light	Medium	Heavy
2	Evaluating the Visions	--	--	Heavy
3	Decomposing the Visions	Light	Medium	Heavy
4	Verify the Decomposition		Light	Heavy
5	Recruiting of Sponsors	Light	Medium	Heavy
6	Determination of Hard Benefits	--	Heavy	Heavy
Validation and Planning				
Step	Description	Management	Operational	Systems
7	Determination of Reasonableness and Cost Estimates	--	Medium	Heavy
8	Development of Value Propositions	--	Light	Heavy
9	Consolidation of Value Propositions	--	--	Heavy
10	Development of Deployment Strategy	Light	Medium	Heavy

Table 10-1

Allocation of Roles by Steps

We have prepared the following table to indicate whose participation should be required for each step, and what their level of commitment should be.

Rule Number	Description
1	**Contiguity** -- Each application must include an acquisition, storage and access component.
2	**Business Focus and Decomposition** -- Each application must be based upon a specific value proposition.
3	**Serial Development of Dependent Applications** -- Applications that are dependent upon the components of another application must be developed one at a time.
4	**Parallel Development on for Autonomous Applications** -- It is permissible to build applications simultaneously, as long as they have no dependencies.

Table 10-2

Correspondence to the Application Rules

In chapter five, we introduced the concept of the data warehouse "application." We said the data warehouse, like the real world warehouse to which we compared it, was nothing more than an empty framework, which we could utilize to store and access data. We further stated that we were going to segregate the different inventories of data within that warehouse into discrete applications. We then proceeded to propose a series of rules about how those applications were going to be defined.

It is critical that the individuals involved in the process of vision development are aware of the above-mentioned rules and their consequences for the overall vision identification and analysis

2a	Every value proposition must be based upon a specific business need.
2b	Every value proposition must have a single, responsible business sponsor.
2c	Each value proposition must define a tangible benefit to the sponsoring organization.

Table 10-3

process. In addition to these general directives, we also defined certain characteristics that we require each of these value propositions to include.

Real Warehouse Decision Making Process

Before we try to begin the development of a warehouse plan, we interview all parties who have stood up and said "I think it would be a good idea." Of course, there is a big difference between a person saying that "It sounds like a good idea." and someone saying "If you could provide me with this functionality, for this cost, we could deliver this benefit."

After you get past the initial flush of excitement and enthusiasm for a warehousing project, you often find that there is little substance behind the apparent momentum.

Wouldn't it be Love-a-ly?

By far, the most common response you get from people when discussing data warehousing solutions, is that there are just an almost infinite number of "neat things" they could do if the warehouse were in place. For example, we were helping a manufacturing company to create a customer information warehouse. This system was designed to reconcile all the different names, addresses and customer information into one central location.

People's immediate responses to this project were overwhelmingly positive. Yes, having this information, in an accurate, usable, easy to access form would be fantastic. Everyone thought that it would be a good idea and the project was approved.

Unfortunately, when we were well into the project, people started to ask, "what will we do with this information, now that we have it?" When this question was asked, the answers were far from what they expected and the project was abandoned.

The problem was that we asked the wrong question! Everyone thinks that something is a good idea if:

- it provides them with something that they do not have, and
- it doesn't cost them anything. It is a very different story when they are made aware of the costs of those benefits.

The question we should have asked at the onset of the project was not:

"Would you like to have ..."?

but rather

"How would you make use of ....."?

If the latter question were asked, we could have determined the real value of the effort.

Great for Somebody Else

When you ask people the "How would you make use of ..."? question, the next thing they usually say is that they would like to have it because -- it would be nice to have. But more importantly, some other department would benefit greatly from such a marvelous tool. This, "somebody else's solution" diversion enables these individuals to defocus from their own operational environment and envision the warehouse as somebody else's problem.

In one case, we were called in to help a large financial institution with their data warehousing plans. The sponsors of the project were convinced that everyone thought it was a good idea. We agreed to help them with this "visioning phase." A team of four analysts spent five days each, interviewing dozens of business area advocates for the warehousing solution. Unfortunately, by the time they finished, not one business person had stood up and said, "if you were to provide me with this solution, it would yield this benefit."

Everyone wanted it, but everyone thought someone else could use it No one was willing to take ownership of it.

Costs of Solutions

When you begin the process of validating peoples assumptions about what the warehouse will provide, there is an overriding tendency towards optimism. What people do not realize is that everything has a cost, and that most things that involve a warehouse involve a lot of costs in a lot of areas.

Financial Costs

The easiest thing for people to accept about the construction of a warehouse, or a specific warehouse application, is that some kind of financial investment is going to have to be made. Unfortunately, the concept of the warehouse is usually presented in such a way that people are led to believe that the vast benefits of the warehouse will greatly outweigh those physical costs, or that somehow, someone else is going to pay for it. We will spend considerable time dealing with the allocation of development costs later in this book.

Time Costs

Another cost that many operational and management areas overlook
is the time that the development of a warehouse will require. The
systems staff paints a picture of what the warehouse will do and
asks for funding. In many cases, the operational and management
areas will assume that once the funding is approved, their cost is
covered. The reality is that management and operational personnel
need to invest a significant amount of their time in the project, in
addition to the funds they have allocated, if the project is ever to
succeed. This touches again on our requirement that systems,
operational and management personnel all understand their roles in
the ongoing process.

The Cost of Change

Though there have been many cases where the managers of the
project had enough foresight to ensure that everyone was aware
of the required time investment; it is the rare organization indeed,
that considers the organizational and procedural impacts that a
warehousing project will entail.

The naiveté with which some people enter these projects is
unbelievable. They are going to spend millions of dollars. They are
going to invest a large amount of time. Yet they hardly ever think
about how the existence of these new systems is going to change
the way people do their jobs. Will certain jobs be eliminated? Will
certain functions become redundant? Will certain computer systems
become obsolete? Many is the project where those questions have
not been asked, until after the new system has been completed. Then
everyone scrambles to figure out the answers to these questions.

The Real Value of Solutions

Besides falling short in their understanding of what the warehouse
initiative is going to cost, it is also quite common to fail miserably at
determining what the value will be. The objective of our approach is
to always tie costs to specific benefits and vice versa.

VALUE, VISION AND FOCUS

Ultimately, whenever we begin to take a look at these kind of issues, we end up needing to deal with questions about value, vision and focus. If we want to create a framework for the diagnosis of these varieties of costs, benefits and different operational units perspectives on the project, we are going to have to be able to understand it all within a common context.

Vision

One of the definitions of the word vision in the dictionary reads as follows: The act or power of anticipating that which will or may come to be; foresight.

It is critical that the developers, sponsors and users of any system, especially a data warehouse system, have an accurate and shared vision of exactly what that warehouse is supposed to be. This shared vision is what allows everyone to understand exactly what the system is going to look like when it is complete. The development of a comprehensive vision guarantees us that what we are building will have value.

Coupled with our desire to get everyone to share the same vision, is the need to get people to identify the focus that the system should address. Focus is described as a central point of attraction, attention or activity. While the vision of the system allows people to picture what it will be like; a clear focus allows them to see exactly how what their actions will fit into that vision.

When we step into an organization where the idea of a data warehouse has been bantered about for any length of time, we inadvertently step into a veritable quagmire of seemingly contradictory and extremely diverse visions. The management group may harbor visions of a data warehouse as the solution to a broad range of strategic business problems. The systems staff may see the approach as a way to reduce the cost of systems maintenance or to deploy systems more quickly. The marketing group may see it as an incredibly complicated and expensive way to accomplish some specific, narrowly focused tactical program that they are trying to put together.

Types of Vision

Of course, there are many different kinds and levels of vision and focus that we must deal with when we begin considering warehousing solutions. We need to understand some of the differences before we can undertake to help people sort through them all.

A Hierarchy of Visions

When we step into a typical business environment start asking people what their vision for the business is and how the vision of a warehouse fits in, we find that these images fall into several categories.

Focus of the Vision

First of all, every vision that a person holds assumes a particular focus, which is usually but not always related to their role within the organization. Some visions are applicable to the overall organization while others apply to specific business areas.

Ask a CFO (Chief Financial Officer) about her or his vision and you will hear things in terms of the current profitability of the company, long term debt, dividends and stock splits. To the CFO, a data warehouse looks like a big expense and he or she will be looking for some big revenues or cost reductions in order to justify its existence.

Ask a marketing manager about their vision and you will hear things about market shares, gross margins and corporate posture. This person has a decidedly customer and sales orientation and their visions will involve making changes in those areas.

Ask a production manager about their vision and they will talk about the cost of production, downtime on the line and operational efficiencies.

Ask a computer systems manager and you will hear about disparate operating systems, production and development backlogs and the need to make the environment more manageable and less complex.

Scope of the Vision

The second thing that every vision will have is a scope. Some visions call for small changes in narrowly defined areas and others call from broad, sweeping revolutions across the entire organization.

One warehousing project might involve the creation of a warehouse which holds copies of data from only two files, which then allows end users to make use of an ad hoc query tool to analyze it. This project would affect few other systems and only a small population of users. Another warehousing effort, like the one we built for a major financial institution, might involve the integration of data from dozens or even hundreds of disparate file sources, and the consolidation and delivery of that data to hundreds or even thousands of users in support of their daily decision making. Clearly the latter would entail a much larger scope.

Hard and Soft Benefits

Not only will a vision have a specific scope and focus, but it will also have a certain hardness or softness associated with it. Soft visions speak in less concrete terms about less tangible kinds of results, while hard visions speak to specific objectives and initiatives occurring within specific time frames.

Corporate Culture and Vision

It is important to bear in mind, when we evaluate the different visions of people within the organization, that different corporate cultures view the visioning process differently.

In some organizations, visions are very direct, concrete things. In these corporations the visions tend to be very hard in nature. In other organizations, it is a taboo to speak of visions in anything but the most general of terms. These organizations tend to proliferate the soft visions.

Not only do different corporations have their own sets of rules and taboos about the vision development process, different business disciplines (i.e. marketing, production, systems, management) also have their own formulas. Our job, in the evaluation of these disparate visions, will be to proceed without violating any of these cultural directives.

Getting a Perspective on Visioning

Clearly, visioning can be done in many different ways. It is very important for us, as we begin to move through this world of different kinds of visions, that we establish clearly in our own minds, what kind of visions apply to the warehouse development effort.

Strategic Corporate Visioning

At the highest level of the visioning hierarchy, is the process we will call strategic long-range corporate vision development. While it is not within the scope of this book to spend much time on this process, it is important that we understand it, and its implications for our objectives.

Strategic long-range corporate vision development is the process by which the people in charge of the corporation set the long term direction. There are several different ways that this process is approached, depending upon the industry the company is in, and the company's current situation.

In general, strategic visioning at this level is a three step process.

First, the visionaries look outward from the corporation and try to develop an understanding of the current and future environment in which the corporation will have to exist. Among the focuses of these kinds of studies are: marketing and the future economic environment; the competitive environment; the legal and legislative environment; the impending financial environment; emerging technology and process improvement options; raw materials and source of supply analysis; etc.

During these studies, the planners develop a business perspective on how to survive and thrive in the future. After this is determined, the planners take an inward look at the business. They identify areas where changes are needed and recommend changes of direction for different groups and operations. In general, they set the direction for the operational units, and tell people what is important and what is not. The final step of this process will be to take the information gained and develop a set of strategic initiatives. They will set goals and objectives for the organization as a whole and for individual groups to meet.

Reduced to more practical terms, in a very real sense, the annual budgeting and forecasting cycle that most businesses go through is a modified version of this strategic visioning process. In fact, in many

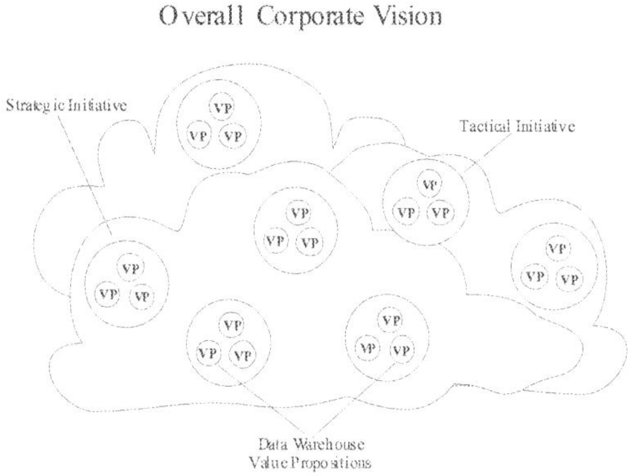

Figure 10-2. The visioning hierarchy

cases, the vision espoused by the budgets that are approved is far more accurate a corporate vision than any kind of "vision statement" could ever be. In summary, where the corporation has decided to put the money, is where they have placed their priorities.

Clearly, there is no role for the data warehouse at this level of vision development. A data warehouse is tool that the business can use to help accomplish the objectives that have been established. In fact, the data warehouse may make it possible for people to develop solutions that would otherwise not be possible. But within the context of our discussions here, the process of vision development we have been discussing does not apply.

Focused Strategic Initiatives

One of the outcomes of the corporate vision development process should be a collection of strategic initiatives. These are goals that strategic planners believe different areas of the business should meet. These initiatives can be large in scope or narrow, but in most cases, they will require the utilization of computer systems to make them a reality. It is here that data warehousing can play a vital role, and it is within the context of one of these strategic initiatives that our warehousing vision development process should begin.

In general, there are three kinds of strategic initiatives that organizations will undertake:

- Improvement of existing operational efficiency
- Redesign of operational approaches
- Creation of new operational approaches

We will consider what is involved in each of these, and how a data warehouse could contribute to its success.

Improvement of Existing Operational Efficiency

Developing strategies and approaches which help make each of the corporations organizational units more efficient represents the "classical" approach to corporate computer systems planning. Indeed, the history of computer systems deployment is a history of business people identifying ways that the computerization of certain tasks can enable them to be executed at increasingly higher levels of efficiency.

A data warehousing approach can be of assistance in the development of some of these types of solutions. In these cases, the opportunity for improvement is made possible by the availability of new kinds of data processing tools. These tools require a data warehouse in order to function effectively. For example, the production control department may realize that, if much of the currently available information was placed in a common data storage area, a lot of new operational efficiencies could be figured out, making use of statistical analysis tools. In these cases, a small, tactically focused warehousing application provides an easy, cost-effective solution.

In many cases, a data warehouse will not represent the best possible solution for certain types of problems. A data warehouse is not an operational system. It is not built to handle the kinds of processing that a traditional OLTP (on-line transaction processing) system is meant to handle. For example, an airline reservation system, or a cash station management system are poor applications of a warehousing approach. These applications are better addressed with different kinds of architectural solutions.

Redesign of Operational Approaches

Over the years, corporations have continually invested in the improvement of each of their organizational unit's efficiencies. In many cases, the introduction of new tools and approaches offers very little real value to those operations. However, what is becoming increasingly important, is the development of applications which cross traditional organizational boundaries and allow businesses to coordinate and analyze the end-to-end operations that drive the business. Often, these initiatives are known as business process re-engineering initiatives. These applications represent an area that the data warehouse can effectively address.

By their very nature, business re-engineering initiatives involve attempting to preserve existing Legacy system functionality wherever possible, while adding on new kinds of cross-system integration of information. These projects represent some of the best applications of data warehousing techniques today.

Creation of New Operational Approaches

Of course, sometimes the planners decide what is needed, is an entirely new kind of business unit or functionality. In these cases, a combination of data warehousing and traditional OLTP, operationally-based applications, will offer the best solution.

It is important for anyone attempting to run the data warehousing vision development project to clearly understand the type of initiative the warehouse will address, and the clear application of the rules we have set out for when the warehouse is, or is not, a good solution.

DETERMINING WHETHER YOU NEED A DATA WAREHOUSE OR NOT

While going through the process of inventorying and validating each persons vision of the warehouse, we will automatically accomplish one of our major business objectives for this phase. That is determining whether the warehouse is a good idea or not.

Before undertaking a project of this kind, we always warn the client that there is a distinct possibility that the end result of our analysis might be that a data warehouse is not a good idea. This can be for many reasons.

Among some of the biggest "show stoppers" we have uncovered in the past are:

1. Infrastructure challenges -- physical infrastructure

In many cases, the corporations computer systems infrastructure will not support the deployment of the technology required to make the system feasible. For example, in some organizations, we have found a great demand for PC-based data mining tools to be integrated with mainframe based data. In some cases, it would be very easy to bring that data together, but cost prohibitive to put the personal computer and networking infrastructure in place. In these situations the infrastructure challenges make the system cost prohibitive.

2. Infrastructure challenges -- operational infrastructure

In other cases we have found that the physical deployment of the warehousing solutions would be possible, but that the organization could not figure out any way to provide the kind of operational support required to make the warehouse feasible. Building a data warehouse entails more than the simple installation of a database server and loading it with data. If ongoing operational support is not going to be available, then a data warehousing solution is not going to be feasible. Organizations that try to build "self managing" warehouses end up either failing miserably or turning their end users into systems managers.

3. Legacy data intransigence

Sometimes, everything about the data warehouse seems feasible until you take a close look at your Legacy sources of data. Sometimes you find out that very little of the data you need actually exists, or exists in a form which is not usable. The intransigence of Legacy data can easily make a warehousing project infeasible.

4. Lack of sufficient demand

Many times, our analysis of the different visions that people hold for the warehouse are so limited in their scope that there is simply no reason to deploy a warehouse solution to solve the problems. If you are not looking to build a warehouse in order to figure out how to share large amounts of data, from diverse sources for access by diverse groups of users; many times you are better off building a simple integrated, single data type of application, as opposed to a full scale warehouse implementation.

5. Data warehouse as redundant step

In some situations, the inclusion of a warehouse architecture into a systems development plan turns out to be redundant. If the warehouse you are envisioning requires either a very high turnover rate (where a large percentage of the data is fully refreshed on a very frequent basis), where no history retention is required, or where the turns are very low (data is refreshed once a quarter or once a year), then there is a good chance that warehousing is too complex a solution for a much simpler set of problems. Many times we find that developers are better off simply bypassing the warehouse, and loading Legacy system data directly into data mining tools. If there is no reason to put things into the warehouse, then you should not use it.

6. Lack of cost justification

The most heartbreaking of all reasons to not use a warehouse is in cases where the need for a warehousing approach shows great merit, but the estimated costs far outweigh the benefits. In those cases, sponsors of the initiative must either give up on the project, or start over again looking to generate more interest in other business areas which might help to leverage the overall solution.

Developing Criteria for the Valuation of the Warehouse

The second business objective for our vision development project, is to determine at the very outset of the project what kinds of valuations or scales will be used to assess the effectiveness of the warehouse. Different organizations have different criteria for measuring an initiative's success. When an organization decides to build a real warehouse, it is because they have determined that there is some kind of a need in terms of inventory management. The criteria for the success of this real warehouse may be something like:

- Elimination of the overstocking of merchandise at the retail level
- Ability to stockpile inventory so that production can attain higher levels of productivity
- Speeding up of the movement of merchandise through the system

Or any number of other criteria

In the same way our overall warehousing initiative needs to be associated with the same kinds of valuations.

Will we consider the warehouse a success if we are able to develop ten new systems that would otherwise not be achievable? What if we can only justify the creation of two new systems? Then is the warehouse a bad idea? Are we looking at a situation where the warehouse is being put into place to relieve the data management burdens of non-data processing personnel? If so, how do we place a value on this kind of effort?

In one organization we found that managers, clerical personnel and engineers were all spending more than twenty percent of their time loading and unloading spreadsheets, formatting queries and in general managing data. In this environment it was getting to the point where people found that they were having less time to do their real work, because more and more of their time was spent identifying and moving data around. For this organization, the data warehouse was the solution to a very large data management problem, not associated with any specific business objective, but dealing with the effective and efficient use of time.

Decomposing the Visions

Equipped with this new insight, we are ready to return to our vision development process. So far, we have begun the process of collecting the visions from different advocates of the warehouse solution, and we have applied some analysis and understanding to the different visions that people have espoused. After we begin to apply much of this discipline to the different visions that people have stated, we must now execute the most difficult part of the process: The decomposition of these visions into their least common denominators.

We have already observed that different visions are going to be stated in terms of varying degrees of scope, focus and tangibility (hard vs. soft). We must try to break each of these down into smaller, more manageable pieces.

Examples of Visions

The following lists a sampling of the kind of "mixed bag" of visions that can typically occur during this process.

CEO -- Corporate Level Vision

"I would like to see this warehouse make it possible for us to reduce our net operating costs by three percent, I don't care how that happens but the board of directors has made that our number one priority for this year."

"This company already has a good reputation as the most friendly, most approachable vendor in our industry. I am looking for ways to increase our level of service to our customers while maintaining our current profit margins."

Marketing Manager -- Marketing Level Vision

" Our company is moving in the direction of one to one marketing. We want to have a personal relationship with each of our customers. In order to do that, we need to have access to all the information that we can get our hands on about those customers. We've got the information. We've got the sales history, returns records and credit ratings, but we can't get at it. We need all that information in the same place at the same time."

MIS Manager -- Information Systems Vision

"Our organization is currently suffering from a nine month production backlog and our users have had enough. I need a way to deliver these new types of data mining applications more quickly and at less cost then I am able to deliver anything today."

Production Manager Vision

"We need a system to help us track products as it moves through our factory. Right now we have dozens of systems but none of them talk to each other. Somehow we need to integrate this information so that we can identify production problems faster, and respond more quickly to changes in conditions."

Testing Engineer Vision

"I need the information in this file ported to a relational database so that I can use my statistical analysis package against it"

Secretary Vision

"I could save three hours of work every week if this information for this status report spreadsheet was centrally located. Right now, I have to get seven different printouts and key all the information back into the system. It just seems silly! All of the information is already in the computer, so why can't we just leave it in there and move it around a little."

Turning Visions into Candidate Applications

Obviously, each of these visions of how to use the data warehouse has a different scope, level and hard/softness factor. Our challenge is to figure out how to break them down.

Fracture Lines (The Visions Decomposition Process)

There are several approaches that have proven to be effective aids in the vision decomposition process. In general, the process is similar to those employed to decompose data models, process models or used in many of the business process re-engineering types of analysis. Some of these include:

1.   Organizational decomposition -- find the owner (departments, roles and responsibilities)

One criteria that can help you to decompose a large vision, is to break it down into the pieces of the solution, belonging to different organizational units or individuals.

For example, a large vision will usually require the cooperative efforts of many different departments. Marketing, accounting, production control and management might all need to do something in order to make it work. In this case, our first cut at decomposition will be to figure out what each of these areas needs to do as their contribution to the ultimate solution. At the next level down, we find that different areas within the department have different roles to play. Marketing might consist of a direct mail, phone solicitation, direct sales and catalog areas. Production control will include inventory management, process engineering and maintenance. We can continue breaking the vision down along these organizational lines, all the way down to the individual person -- if we must.

2.   Functional (process) decomposition -- what are the steps in the process

The functional decomposition process is used frequently in the development of specifications for computer systems, or in the execution of business process re-engineering exercises. These approaches go under many names, but they include things like brown paper analysis, functional decomposition, task analysis, process flow engineering and a wide variety of others.

While many of these approaches may end up being too formal and involved, the general process is the same; break down the big processes into smaller ones.

3.   Financial decomposition -- how is the cost allocated

Another good clue to figuring out how a vision might be broken down into smaller pieces is to apply some financial criteria to your analysis. How is money involved in the process, and how does it move from one part to the next.

Noun	Breakdown
Organization	Marketing, Accounts Payable and Management
Production Backlog	Marketing and Production Control Applications
Users	Marketing Users
Data Mining Products	SAS, SPSS and Excel

Table 10-4

4. Syntactic decomposition -- verbs and nouns

Another technique for reaching a quick answer is to apply the verb and noun rule. Write a description of the vision so that everything about it is clearly defined. Then start to figure out where each of the verbs and nouns are in the sentences. Each verb and noun is fully decomposed, or can be broken down into smaller verbs. When the verbs and nouns can no longer be broken down, you will have isolated the full population of discrete candidate applications.

Noun	Breakdown
We	A group of three engineers in the same department
Information in this file	A specific set of data is identified
Relational database	The place to which they want the data ported
Statistical analysis package	Lotus spreadsheet

Table 10-5

For example, if we were to take our MIS Manager vision "Our organization is currently suffering from a nine month production backlog and our users have had enough. I need a way to deliver these new types of data mining applications much faster and for considerably less cost then I am able to deliver anything today."

We would find the nouns:

- organization
- production backlog
- users
- data mining applications

Break each one down by going back to the MIS Manager and getting more detail about what is specifically meant by each phrase.

The table below shows how each of these nouns was then decomposed

This very general vision could be decomposed into a collection of candidate applications for each of the areas listed (marketing, accts. payable, management, production control) using each of the tools listed (SAS, SPSS and Excel) . In likelihood, the real candidate application probably has something to do with some specific needs of the marketing area (since they show up three times in the list).

In this case, we would probably decide to go back to the marketing group and determine what is really needed.

If we apply the same technique to an already decomposed vision, we should get the same result as we started with. For example our testing engineers vision "I need the information in this file ported to a relational database so that I can use my statistical analysis package against it"

When we have completed the decomposition process, our end result is no longer a collection of unrelated visions, but is now a list of candidate warehouse applications.

Verifying the Decompositions

After we have applied the decomposition techniques that seem to make the most sense, we need to find out if the decompositions still make sense. There are several criteria we apply in order to validate this decomposition.

1. Does each candidate application make sense as an autonomous project?

2. Will it involve aspects of acquisition, storage and access?

3. If it does not include all three, are there other candidate applications that include what this application needs?

4. Do the candidate applications seem to make sense from a business perspective?

In many cases we will have to go back to the people interviewed, and validate that our understanding of the original problem and our subsequent breakdown were accurate.

Rejection Criteria

As a part of this process we will also develop a list of rejected candidates. Candidate applications will be rejected for many reasons.

1. The application does not make sense for a warehouse application. Perhaps it could be pursued as an independent project. Sometimes, the candidate application might not even require the use of any computer facilities at all.

2. The candidate application will obviously cost a lot more then the value it will bring. This will include those "pet projects" that some people harbor, where the value delivered will be much lower than other solutions might provide.

For example, one vice president we approached wanted us to integrate twelve different reports that he had to review into one report. While we certainly could have developed a warehouse to do this, this executive would be the only user of the system. In this case, it would be considerably more cost effective to hire part-time office help to do these basic tasks, than go through the trouble of engineering a warehouse type solution.

RECRUITING OF SPONSORS

Now that we have collected the visions, evaluated them, decomposed them and verified their practicality and applicability, we are ready to begin the process of finding business areas sponsors for each.

Until now, we should (at least theoretically), have been able to conduct our investigation without regard for the politics, organizational and environmental constraints that we might encounter. It is at this point that we attack these problems head on. Remember that some of the biggest problems we face when trying to develop a warehouse are problems in the areas of focus, ownership and economic return on investment. The assignment of a sponsor to each of these initiatives will provide us with the means to eliminate many of those problems.

THE ROLES OF THE SPONSOR

When we begin looking for a person or organizational unit to sponsor each value proposition, we are looking for someone to take responsibility for several things. We need a person or organizational unit that:

1. is interested in what the value proposition has to offer, and sees a lot of benefit for him or her self and his or her group.
2. has a vested interest in the successful and timely completion of the application.
3. is willing to take responsibility for the benefits the value proposition is supposed to deliver.
4. is willing to take responsibility and provide leadership in the resolution of the many different data identification and delivery problems that we are going to encounter.
5. is willing to provide the business expertise necessary to pull the application together.
6. is able to provide a solid cost justification for the premises of the proposition.

It is during the stage of sponsor recruitment that you find out whether the value propositions you have been working with have any real value or not. It is not uncommon to come up with a long list of impressive candidate applications, only to find that, although they would clearly provide benefit to the company, no one is willing to take ownership for them. In many cases the issue of ownership is straightforward. For example, a tactical application which enhances the capabilities of the human resources department can clearly only be sponsored by that department. In other cases, especially in those situations where the candidate application crosses organizational lines, it can be very difficult to figure out who would most appropriately handle the benefits.

A person might ask, "Why make such a big deal about the sponsor recruiting process?" Surely, if a value proposition shows the potential for big savings or big process improvements, everybody will jump on it. Unfortunately, that is not the case. We must remember that the candidate applications elicit several different kinds of consequences. Certainly they will offer some value to the company. But what is unclear, until we begin the sponsor recruitment process, is exactly what kinds of hidden costs might be involved.

In some cases we have found that value propositions actually frighten or threaten people. They are afraid that if they admit that the assumptions of the value proposition are correct, it reflects badly on them. The thinking goes...if these people could identify a way for me to improve my processes, then I must not be doing my job. Although this kind of paranoid thinking is far from accurate, it still appears from time to time. Another situation that can sabotage the best of value propositions is when the value propositions in question open up issues of political discord. This kind of discord can take two forms:

1. Inter-operational unit rivalry
2. Operational vs. systems animosity

Inter-operational Unit Rivalry

We have already alluded a bit to this type of rivalry. In general, this happens when different organizational units feel that the value proposition and the benefits and improvements, are something they should enjoy. In some situations you can actual run into people trying to set things up, so that another group absorbs the cost while their group enjoys the benefit. It is important to remember that any change to the typical corporate business environment is going to represent a chance for all of the political agendas to come out. Many a project has been sabotaged by this kind of maneuvering.

Operational vs. Systems Animosity

Another kind of rivalry manifests itself in value propositions between the operational units which need the system and the computer systems support department. In some organizations, the relationship between the two groups is so strained that no systems project can be considered without taking all the historical baggage into account. This animosity usually takes the form of some kind of power play. The operational people may feel resentment because they have been forced to live with a long history of ignored requests for system enhancements and long wait times for new systems. The thinking of these individuals may be "Why should I work on this value proposition with you, when you have been unable to meet even the simplest of my requests in the past"? or "How can you have budget money for this, when you don't have it for my other projects"?

In the worst cases, the proactive advocacy of a data warehousing solution by the systems area is interpreted as a political come-on; a way to raise budget dollars for systems, or a way to shift focus from the other problems in the systems areas. There are even organizations where the systems area maintains a not-so-well-hidden agenda which views the building of a data warehouse as a means for systems to wrest control from independent user areas. This will force everyone to abdicate their data and their systems options for the sake of a single, monolithic, centrally (I/S) managed, data warehouse.

A Necessary Step

Despite all the problems that recruitment of sponsors is going to create, it is a critical step in the process. Resolving the political, organizational and budgetary issues that appear when you begin looking for sponsors is critical to the success of the project. Many times, enthusiastic advocates of data warehousing solutions have "pushed through" the projects by gaining higher level corporate sponsorship, attempting to bypass the "in the trenches" political and organizational in-fighting.

While this might seem like a solution, it really only postpones the turf battle. It is better to get all political and territorial issues resolved before the warehousing project begins, than to allow those issues to fester under the surface, waiting for the chance to explode on the scene, invalidating most, if not all of the work that has been done.

Do Not Create Corporate Sponsored or I/S Sponsored Value Proposition Initiatives

For these reasons, we strongly recommend that people not try to get support for individual warehousing value proposition initiatives from upper management. We have also found that I/S sponsored value propositions usually fail.

Certainly, you need to have I/S and upper management support for the overall data warehousing process and project, but this support is for the warehouse itself. Individual applications must have individual business area sponsors, if they are going to succeed.

DETERMINATION OF HARD BENEFITS

After we have successfully identified a sponsor for our value proposition, our next step is to work with that sponsor to develop an idea of the potential hard benefits associated with this proposition. Until now, our assessment of benefits has been very high level and general in nature. We need to get specific about what this value proposition is going to deliver.

The nature of the benefits we intend to associate with a given value proposition and the way it is presented will be the key to the overall success of the project. The single biggest factor providing focus for the people associated with the project, is a clear understanding of which benefits the application is being asked to deliver.

Benefits and Focus

While at face value the above statement may seem to be overly strong or dramatic, when you get down to the nitty-gritty of systems development, a common understanding of the drivers of the system will ease the process greatly.

Few people realize the volume of issues that appear while you are in the process of addressing the thousands of details that make up a modern application. Time and time again, programmers, analysts and users are going to be forced to make hard decisions and compromises about what they should and should not do. In a large number of the cases, a clear understanding of the potential benefits will provide them with an answer.

There are actually several different ways that the benefits of a system can be determined.

Savings

Probably the most commonly mentioned justification for a system is explained in terms of some kind of savings. There are many ways that savings can be calculated and rationalized.

Time Savings

Sometimes the data warehouse provides no additional functionality at all. What it does provide in these situations is the ability to do certain kinds of operations more quickly, saving time. We built a data warehouse for a grocery wholesaler. The buyers for this origination were spending an inordinate amount of time pulling together information about each of the products they were managing. In fact, each buyer spent over half their time simply plowing through a vast assortment of reports and on-line systems, making redundant phone calls to suppliers and retail outlets; just to figure out how each of their products was doing. In this case, the data warehouse simply provided the same information in less time. The direct benefit of this system was calculated as a percentage of the buyers time.

Ripple Effects when Time Savings are Concerned

When you save someone the time needed to perform a task, you create more value than simply the amount of time they spend. You also create a whole range of dependent benefits.

1. When a professional who is paid to do a certain kind of job ends up spending a lot of time doing trivial and redundant data processing tasks, they not only lose time, they become de-focused. By saving the time, you also increase the overall effectiveness of each person, because they have more time to do their real job.

2. Another chain reaction benefit to time savings occurs when the timeliness of a given operation is critical. For example, not only were the buyers in the example cited above able to spend less time investigating their product groups, they also got their analysis done much more quickly. In a business where making decisions quickly is critical, the chain reaction value can be great. For example, what good is it to find out that you had a load of lettuce sitting on the loading dock for four days, when it gets spoiled after two. When calculating the benefits that this kind of process improvement can have, you must take these dependent benefits into account as well.

Money Savings

Another way that people appraise the value of an initiative is to look at the amount of money it is going to save. In many situations the value proposition has some straightforward savings associated with it. For example, at one large financial institution where we installed a warehouse, we were able to justify the elimination of over 30 redundant clerical positions. Other systems that we have installed have resulted in the reduction of scrap, speeding up of the assembly process and elimination of redundant processes. All of these translated easily into hard savings.

Computer Resource Savings

Sometimes, some of the benefits of the warehouse can be attributed to savings in the computer systems area. Reduced disk utilization, reduced CPU costs and sometimes even the elimination of redundant systems. All of these can add up to respectable savings. For a large brokerage firm, we installed a system which made it possible for brokers to handle twice as many transactions a day, more accurately and more comfortably than they could before (meaning that each broker could do twice as much business).

Revenue Generation

Of course, a data warehouse often provides an organization with the ability to generate revenue in ways that were not previously possible. For example a clear revenue benefit can be provided by the installation of a marketing data warehouse to provide the company with the ability to run direct marketing and phone solicitation departments that it previously could not service.

Profitability Improvement and Efficiency of Operations

The ability to integrate information from a variety of disparate sources often provides companies with creative ways to improve overall profitability. Many of the "third generation" data warehousing solutions that we built, have provided companies with the ability to manage their processes in ways never before possible. For example, studies with many different manufacturing companies have shown that a data warehouse provides the perfect means to integrate manufacturing processes. For more information about this kind of operation, see the appendix on third generation data warehousing applications.

Hidden Benefits

Occasionally, companies find that with the implementation of data warehousing solutions that they have created benefits that they had not anticipated.

Accuracy -- These have included incredible improvements in the accuracy of existing systems with concomitant improvement in the overall decision making process.

Fraud Detection-- In some rare situations, the developers of data warehouses have uncovered cases of computer systems related fraud that remained undetected because of the quagmire of conflicting data systems that auditors needed to wallow through.

Redundant Processes -- It is not uncommon for a warehousing initiative to uncover systems and departments whose functionality is being duplicated in other operational areas. By mapping the data out, these processes can be identified and reduced.

Marketing Values

The benefit that a warehousing application can provide need not be limited to the operational and financial kinds of benefits that we have been discussing. In many cases, warehousing applications

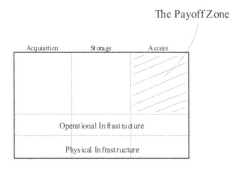

Figure 10-3. The "payoff zone" of the warehouse

provide companies with the ability to accomplish things in the less explicit area of marketing position improvement. Benefits such as: increased market share, retained market share, improved customer relationships, one-to-one marketing posture and more profitable marketing initiatives are common applications of the warehousing approach.

DATA MINING TOOLS AND BENEFITS

Although we will be spending a considerable amount of time talking about data mining and the access component of the warehouse in later chapters, it makes sense at this point to introduce a few of the fundamental concepts associated with data mining and value propositions. First of all, it is important that we realize when we are talking about the data warehouse and value propositions, that it is only in one small area of the warehouse that those payoffs can be realized.

The pay-off zone for a data warehouse consists of all of those data mining applications within the access component. When we examine the realm of products and applications that function within this payoff zone, we find that the applications that operate in this area are one of three types:

1. Holistic solutions
2. Analytical solutions
3. Operational systems

Holistic Solutions

Many applications for the data warehouse involve the development of holistic solutions. We include in our definition of holistic applications any kind of system that allows people to get a more comprehensive, more accurate view of some aspect of the business. For example, a holistic customer application will make available to the user the full extent of the history and characteristics of a given customer. From one screen, the user can see a history of all of the sales made to that customer, a listing of all of their service calls and complaints, and a history of all marketing materials sent to them and all promotions run in their geographical area.

On the other hand, a holistic production control application will provide the engineer with all of the information available about the progress of a given lot of materials through the manufacturing process, the status of the material at each phase of manufacturing, the results of different tests applied to that lot, and related information about each of the components that went into that lot.

A wholesale or retail organizations holistic application might track the movement of goods, along with the associated costs as product moves from manufacturer to warehouse to sales floor. The system can also provide cross reference sales information, comparing different lots of like material in different stores.

Analytical Solutions

The second type of applications provided by data mining fall under the category of analytical solutions. These products allow users to analyze collections of data in way previously not possible. With analytical solutions, users can identify trends, make more accurate predictions and optimize decisions about pricing, scheduling, and process control by applying the insights that the analytical products provide.

Operational Systems

Although we have stated several times that a data warehouse itself could not function as a operational system, we also stated that by making use of feedback mechanisms and the work area, that it would be possible to stack operational systems on top of the warehouse. These systems are typically dependent upon the warehouse for the bulk of their usable data, but can also be considered to be functioning as independent of the system itself.

Each of these types of solutions offers a different kind of benefit to the sponsoring organization and our definition of the value proposition needs to take all of them into account.

DETERMINATION OF REASONABLENESS AND COST ESTIMATES

After we have developed a comprehensive definition of what the benefits of the proposed application will be, we need to come up with some estimates of what it is going to cost to deliver those solutions. To say that cost estimation is an art more than a science would be a gross understatement. Clearly, there is no way to accurately estimate system costs without a great deal of information about the system itself.

Unfortunately, few organizations can afford to do exhaustive cost estimating before actually trying to get approval for projects. Our best alternative is to develop a discipline for estimating warehousing costs which will at least minimize the risks of running into problems. This estimation process will take a worst case scenario approach. We will assume that everything involved in the process will be at the extreme end of the range, thereby minimizing our risk of underestimating the costs. This phase of the vision development process is the most time and resource intensive of all the steps.

During this phase we need to determine things like:

- Where will the data come from?
- Who will use the information and how?
- What will it take to deliver the data?
- Systems Integration Issues (HW, network, application software, tools)

And a score of other issues

Our approach to developing these estimates will be four-fold. First, we will develop physical infrastructure estimates of exactly how much disk space and computer power we estimate will be required to support the system.

Second, we will develop estimates of what kind of operational support will be required, and how long it will take to put that operational support in place. Third, we will examine the nature

Industry - Category Discipline	Manufacturing				Retail				Financial Services				Telecommunications			
	Automotive	Computers	Consumer Goods	Industrial Goods	Department Stores	Clothing	Grocery	Direct Marketing	Banking	Investments	Real Estate	Insurance	Cellular Local	Telephone	Long Distance	Satellite
Marketing																
Production Control																
Accounting																
Logistics and Support																
Customer Service																
Human Resources																

Table 10-6

and complexity of the data analysis and delivery effort; developing estimates for how many people and how long it will take to develop the application data stores. Fourth, we will analyze the data access and data mining requirements and develop estimates for the activity required to bring that into existence. Finally, we will put these estimates together for the development of a full application plan and cost estimate.

Before we can provide a comprehensive approach to this process, we are going to need to examine the physical, operational, data discipline and data mining characteristics of the system in a lot more detail. Therefore, we have postponed our exploration of these issues until the end of the book. The reader is encouraged to turn to the appendices of this book for more specific information in these areas.

Development of Value Propositions

After we have succeeded in gaining sponsors, developed a benefits statement and derived our estimated costs, we will be ready to create our official value propositions. These value propositions must explicitly summarize each of the steps we experienced in developing them, and summarize for management, the operational sponsoring areas and the systems area exactly what is to be done and why.

Categories of Value Propositions

Throughout this chapter, we have referred to many of the different ways that visions and value propositions could be categorized and cataloged. While there is indeed a vast assortment of these propositions, what we should be able to categorize any value proposition based upon several distinct parameters.

The Industry Category / Discipline Value Proposition Grid

What we find, when we actually begin to isolate the individual value propositions that different companies develop is that patterns begin to occur. In general, all of the value propositions for a given business discipline area (marketing, production control etc.) tend to share a lot of the same characteristics across all industries, and the value propositions for related industries tend to be similar. Basically, what this tells us is that value propositions are significantly dependent upon the industry that the company happens to be in, and upon the business discipline to which it is related.

As we go through the process of understanding more and more of these industry and discipline driven value propositions, we should be able to develop an understanding of the pattern that underlies them all.

The Value Proposition Format

The appendices in the back of this book provide you with a sample value proposition. Included in this document is all the information anyone would need in order to quickly find out what the value proposition is, how it is rationalized, what it should cost, and how long it should take to develop.

Consolidation of Value Propositions

Once we have formalized our understanding of each of the value propositions that we have collected. We are ready to begin the consolidation process. We have many objectives for this consolidation process.

1. We want to develop some estimates for the overall size of the fully implemented data warehouse.

2. We need to be able to begin to develop cost and time estimates for the overall effort.

3. We want to begin organizing and prioritizing the value propositions, and group them into different phases of development.

With this information in place, we should be ready to develop a full blown warehouse deployment strategy.

Sizing the Warehouse

The process of warehouse sizing involves little more than simply adding up all of the sizing estimates from each of the value propositions that we have successfully produced. The net result of this process will be full disk estimates, computer CPU estimates and all the other kinds of physical and operational infrastructure issues that we have captured.

Developing Overall Cost and Timing Estimates

The development of overall cost estimates however, is a slightly more complicated process. The sum total of the estimates for each of the value propositions will not be the same as for the real development plan. Our actual, full systems costs might be higher or lower depending upon our deployment strategy. At this stage of the process however, we need to summarize the estimates from each of the value propositions and use that information as input to our deployment strategy and ultimate costing model.

Organizing and Prioritizing the Value Propositions

After we have developed our overall system estimates, our next step is to figure out how best to deploy each of the applications proposed. Obviously, the more value propositions we intend to implement, and the more interdependency we have between them, the more complicated the process becomes. When we begin to organize the value propositions, we will probably want to develop several different groupings, in order to look for efficiencies.

Value Proposition Grouping Strategies

One way to group value propositions is by sponsoring organization. Under this mode of operation, we group all of the same business areas propositions into the same phase or cluster of applications. Another way is to group them in the order of priority. Which ones have the most strategic importance?

Yet another way this process can be approached is to prioritize them by cost/benefit ratio. The value propositions with the best payback get done sooner.

In some cases, the propositions might need to be grouped by infrastructure requirements. Some may require a very large investment in workstations and network implementation, while others might require little or no investment in that area.

In all cases, we must consider the dependency between applications. In some cases, there may be several value propositions with very little inherent value in and of themselves, but a great many other value propositions depend upon its existence in order to succeed. In general, what we want to accomplish through the grouping process, is to come up with a logical sequence of events that allows us to group propositions in a manner that maximizes:

1. Physical and operational infrastructure costs
2. Serial dependencies
3. Business priorities

Limited Investment to Start

In some cases, the organization may decide to take a piecemeal approach to value proposition roll out. In these situations, the organization bypasses the development of an overall rollout plan and opts instead to simply take on one or two of the most promising propositions and use them as pilot, proof of concept applications.

Development of a Deployment Strategy

Given our value proposition deployment plan, we are ready to put the full blown warehousing plan together. During this process we will need to:

- Select architecture (platforms, network configuration)
- Develop high level architectural specifications document
- Determine the location
- Report on high level cost estimates
- Report on the prioritization of all value propositions

In the next few chapters, we will take a closer look at the data disciplines which drive the actual process of application development, after which we will see how the output of the data discipline process can be used to drive the development of our infrastructure. With that complete, we will be able to actually develop a case study involving several value propositions, and begin considering some of the lowest level detail of how the warehouse is actually going to be created.

CHAPTER 11

VALIDATION AND ESTIMATION

While we know that cases of short-cutting are legion in the history of data processing systems development, this knowledge does little to help us in organizing our project to prevent falling into the same traps. Actually, we are faced with another paradox when it comes to this issue. Experience has shown that the dedication of a large number of resources to the analysis and design process usually ends up with little to show for it. On the other hand, the simple advocacy of a "just build it and we'll figure out the details later" is just as dangerous. We must figure out where the middle ground lies.

When you look at all these different problems and consider them as a whole, you can come up with some fundamental conclusions. Underlying all of them is one of two factors. Either the developers of the system:

- Failed to validate the assumptions they made about what the system would or could do, or
- They failed to develop accurate estimates of what it would take to bring the project to completion.

Obviously, there is a serious overlap between validation and estimation issues; in fact, you cannot accomplish one without the other, but for the rest of this chapter, we will concentrate on the validation process, and spend the next chapter on the topic of estimation and project planning.

LEVELS OF VALIDATION EFFORT

We actually have several places within our framework for systems development where we must deal with validation issues. The first is at the highest level, during the development of the overall warehouse plan. Validation at this level is concerned only with the viability of the solutions proposed at the highest level. When validating at this stage we will be only minimally concerned with specific technical and business issues, but will concentrate instead on the feasibility of the overall warehouse's objectives.

The other place where validation will need to occur is in each of the applications that are going to be developed. This level of validation takes a lot more technical detail into account and is actually an important part of the application development process.

VALIDATION AND ASSUMPTIONS

The first concept that we must understand is systems assumptions. The objective of the validation step is to examine each of the assumptions that have gone into the development of the systems vision, and determine whether they are valid or not. There are several things which make assumptions tricky. First, whenever dealing with a large systems project, there are a lot of assumptions that people make. Secondly, different people can make different assumptions. Thirdly, when different people make different assumptions there is no way to know if they are in agreement. Since everybody is assuming, nobody sees any need to talk about it. The fact that people are making different kinds of assumptions, in and of itself is not a bad thing. It is certainly possible for things to work out as long as the disparity between the assumptions is not too great. A much bigger problem arises when special kinds of assumptions occur. Two categories of problem causing assumptions occur when people:

1. Make the assumption that somebody else understands it, or has taken responsibility for it.
2. Fail to communicate the confidence level associated with the assumption, assuming somebody else is taking care of it.

This is an obvious consequence when people begin to make assumptions. You assume that everything has been taken into consideration when it really hasn't. The cases of misplaced assumptions occur frequently throughout the systems development process. The problems associated with this condition tend to get worse as the project continues. Usually, the revelation that something has been missed occurs slowly over time, as people begin to realize that there is a problem. Usually by that time it is too late.

THE CONFIDENCE LEVEL OF AN ASSUMPTION

The other thing about assumptions is that there are usually levels of risk associated with each assumption we make. We assume that the sun will rise in the morning with a high confidence level. We assume that users can learn how to use a new data mining tool with less confidence. As the risks associated with our assumptions grow, it is imperative that those risks be identified and addressed during the validation phase. Anyone who goes into the development process while harboring serious doubts about the viability of a solution is setting themselves up for failure.

Our objective should be to enter infrastructure development and applications development with an exceedingly high level of confidence (at least eighty percent), and it is the job of the validation process to ensure that is exactly what happens.

THE VALIDATION PROCESS

The validation process therefore has several things it needs to accomplish. It must:

1. Be systematic and thorough, thereby guaranteeing that all the important assumptions have been identified and documented. One of the biggest objectives of the validation process is to make sure that everything important has been

considered and reviewed by everyone involved in the process.

At the same time, the validation process must:

2. Evaluate and minimize the risk associated with systems development. Another important function of this process will be to clearly flag those areas where the risk is higher than acceptable, and to develop mechanisms which will minimize that risk.

When it comes to identifying assumptions and minimizing risk, there is something else that we are going to have to do during validation. The only way that we can evaluate what the assumptions mean, and the risk associated with each one, is to gain some assurance that we truly understand how it is going to be executed (define-ability) and that the effort required for development can be accurately estimated (estimate-ability).

We must also remember that in the area of risk, we really have several types of risk to worry about. We must be concerned with:

Functional Feasibility -- Whether the proposed solution can work. This applies to both business/operational functionality. For example:

• Is it possible to get the marketing department to change the way they do things in order to make use of this system?

And technical functionality

• Can we build a system that can handle these volumes of data and deliver it to the users in a reasonable time frame?

Delivery Feasibility - Can the solution actually produce the results we want? For example, if the system is put in place do we really believe that sales revenue will increase by twenty-five percent?

Developmental Feasibility - Can the solution be developed on time and on budget. Does the proposed development staff have the expertise, experience, tools, budget and management structure to actually complete the system?

It is a common occurrence for people to dismiss different capabilities or functionalities as doable, when in fact they really have no idea about how it will be done. They simply assume that somehow, someone will figure it out.

In general therefore, we want the validation process to answer the following questions about each aspect of the warehouse solution:

1. Is it feasible? Are the assumptions valid?

2. Is it definable? Can you define each of the steps involved in its development and operation?

3. Can it be estimated accurately? Is it defined well enough so that you can generate relatively accurate estimates as to effort level, time tables and other costs?

4. What are the risks? For those situations where the risks are high, can we identify them and minimize them before committing significant resources to the project?

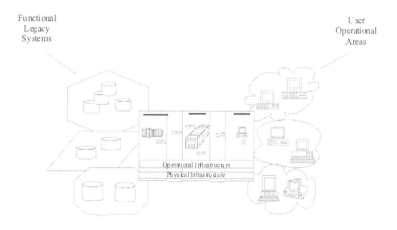

Figure 11-1. The warehouse framework

A SYSTEMATIC APPROACH TO VALIDATION

Since we want our approach to be thorough and systematic, we will make use of the warehouse framework which we have been defining throughout this book as the starting point for the process. We will envision the warehouse with its three components and multiple layers and consider the validation process from two perspectives; validation as it relates to the overall warehouse project and validation of the individual applications.

Notice that in addition to the basic framework itself we have added two things. First, extending from the data access area we have shown the different grouping of users within operational clusters. It is our assumption that each application has been designed to meet the needs of a different operational group, and the risks and feasibilities associated with these business operations must also be included in our analysis.

At the other end of the warehouse we have included the different functional Legacy systems areas. These areas too have an impact on our validation process. There are two kinds of validation that we need to consider. The first type occurs when we are developing our initial vision of the overall warehouse; this occurs in those situations where the warehousing project is going to have a very wide scope and involve the implementation of several applications. When the warehouse infrastructure under consideration is large, this will be a process all by itself. The other kind of validation to take into account is the validation of each of the applications that are going to be implemented.

Validation of the Overall Warehouse

When we begin wrestling with the issues of overall warehouse validation, we must take a decidedly "big picture" perspective. From this view we are not concerned with the minute validity of individual value propositions and their assumptions, but with the overall warehouse approach as a viable solution.

Overall Operational Validity

When we consider the operational validity of the data warehouse, the question we need to answer is "Do I have a high degree of confidence, based upon what I know about the different value propositions proposed for utilization within the warehouse to believe that investment in a warehouse is justified"? In other words, has the vision development process convinced you that the warehouse is a good idea?

While it would certainly be nice to know all the details about how each of the proposed value propositions are going to be executed, it is really not essential that we validate each of them at this stage. All we really need to do is validate that:

1. Each value proposition has merit (shows the potential for providing value).

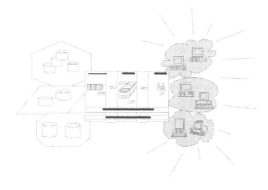

Figure 11-2.   Validating operational assumptions for the overall warehouse

2. Each value proposition exhibits at least prima facie evidence of being feasible, definable and estimable.
3. The value propositions represent no major risks in their assumptions.
4. The warehouse solutions provided will be able to be operationally integrated into the existing business areas.

The process of validating the operational assumptions for the warehouse, at this level, are therefore almost completely business and organizationally based. If the preponderance of evidence indicates that the different groups involved see a value in the warehouse, can

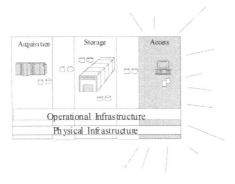

Figure 11-3. Validating access component assumptions

envision themselves making use of it, and are willing to propose benefits in hard terms; then the warehouse is certainly validated from this perspective.

Validating Data Access Assumptions

Viability of access assumptions

Our first and most basic assumption about the data access component of the overall warehouse is that all users will be able to gain access and make use of the warehouse through the use of their existing workstations, terminals and supporting network infrastructure, or that the organization will be able to afford and/or cost justify making that possible.

The only way we can hope to validate this assumption is by developing an inventory of all proposed future users of the warehouse and ascertaining whether that capability exists or not. If it does exist, then we simply need to validate that the anticipated work loads will be attainable by the system. If it doesn't, then we need to figure out what it will take to bring these workstations up to the required level, and determine whether doing so is going to be cost effective.

Obviously, there is a significant amount of overlap between ascertaining the validity of this component and developing the corresponding estimates of cost involved. We will save the rest of our discussion about this aspect for our section on estimation.

Utilization Assumptions

Our second assumption will be that those users have the ability and desire to make use of the different data mining and other data access mechanisms envisioned or that the ability and desire can be developed.

It is a serious mistake to assume that just because the developers of the system or the managers within the organization think that a solution will be capitalized on by the users without verifying this fact first hand. I will never forget the experience I had as a fledgling system designer for a manufacturing company. I was given the mission of implementing a change to the existing loading dock tracking software in order to include some new functionalities. After six months of effort, the new solution was implemented. It was beautiful, sophisticated and met all the requirements. Everyone at the home office thought it was great. Unfortunately, when we implemented the change out in the factories, we ran into a serious problem. It was too complicated for people. The solution confused them and frustrated them. Finally, they actually got the

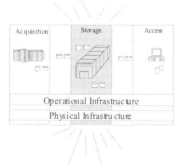

Figure 11-4. Validating storage assumptions

union involved and my eloquent solution was replaced with a much simpler, more user friendly solution.

At another organization, many years later, we made the same mistake. We assumed that the terms Windows and user friendly were synonymous, so we proceeded to develop a beautiful user interface for the warehouse. It had icons, menus, everything driven by the mouse.

Unfortunately, the user community was comfortable with their old 3270 menu driven screens. The supposedly "user friendly" interface was intimidating and frightening. We ended up needing to add three months to the project schedule in order to give everyone a chance to become trained and comfortable with the new approach.

The two examples just sighted represent minor changes to the system when compared to the changes in operational procedures and user interfaces that most sophisticated data mining effort entail. As a consequence of this, it will be crucial that this aspect be evaluated, and our assumptions about user acceptance validated before proceeding.

Validating Storage Component Assumptions

Platform Viability

The next evaluation we need to perform is for the storage component. Our principle assumption about the feasibility and costs of building the storage component are that the platform in which we choose to house the storage component can store the volumes of data that the warehouse will eventually hold, and will be able to provide end users will timely access.

This is another area where the traditional approach to data processing is really stuck. According to the rote method of database design, the only way to know whether a database can handle the data you expect it to, is to develop detailed models of all of the data and volume estimates for each one. We can then determine all the different ways that people are going to access it. In other words, you must practically complete building the system before you can develop estimates!

While it is very difficult to argue with the premise that the best and most accurate estimates can be developed when you have as much information as possible about what you expect the warehouse to do, it is also not feasible in most situations. Therefore, the issues of

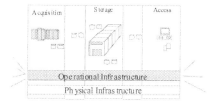

Figure 11-5. Validating acquisition assumptions

estimation and validation for the storage component are going to have to be managed through some kind of compromise solution.

While it is not possible to validate the viability of the selected platform without information about volumes and access rates, it is possible to develop high level estimates of these things without the benefit of all of the detail. In our case, we will assure our viability and develop our capacity estimates through the use of generalization and approximation techniques which we will detail in the next chapter.

In this case, as in all cases of validation having to do with warehouse capabilities from a physical perspective, we will rely heavily upon the estimation process to provide us with our validation.

Validating Acquisition Component Assumptions

The final component of our warehouse is the acquisitions area. The acquisitions area is responsible for taking care of the process of extracting data from Legacy systems, preparing it and staging it for loading into the warehouse. Our principle assumption about the warehouse in this regard will be that it is possible to perform each of the acquisition processes in a reasonable amount of time.

Data Sourcing and Mapping Viability

One of the biggest assumptions that people make about acquisition is that:

1. The data they are looking for exists.
2. That the data can be easily extracted.
3. That the data can be used within the warehouse.
4. That there are resources available who understand the Legacy system or externally defined data and who can assist in the process of understanding it and working with it.

Let's consider some of the ways that these assumptions can be invalidated.

Data Existence

As we have mentioned on several previous occasions, often times people make assumptions about exactly what data is available and where it can be found. In too many cases, these assumptions are discovered to be invalid.

While the principle area of concern is when we talk about validation of the existence of data for individual applications, on a much higher level; we need to, in the early stages of overall warehouse development, get some assurance of the likelihood that the data we are seeking exists on the system.

The validation of data existence at this level can easily be accomplished by determining exactly what types of data users will expect and where they think it can be found, before talking with the people responsible for the management of those systems for verification.

Data Extraction

Another assumption we will make is that the data can be obtained from the sources provided. Unfortunately, this is not always the case. Sometimes, Legacy systems are so complicated, or back logged with work, or are making use of so many resources already, that it is determined that the data simply cannot be provided. If this kind of issue can arise, it must be identified at this time.

Data Utilization

One of the most frustrating things that can happen is when users identify desired data and the data is located; but the owners of the data are not willing or able to allow the data to be used. An interesting case occurred recently, where a government organization tried to make use of another governmental agencies lists to help track down traffic violators. A person apprehended through this new system argued that the transference of the list from one agency to another was a violation of his right to privacy and the agency was forbidden to use the information again.

In addition to those cases where the ability to use data has been legislated away, or cases where the organization owning the data simply does not want to share it, (as is common in the case of mailing lists, where one organization does not want another to use their list because of the impact it would have on the recipients of the mail) or want to sell it for more money than the requesting organization is willing to pay (as in the case of purchased or rented lists).

When any source of data that is critical to the operation of the warehouse is owned or managed by a group other then the one building the system, then the validity of our assumptions about utilization must be addressed.

Data Understanding

Another place where people's assumptions fall short occurs when we assume that there are people available to help us understand what the data is, how it works and what it means. Unfortunately, in today's lean, mean data processing organizations, we often find Legacy systems that have been left to "run themselves". The staff that understood the system has long since retired or moved on to other jobs. If we make assumptions about the availability of these resources, then we had better get some assurance that when the time comes, assistance will be there.

Validating Application Development Assumptions

In general, most of our assumptions about application development will be made in regard to the development of each application.

However, we will need to make certain assumptions about how the overall process is going to be managed and run. Our own assumption is that the approach that we have laid out for value proposition development, the layering and serialization of application development, and the availability and commitment of staff to the execution of these plans.

From the perspective of the overall warehousing project these assumptions need to be stated, and assurances gained from all parties involved that these procedures will follow. It would be an incredible waste to go through the entire process of vision development, validation, estimation and infrastructure development only to find that there is no commitment to the methodology proscribed.

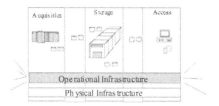

Figure 11-6. Validating operations infrastructure assumptions

Validating Operational Infrastructure Assumptions

We will also find ourselves making assumptions about the operational infrastructure that will support warehouse operations. Each individual will be counting on this infrastructure to make using the warehouse easier. At the same time, we don't want to build more robustness into this layer than is necessary. To validate our assumptions in this regard, we need only to develop a general understanding of how it will work, develop a rough estimate of what it will cost to develop, and reach concurrence from all participants that this functionality is desirable and reasonable.

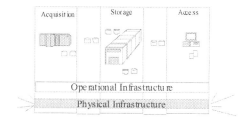

Figure 11-7. Validating physical infrastructure assumptions

Validating Physical Infrastructure Assumptions

The final area where we will need to perform serious technical validation is physical infrastructure. While the viability of the data identification process and the ability of the platforms to support their designated functions will have been validated in previous steps, we must also develop assurances that the overall infrastructure can handle all the different operations envisioned.

Data Transport Assumptions

While our evaluation of the acquisition, storage and access layers weighed the ability of each component to accomplish its objectives, we have yet to examine whether the infrastructure will be able to handle all the different kinds of data transport it must support. How will data move from Legacy systems to the acquisitions area? How will acquisitions processing be managed? How will data move from the acquisitions area to the storage area? And what about the staging and work area components?

The assumption that the networking and other kinds of data transport mechanisms will be in place to move data from the Legacy system to the access area must be validated. Many times people have discovered too late, that major changes to platforms and networking arrangements must be made in order to support the initiative.

Data Storage and Location Assumptions

The other place where assumptions can leave you short occurs when people dismiss the process of storing, processing and moving data through acquisition. If a series of programs must be run that need to read and write from a progression of multi-million row files, it is essential that enough disk space be available to make that

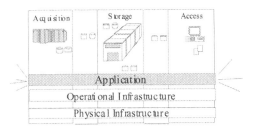

Figure 11-8. Validating individual application assumptions

progression doable.

Application Validation

While the aforementioned validation steps will help us to gain some assurance that the overall warehouse will be a success, we must also apply those criteria and some additional ones, when validating each of the individual applications.

Validating the Operational / Business Assumptions

Before beginning the development of an application, we are going to need to validate that the business assumptions upon which it is based are valid. It is one thing to say that a new application sounds like a good idea, and it is another to say that we hope certain things will happen when the application is complete, but it is an entirely different matter to be sure that the assumptions represented are reasonable. for example, one group proposed that by having access to different types of purchased list and historical sales information that they would be able to improve marketing efforts by over twenty-five percent. Their assumption was that more ready access to the information would result in better decision making. Unfortunately, after suffering and great expense, when the system was finally activated it was discovered that the actual quality of the decision making was worse than it had been under the older and more disciplined methods of data analysis.

Somehow, for each value proposition that we consider, we need to gain some assurance that the assumptions are accurate.

Validating Data Assumptions

While at the higher level of validation we were only concerned with the general question of whether data would be available or not, when we get down to the specific application, we need to ensure that all data required to get the job done will be available. The steps that we outlined earlier -- about validating the data aspects of the access, storage and acquisitions components must be applied, to a far greater level of detail, when we find ourselves focusing on an individual application.

Validating Technical Performance Assumptions

In the same manner, we must also apply a great deal more rigor to the validation of the technical assumptions made for each application. Hopefully, in the process of validating the technical assumptions for the overall project, we have already addressed whatever an individual application might need. If not, then it will have to be addressed at this time.

Checklists

In order to assist us in the process of validation at both the overall and individual application level, we have found that it can be helpful

Area to be Validated	Assumption to be Validated	Comment
Value Propositions		
	Has merit	The value proposition will provide real value to the organization.
	Feasible	The solution can be executed.
	Definable	We can figure out how it will be done.
	Estimable	We can estimate what it will cost.
	Low risk	There is a low risk factor.
	Can be integrated into operational environment	That the solution will integrate with other operations in the business.
Data Access		
	Users will have ready access	Workstations and network are in place (or the cost has been factored in).
	Users can utilize the solution	Users will be able to use the tools delivered.
Storage		
	Platform can handle volumes	The database can operate with these volumes of data.
	Platform can handle access rates	The database can support the number of users and number of transactions proposed.
	Platform will fit in the environment and be supported	The platform will be supported by organizational support staff.
Acquisition		
	Data exists	The data needed can be located.
	Data can be readily extracted	It will be easy to extract data from Legacy systems.
	Data will be in a usable form	The data will be usable (it will not require an inordinate amount of effort to cleanse it and prepare it for access).
	Expertise and support available for Legacy systems	Staff familiar with Legacy systems will be available.
Application Development		
	Staff will be available	Staffing levels will be sufficient.
	Staff will be competent	The staff will know the technology, application and approach being used.
	Staff will be dedicated	Staff will be allocated sufficient time to give good support.
Operational Infrastructure		
	Solution is understood	Do we understand what the operational

Table 11-1

to maintain several checklists . Since the major objectives of the validation process are to identify all of the assumptions that have gone into the development of the solution, to ascertain the validity of each and to be sure that the nature of those assumptions and the risk associated with each is communicated to everyone involved, the following lists have proved to be instrumental.

Validation Checklists

The following validation checklist summarizes the validation issues that we have identified so far. It should be used as a minimum starting point in assuring that all aspects of the warehouse's development are being explored and to ensure that there are no hidden, high risk assumptions.

Critical Assumptions Checklists

In addition to the maintenance of the Validation Checklist, it is also standard practice on projects of this nature to maintain a list of the critical assumptions that people have made about the project. The critical assumptions list serves as a way to highlight areas of concern, and should then be used as the means to guarantee that everyone involved in the process understands what is being developed.

The Estimation Process

Many aspects of the validation cannot be developed without a significant amount of specific information about exactly what the proposed warehouse is supposed to be able to do. The development of this information is referred to as the estimation process. Because estimation and validation are so closely related, we can almost consider them to be two parts of the same process. However, when we talk about estimation, we need to realize several things about the process.

First, when we begin talking about estimation in this environment, we must realize that there are actually several kinds of estimates with which we need to concern ourselves. Secondly, we need to develop a better understanding of the estimation process itself.

Estimating Warehouse Development

There are actually four kinds of estimates that we need to develop in a typical warehouse development environment, and several more as we need to propose benchmark, prototype and proof of concept projects.

The major areas where estimation is done:

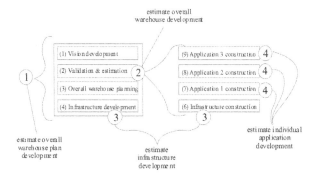

Figure 11-9. Areas of warehouse development estimates

1. The time and effort required to develop the warehouse plan. (The effort required to perform the vision development, validation and estimation, planning and infrastructure development steps).

2. The time and effort required to build the overall warehouse itself. (This is the output of the validation and estimation step).

3. The time and effort required to build the infrastructure. (One of the outputs of the infrastructure development step).

The time and effort required to develop each individual application, and additional estimates for

4. Benchmark, proof of concept and prototype development efforts.

Before we can begin to take a look at the requirements for developing each of these estimates, we need to take a step back and consider the process of estimating itself. An estimate is a discipline we follow that enables us to develop a reasonable idea about what is required to accomplish different tasks. In a very real sense, an estimate is a qualified guess. Since an estimate is nothing more than a guess, then how in the world are we going to determine whether it is accurate.

You Cannot Estimate what you Cannot Define!

Of course, one of the biggest assumptions we will make before going any further in our discussion of the estimation process, is that the managers of the project have set out to eliminate as many unestimatable factors as possible. All of the estimation effort in the world is wasted if we proceed with the execution of a project plan that includes large inexplicable gaps.

For this reason, we have thoroughly defined the warehouse development process, and demanded that things be done in certain ways and in a certain order. It is also for this reason that we have completed the validation phase. The main purpose of the validation phase is to identify those places in the project plan where it is not possible to develop estimates, and take actions before estimation begins to make their development possible. A couple examples of

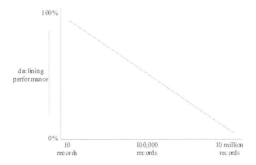

Figure 11-10. Gradual decline in performance as the database volume increases

how these "black holes" in a project plan can cause the rest of the projects estimates to be invalid should help illustrate our point.

Database Access and Scaleability Assumptions

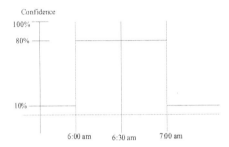

Figure 11-11. Step function decline in database performance

One of the "black holes" that has scuttled many a warehousing project can be found in the area of database accessibility and response times. When making decisions about whether a database can support the volumes of data and access requirements that they think the warehouse is going to need, most inexperienced developers assume that there is a straightforward tradeoff between the amount of data that the database can handle, and the ability of that database to support it. This assumption can be viewed in terms of a graph, showing the gradual decline in system performance as a direct function of the increase in data volumes.

Unfortunately, the above-mentioned assumptions have proven to be a mistake. In reality, as the volume of data increases, all databases hit break points where performance drops off drastically for no apparent reason.

This step-function curve drastically changes our assumptions about what a database can handle. What is even more frustrating is that unique combinations of hardware, memory, disk devices, data base software, data volumes and application access all force these step functions to occur at apparently different and random points along the curve. Often the only way to know if a data base can handle a projected work load is to try it. This represents a significant drawback to our ability to estimate costs and development times in a warehouse environment of high data volumes, and it is impossible for us to develop estimates without a mechanism for making that determination.

Software Connectivity Assumptions

Another type of "black hole" can occur in the utilization of unique combinations of software, hardware and networking environments. Unfortunately, most environments combine a vast assortment of non-standardized network and software arrangements that hamper our ability to confidently estimate how well something will work.

There have been many situations where the end users have selected a data mining tool, and the development team proceeded to execute the project plan which would deliver the application. Much later in the process, people realize that the software product chosen will not work in the targeted environment, and that the cost of making the product usable is not acceptable. This kind of misfire can wreak terrible chaos on the overall project plan. When it is discovered that the tool might not work, the entire development effort must be halted while the problem is investigated, causing serious backlogs in the project plan. When it is discovered that a different tool must be used, the project must be re-launched, taking the new tool and its idiosyncrasies into account. Our assumption therefore, will be that the developers of our estimates have done everything possible to eliminate risk, stabilize the infrastructure and validate assumptions about the system, before attempting to develop estimates. Our approach to estimation will therefore assume that these things will not occur, or will be appropriately addressed if they do occur.

Sources of input into the estimation process

Experience and History

Ideally, one of the most reliable sources about how long something is going to take, or how much it is going to cost is to find someone who has done it before; get this person to use their knowledge to help develop your approximations. Unfortunately, in most cases, the systems being developed are so unique, that there is little experience that people can draw upon to help in the process. When estimation based on experience falls short, you must try to do the job by other means.

Existing Systems Inventory

The second source of potentially helpful information is to look at existing systems within the organization which perform equivalent or related functions. Developers of estimates will often get their best information about transaction rates, user characteristics, data volumes and activity levels by examining these characteristics for existing systems and using that information to develop the estimates for the new system.

Models

Of course, the final source of information for our estimates will be models. Models and methodologies are formally or informally defined techniques and approaches that people have used in the past, which try to simulate the behavior or characteristics of the system on a conceptual level, allowing us to apply mathematical techniques in developing meaningful estimates. Perhaps the best known of the estimation modeling techniques is function point analysis. Under function point analysis, the estimator examines the functionalities that they system is expected to perform, and translates those into function points. The function points can then be added up, and algorithms applied, to derive estimates of development times and levels of activity.

Derivation, Extrapolation and Multipliers

The key mechanisms in the estimation process are derivation, extrapolation and the use of multipliers. Derivation and extrapolation are the mathematical process of taking a given set of information and applying mathematical processes to them, enabling us to project what the ultimate, size, shape or duration of something. In less sophisticated situations, the estimator will develop simple multipliers, allowing them to derive the expected requirements that a system may have.

Confidence Levels and Costs of Estimates

Before we consider the estimation process, there are two more prerequisites: the confidence level of the estimate and the cost. Confidence level is much more then the simple assignment of a probability to an estimate. There are actually several components to it. In the simplest case, I might say that I am 99.9 % confident that the sun will rise tomorrow. What is assumed in this statement is that there is a .1 % chance that it will not. In this situation there are only two choices, either the sun rises or it doesn't; so a one dimensional confidence level is acceptable. But what if I were to say that I am 80% confident that the sun would rise between 6 and

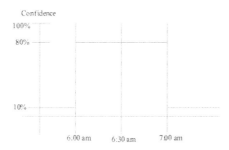

Figure 11-12. Probability chart for the sun rising

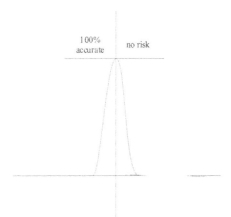

Figure 11-13. A 100% accurate cost estimate

7 a.m.. Meaning that there is also a chance that it will rise before 6 or after 7 a.m. In this situation there is more than a simple binary (yes/no..on/off) choice. In cases like this, it is typical to express probabilities as a function of a curve.

This figure shows a typical probabilities curve. It tells us is that while the greatest probability is that the sun will rise within a half hour of 6:30, (the center line of the curve); there is an 80 % chance that it will be between 6 and 7 a.m. (the left and right quartiles); a 10 % chance that it will be before 6 a.m.; and a 10% chance that it will be after 7 a.m. By exploring and reporting probabilities in this way, we are able to communicate a lot more about what the real probabilities are.

The Perfect Estimate

Let's just say that it will be our objective to develop the perfect estimate. An estimate with a 100 % confidence level and absolutely no risk or variance.

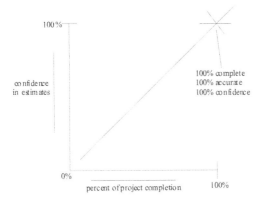

Figure 11-14. Accuracy and confidence increase as more of the project gets completed

No problem. How did we do it? We simply finished the project, and wrote down everything it took to get the it done. Of course, if we had to finish the project before we could estimate its cost, we would not need estimates in the first place. However, this revelation tells us two very important things about the estimation process. First of all, what is clear is the more of the project we have completed, the better and more accurate our estimates will be.

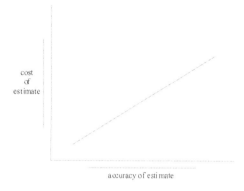

Figure 11-15. Relationship between the cost of an estimate and its accuracy

The conclusion that we can draw from this, is that the longer we can postpone the estimation process, and the more we can find out about what we want to do before we start, the better the estimation will be. The second thing that we learn from this relationship between estimates and percentage of completion, has to do with the cost of the estimate. Of course, the estimate will be extremely accurate but the cost of that estimate will be very high. It will in fact be the cost of doing the entire project. This establishes our second relationship; the one between estimate accuracy and cost.

Generally, the more we spend on estimation, the more accurate the estimate will be. This relationship between cost and accuracy is not always valid. It is certainly possible to spend a lot of time and money on the development of estimates that are of a minimal value. This presents us with our third characteristic of an estimate to consider; its value.

The Value of an Estimate

For every given estimating situation, we must weigh the cost (in time and money) to develop that estimate against the accuracy that the estimate will give us (including its ranges of confidence levels) and the ultimate value it will provide. While it would certainly be nice to have extremely accurate estimates, there are many situations where the information is not worth the price. There have been many situations where organizations have spent unbelievable amounts of time and money in their attempts to determine whether a given platform or database product could handle the anticipated workloads. In many of these cases, the organizations have dedicated so much time and effort to the estimation process, that they found it would have been less expensive to simply build the infernal system and try it from the beginning.

Overcoming the Need to Over-Estimate Things

Because there has been such an abysmal history of systems failure in our past, many people have started to try to compensate by overestimating. Our objective is to take an approach that attempts to balance the extremes.

Things that Need Estimating

While we have already identified the parts of the overall development process which require estimation, we have yet to consider the types of estimates that we will need to develop. There are several:

1. Estimate of the time it will take to complete a task or project (The wall time estimate). This estimate answers the question "When will it be done?"

2. Estimate the amount of time that people will have to spend on the execution of the tasks. (The CPU time estimates). This estimate answers the question "How many hours will how many people actually spend working on this task or project?"

3. Estimate the sizes, types, costs and capacities of the physical resources that will go into the construction of the system. (The hardware/software estimates). These estimates answer the question " How much will I need to spend on hardware and software to build this system?"

Of the five areas of estimation that we have defined for this approach, all require the first two types of estimates mentioned above. Some require that Hardware/Software Estimation be done.

Confidence Levels and the Areas of Estimation

While we certainly would like all of our estimates to be as accurate as possible, it is important for us to keep the costs of that accuracy in mind, and develop a criteria for their development which is appropriate to our objectives for the process. When making this evaluation, we want to stay cognizant of not only the costs and confidence levels of the estimates, but of the consequences and risks involved in the creation of less accurate estimates. For each area of estimation that we consider, we begin by identifying the reason for developing the estimate, and the overall objective of the estimation process.

Overall Warehouse Planning

The process of planning the overall warehouse involves no estimation of hardware and software whatsoever. It is entirely a thinking, writing and communicating process. Therefore, the risks involved in the development of inaccurate estimates in this area are minimal. The big challenge in this area is to determine how to reconcile the differences between the wall time and the CPU time (actual activity time) involved.

The problem with estimating the planning process is that involves investigating, interviewing and consensus building. That means that the really important things happen when the managers, operational personnel and systems people can get together and hammer things out. The second kind of time lag occurs when people need to find out "how things work," or what the capabilities of new components might be. Again, the people doing the planning are totally dependent on the availability of vendors, sales people, and people working on other systems to provide them with the information they need.

The actual ratio of the time spent waiting to the time spent working in this environment can be great. At a minimum you will need to assume at least a fifty/fifty ratio between the two, and it can easily turn into twenty-five/seventy-five ratio. In other words, we may assume that it will take a one week effort to successfully complete vision development. However, the unavailability of key people and other inflexibilities in people's schedules can easily turn that one week into four weeks. Our estimates for the execution of this phase of the project must therefore be based upon realistic expectations for the availability and dedication of the parties required. If enthusiasm is high and the resources are available, then a relatively tight estimate can be utilized. If part of the process is to educate people on something they know nothing about, or to work with people who are less than enthusiastic, then you will need to allocate more lag time. Estimates for the execution of this phase can usually be measured in weeks. Exceedingly large projects may reach the several months range, if resistance to the project, or the complexity of the issues becomes very high.

Developing Estimates for the Overall Warehouse Development Effort

The second area where we are going to need to exercise good estimating practice is in the area of estimating the overall development effort (part of the general planning process).

The estimates developed during this phase must provide us with information about:

1. The overall time it will take to finish the warehouse.
2. Some idea of the times required to complete each application (value proposition).
3. The hardware, software and network infrastructure required to support the warehouse.
4. The effort required to deliver the systems (the people and time they spend on each project).

Estimating the Time and Level of

Effort for the Overall Warehouse

There is no easy way to come up with these numbers, especially as early in the process as we are going to need them. There are several things we should keep in mind before beginning the process. Somehow we need to develop an approach that allows us to determine the best possible overall appraisal of the effort, without forcing us to actually design each of the systems. An approach that has proven effective in the past involves the following steps:

1. Identify each of the value propositions to be included within the scope.

2. Separate the applications into the different major categories of effort that they should entail.

3. Develop high level estimates of the level of activity for each component of the warehouse (acquisition, storage and access) by developing an understanding of the screens required, volumes of data required, access rates and development effort for one of the projects from within each category.

4. Extrapolate the overall level of effort from these samples.

Categories of Level of Effort Applications

While each warehouse application is going to be unique, it is also true that the different types of warehouse applications tend to cluster into the following different groupings. They can be categorized by:

1. Acquisitions component size and complexity

In general we can evaluate any data warehousing effort in the area of acquisitions activity as involving:

- No effort -- For those cases where the acquisition of data will have been accomplished by the development of a previous application.

- Low effort -- A low number of input files (1-5) and a low level of data transformation required.

- Average effort -- A medium number of input files (5-15) and a reasonable level of inter-file coordination and synchronization requirements.

- High effort -- A large number of files and a lot of complexity in the data preparation process.

2. Storage component size and complexity

Storage component development activity is easily measured and estimated in simple terms. How many tables will there be? How big will they be? And what kinds of access will they be required to support? Armed with this information, it should be a relatively straightforward task to develop good, rough estimates of this activity.

3. Type of application

Probably the most difficult thing to estimate at a very high level will be the effort required to deliver the applications portions of the system. Applications will be of the following types:

*   Customized solutions, written using application programming languages and graphical user interfaces.

*   Solutions which involve the direct linkage of data mining tools to the warehouse storage area.

*   Solutions which require the building of data chains and the feeding of the data from those chains into data mining tools.

In cases where a data chaining mechanism will be required, the development of that facility, the first time, will suffice to meet the needs of all future applications that require it. After we have ascertained the characteristics of each of the applications according to these criteria, we can pick the critical components to drive our estimation process, and determine realistic development levels for those areas. When those estimates have been completed, we can use the information to extrapolate our final, overall development effort.

Not only must we include an estimate for the development of each of these applications, we must also provide a reasonable estimate of the effort required to establish the infrastructure. In order to do that, and complete the estimates we have already initiated, we are going to need some relatively dependable physical system estimates to drive the decision making process.

Thoroughness in the Area of

Physical and User Requirements

Experience has repeatedly shown that when you are developing estimates for the construction of warehouse environments that involve the use of user workstation and client server technologies, that the number of technical and managerial issues that need to be addressed can be astronomical. The following checklists have been developed to assist people in ensuring that all the issues of personnel and technical capability have been addressed.

Platform	Selection	Installation	Development Support	Production Support
Hardware				
CPU Size				
Chip Type				
Internal Architecture				
Disk Requirements				
Cost/Maintenance				
Branding/ Dependability				
Operating System				
Topology/Geography				
Utilities				
Full system Backup/Recovery				
Disaster Recovery				
Machine Security				
Network				
Topology (Where & How)				
Hardware (Cabling, NIC...)				
Typology (Ethernet, Token Ring)				
Protocol (IPX, TCP/IP...)				
Network Operating System (Novell, LAN Mgr...)				
Capacity				
Transaction Rate				
Volumes				
Throughput				
Bandwidth				

Table 11-2

Technology Inventory (Master List)

The first table provides a checklist which identifies the different kinds of hardware/software that need to be included in our estimates, with columns indicating the critical functions that must be performed in relationship to each other. For example, in the selection of hardware, we must allocate cost for the purchase of the item, leave time in the plan to allow for the time needed to make the proper selection, go through the process of installation, provide for ongoing development support, and provide for support of the hardware in the ultimate production environment.

Data Architecture Checklist

In the area of databases, we need to be sure that we have addressed all issues having to do with the topology of the data architecture (size, volume, location etc.) as well as the modeling, administration and software support issues.

Operational Requirements Inventory (Master List)

Data	Estimate Development	Ongoing Support
Topology		
Sizing		
Volumes		
Access Rates		
Location		
Logical Data		
Models		
Dictionary/Repository		
Database Administration		
Database HW		
Database Middleware		
Database Software		
Software		
Windows		
OS/2/Windows/XWindows		
Environments		
PowerBuilder		
SmallTalk (et al)		
etc.		
Languages		
C, C++, Basic		
Visual Basic etc.		
Tools		
Word Processing Tools		
Spreadsheet Tools		
Graphics Tools		
Personal Databases		
Personal Utilities		
Applications		
Custom Developed Systems		
Pre-packaged Systems		
E-Mail, Work Flow etc.		
Suites and Families		
Application Architecture		

Table 11-3

This next checklist can serve as a starting point to help us ensure that all the operational information for validation and estimation has been collected.

Operational	
Who will use the system?	
Users	
User departments	
User types	
User classes	
User functions	
Functional areas	
Where will the users be?	
Topology	
Geography	
When will they use the system?	
Timing	
Cycles	
Work patterns	
What will they do with the system?	
Functions	
Transaction types/classes	
Operation types/classes	
Application types/classes	
Desktop load types	
How often will they use the systems?	
Rates	
Temporal parameters	
Transactional drivers	

Table 11-4

Administrative Issues Checklist

Our next checklist takes a cross section of the other issues, and identifies key issues in the execution of administrative functions.

Administrative		
Who will support		
Selection		
Installation		
Development		
Ongoing support		
Backup/recovery		
Security		
Monitoring and tuning		
Troubleshooting		
How will we manage		
Standards		
Procedures		
Policies		
Roles		
Responsibilities		
Developmental		
Design		
Methodology		
Case		
Models and tools		
SDLC		
Architecture		
Application		
System		
Project		
Environmental setup		
Version control		
Software migration		
Test, development, production migration		
Tool selection		
Staffing		
Training		
Hiring / contracting		

Table 11-5

CHAPTER 12

BUDGETING, BIDDING AND STAFFING

The last set of topics we will consider in the overall warehouse construction are the budgeting, bidding and staffing processes. While the framework we have been describing up to this point certainly provides the reader with a lot of helpful structure, it is important that we include within this framework some understanding of the process of financing and managing it.

TO BUILD OR TO BUY?

The first thing to consider when trying to decide how to finance the construction of a large scale system is to determine whether you are going to build the entire data warehouse on your own, or get some help. Outside assistance in data warehouse construction can come from several sources, but the principle sources are hardware vendors, software vendors and consultants.

Hardware Vendors

There are many ways that you can use hardware vendors to help leverage your data warehousing development efforts

1. Bundled solutions

As data warehousing becomes a more popular alternative, innovative vendors of hardware products have begun to create "data warehousing packages," which combine specially developed hardware arrangements combined with specifically designated software to offer the would be data warehouser a "ready to use" solution.

These kinds of packaged solutions offer many advantages. The purchaser is assured of getting a well coordinated collection of products. Many infrastructure and operational issues will have been worked out in advance. The big risk in these situations can be avoided if the person investigating the options ensures that he clearly understands the strengths and limitations of the package.

2.   Hardware vendor provided consulting

 In addition to providing assistance with the technical aspects of the construction process, many hardware vendors have added consulting support services to their staffs in order to provide customers with a more complete solution. For the most part, these services should be considered in the same vein as "normal" consulting activities. (see below)

3.   Software vendors

The second place where help in the warehouse construction process comes from is through the vendors of data warehousing software products. There are several categories of product we need to consider.

4.   Acquisition component products

In this category, we include all products designed to assist the developer of the warehouse in the process of analyzing, converting and transporting data from Legacy systems to the storage area. There are several types of product in this category:

- Data movers - These products automate the process of moving data from one place to the next. By making use of a separate platform and network connectivity between the platforms, these products allow the user to input specifications for the data to be moved, where it is to be moved, and when. The product takes care of the rest. The Info-Pump is a good example of this kind of product.

- Data analyzers - These products assist people in the process of understanding where their data is and what it means. They are usually tied in with existing data dictionaries and other types of repository support software, but can save many days of analytical effort when used correctly.

- Data cleaners - Software in this category actually makes it easier to clean up data. It uses special rules and routines to check for the validity , accuracy and compliance level of each field within the database. Data cleaners often include adjustment software which cleans up the data automatically, after it is discovered.

At the most sophisticated end of the spectrum are the highly intelligent, specialized data cleansing products like PostalSoft, which reads in name and address information and makes use of sophisticated soundex , postal standards and merge/purge processing to clean up files for mailing.

At the more general purpose end are products like Vality, which uses reference files and search criteria to validate and cleanse individual fields.

5. Storage component products

- Databases - Of course, no data warehouse would be possible without a database management system software packages to run it. These packages ultimately turn out to be the "heart and soul" of most data warehouse applications.

  Products in this area include the "big databases", the most popular in the industry including DB2 on mainframe and Oracle, and Informix and Sybase in the UNIX arena. Also included are products that deal in specialized industries or in the delivery of specialized database services, like Red Brick and Ingres.

- Data accelerators - As an adjunct to the normal database software, many people have begun purchasing accelerator products. These products work as add-ons to existing database technologies and make it possible for queries to be executed in a fraction of the time that a normal query would take. These products are especially important when databases get extremely large.

- Repositories - repository products provide a software-enabled framework which makes the management of the warehouse storage area easier. Repositories make use of special indexes and table control tables which store Meta-data (information about the information in the warehouse). The utilization of a repository product can make management of the actual warehouse, the

data extraction, and data chain building processes easier.

6. Access component products

    - Data mining products - The driving force behind many
      warehousing initiatives today is the ability to attach
      high powered data mining tools to it. In the last sec-
      tion of this book, we will spend a significant amount
      of time considering the products in this category.

    - Middleware - Of course, all of the data mining tools in
      the world are useless, if we don't have a mechanism in
      place to make it possible for us to hook them up to the
      warehouse. While in some situations we will be able
      to make direct connections between user workstations
      and the warehouse, in many cases we will need the
      assistance that middleware products can bear to help
      make those connections inexpensive and user friend-
      ly.

7. Operational infrastructure products

The final category of products that can be purchased provide us with
the ability to manage the entire operational layer of the warehouse.
Several vendors of data warehouse management packages include a
variety of services and mechanisms which can provide the kind of
operational support we have described throughout this book.

PERCENTAGE OF BUDGET ANALYSIS

After we have determined the products to include in the development
of our warehousing solution, our next step is to begin determining
how to allocate the costs for each of the development steps. While
the development of the hard numbers required to do this should
be a product of the estimation process, there are some things
about the overall ratio of costs allocated that can be helpful both
in understanding the budgeting process, and in validating that our
estimates are accurate.

The Easy Warehouse - Budget Analysis

We begin our investigation of budget ratio analysis by considering the simplest and easiest kind of warehouse development case, in order to get an appreciation for the issues.

The simplest kind of data warehousing solution that we could envision might be where a group of users has identified that the information on a list of potential customers (available from one of the Legacy systems within the organization) contains information to which they would like to gain ad hoc access. Their intention is to perform ad hoc queries against the information in that file to investigate the different characteristics that the customers might display. No special data analysis or identification work will be

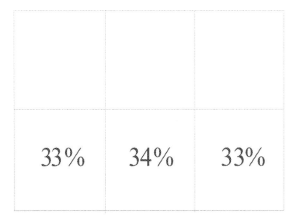

Figure 12-1. An "easy" warehouse - % of budget

required, and the users will simply accept the data as it is extracted from the system.

The process of delivering this warehouse solution, therefore, assuming that the infrastructure (physical and operational) is in place, requires that we read the file into the storage area, and then provide the end users with a query tool to access it.

Our allocation of the expense for the delivery of this system might look something like this.

- Acquisition Development - Thirty-three percent
- Storage Development - Thirty-three percent
- Access Development - Thirty-three percent

Sophisticated User Analysis

We can now begin to change the variables involved and see what kinds of impact it will have on this allocation.

If we take the first case, where the acquisition, storage and access components were all relatively simple, we saw that the percent of budget was allocated rather evenly. Now let's consider what happens when the end users decide that they would still like to use the same data, but plan to be more sophisticated in their use of it. For example,

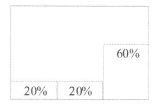

Figure 12-2. Sophisticated user access

they may decide to use a multi-dimensional database or a neural net for better processing. In this case our allocation of the funds for the project will be different, more like:

- Acquisition - Twenty percent
- Storage - Twenty percent
- Access - Sixty percent

Complicated Input Data

In a third case, we will assume that the users only require the simple access mechanism we assumed in the first situation, but now the

Figure 12-3. A complicated acquisition process

data they want to see is much more difficult to get at. It might for example, require that we pull data from three or four different files. And we might need to merge, purge and sanitize much of it before it can be loaded. In this case, the percentages would be reversed:

- Acquisition - Sixty percent
- Storage - Twenty percent
- Access - Twenty percent

Figure 12-4. "Heavy" storage requirements

Large Volumes of Data

In the last situation we will consider, we will assume that the data to be used in the warehouse is easily attained, and that the users access will be simplistic. However, the volumes of data we need to work with are quite high, and the relationships between tables are made more complicated. In this case, our allocation of budget will become skewed at the center.

- Acquisition-Twenty percent
- Storage-Sixty percent
- Access-Twenty percent

By taking the total estimate of the requirements to develop the warehouse, breaking it out, and viewing it in this manner, we begin to gain some valuable insight into the real effort needed to develop the warehouse.

Reality Checking

The first thing we can do when we distribute the budget along these lines, is determine how realistic the plans for the warehouse are. If the allocation of budget is skewed in one way or another, that may be a sign that someone has made an omission in the overall

Figure 12-5. A "typical" high-low-high ratio pattern

estimation process.

In general, unless there are some special circumstances or situations to be addressed, the ratios for allocation of the budget to the warehouse by component should show either:

- A lower storage component budget then the other two, or
- A clear pattern of ascent of descent from one component to the next.

Storage Component as Lower Percentage of Budget

Probably the most common allocation of budget for a warehousing project follows this high, low, high kind of allocation.

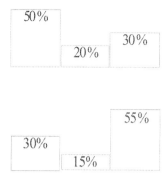

Figure 12-6. Variations in the high-low-high pattern

Figure 12-7. Incline and decline patterns

This pattern indicates that there is a high degree of activity required to find and prepare the data, and a comparable level of activity in the preparation of data mining solutions. In general, a high level of activity on the data acquisition side is usually accompanied by a high level of activity in rendering that data usable.

The storage component development budget is much lower, because the hard work is being done by the other two development areas. By recognizing this high, low, high pattern, we are not saying that the acquisition and access components will have the same percentages of budget, but they will both be higher than the storage component.

Clear Patter of Ascent or Descent

Sometimes, conditions are so extreme at one end of the warehouse, that the pattern will resemble an incline or decline pattern. This can happen when the volume of work required to develop the acquisitions component is very high because of Legacy system conditions, and there is a corresponding simplicity on the access end, or vice versa.

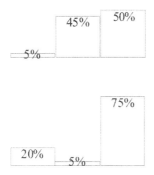

Figure 12-8. Radical variances - a warning signal

USING THE RATIOS AS A
REALITY CHECK

By examining the ratio allocated to each component, we can get a reality check on how reasonable the development effort will be. For example, if we show a low acquisitions allocation, but we know that the task is very complicated, we should question the estimates developed.

Radical Variance in the Allocation of Budget

We must be vigilant in looking for cases containing a radical variance in the allocation. If any component is being allocated a significantly lower percentage of resources than the others, that is a very good indication that something has been missed.

Staffing and Allocation Ratios

Another useful insight that our analysis of budget ratios can give us, is to serve as a starting point for the development of staffing requirements. Clearly, our allocation of people to the job of developing the warehouse should correspond to the level of effort projected for each component.

It is amazing how individuals can develop plans and budgets, and then simply throw personnel at the tasks involved, without really considering the requirements to get the job done.

When it comes to data warehousing, different organizations and different situations can bias people towards the over or under staffing of key positions.

In an environment that is heavily database and data-oriented, we often find an over-staffing of the storage component development. In environments where working on Legacy systems is considered as punishment duty, the allocation of resources to the acquisitions component tends to be de-emphasized and as a consequence, greatly understaffed.

In environments where the focus is on the development of user-friendly solutions, we find an emphasis on the access component.

Before considering the specific skills and level of experience required for warehouse construction, it is critical that we ensure the staffing approach is balanced. The best way to ensure the balance is correct is to base it on these budget ratios.

Other Under-Staffing Dangers - Complete Warehouse Solutions

The one type of product or offering that should make the purchaser

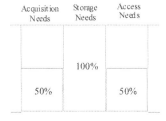

Figure 12-9. Percent of needs met by warehouse package solution

the most wary is the "complete" warehouse solution offering. These packages or offerings claim to provide the buyer with everything they need in order to run their own warehouse. Just buy their product and the rest is automatic. At least, that is the claim.

Unfortunately, the reality of the situation is usually far from that simple or straightforward. We can use the budget analysis ratios we have just discussed to validate or disclaim the merit that a proposed "total" warehousing solution will have.

Acquisition	Storage	Access
	Application 4	
	Application 3	
	Application 2	
	Application 1	
Operational Infrastructure		
Physical Infrastructure		

Figure 12-10. Layers of the warehouse

The first step in considering the purchase of a warehouse solution, is to develop an understanding of what the product does, and determine what percentages of the overall warehouse functionality it will really provide.

For example, a good, broad-based solution might concentrate on the management of the storage component, while providing support for fifty percent of our acquisition needs, and fifty percent or our access needs.

Having developed this analysis, we can then start to estimate what the real warehouse solution is going to cost.

Allocation of Percentages by Layer

Another kind of ratio analysis that can be useful, both in the validation of estimates and in the development of staffing requirements, is

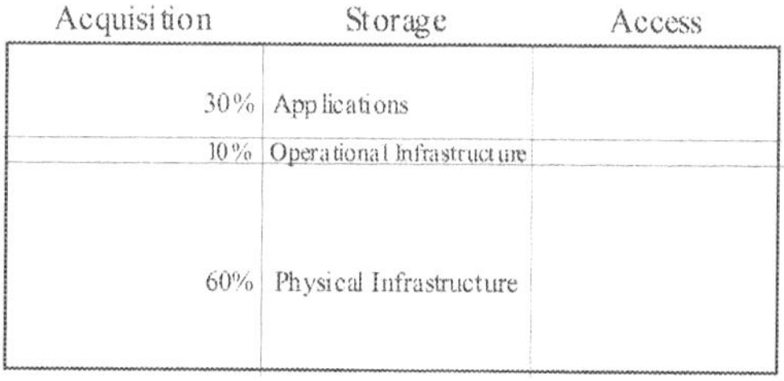

Acquisition		Storage	Access
	30%	Applications	
	10%	Operational Infrastructure	
	60%	Physical Infrastructure	

Figure 12-11. Over-budgeted physical infrastructure

allocation by layers. You may recall that the warehouse consists of several layers, the physical infrastructure, the operational infrastructure, and each of the application layers.

By determining how much of our overall budget is to be spent on physical hardware and software, vs. operational software vs. applications software and databases, we can get a much better idea of what the project is really about.

Warning Signs

Some of the warning signs that our project is out of synch with our objectives will become apparent when the allocations across these layers becomes skewed.

The Operational layer should always represent a small percentage of the overall budget, but not so small that it is non-existent.

If the cost of providing the infrastructure for a warehouse is significantly higher than the cost of the development of the solutions, there might be reason to suspect that the project is ill-proposed.

More importantly, when considering the purchase of packages and bundled hardware solutions, it is critical that we develop estimates for the activity needed to complete the warehouse, after the vendors have left.

The Hidden Costs of Warehouse Development

Hopefully, the different forms of budget ratio analysis that we have considered will provided the prospective warehouse developer with a good idea of exactly what it is going to take to complete the system. In too many cases, people habitually underestimate the real level of effort required to identify, cleanse, synchronize and load the data into the warehouse. This is especially true in those cases where the vendor offers a "complete" solution.

The danger in these situations comes when people allow the vendors to "guestimate" the level of effort that the execution of the data

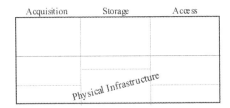

Figure 12-12. Ratio of physical infrastructure budget by component

disciplines is going to require. When these disciplines are estimated lightly, people discover all the subsequent data integrity and synchronization problems too late in the process to do anything about them. Failure to budget adequately for data preparation and mapping is the principle source of most warehouse budget mistakes.

Physical Infrastructure
Ratios Across the Components

The last kind of ratio that we will look at, is the ratio of the overall physical infrastructure budget that has been allocated to each of the warehouse components. By developing these ratios, we have the final piece of information that we need for effective staff decision making.

These ratios typically map out into two patterns. The physical infrastructure requirements for the acquisitions component are usually pretty low. For the most part, people will try to leverage existing Legacy systems platforms as much as possible to support them.

In a great number of cases, the allocation for the storage component will be the highest. In those cases, people intend to purchase separate dedicated platforms to support the activity. In other cases, the storage component will be managed via an existing platform. Obviously, in those cases, the ratio will be low.

The budget for the development of the Access component can be non-existent, or the highest expense, depending upon whether or not the users already have workstations and network connections in place. In all cases, our understanding of how these ratios play out give us a good idea about how resources need to be deployed to carry out the plan.

Staffing Requirements

Provided with the information that we obtained from the estimates, and each of the different types of ratios that we considered, we can turn our focus to ensuring we have put a staff in place that is capable of delivering the warehouse, on time and under budget.

The Size of the Project

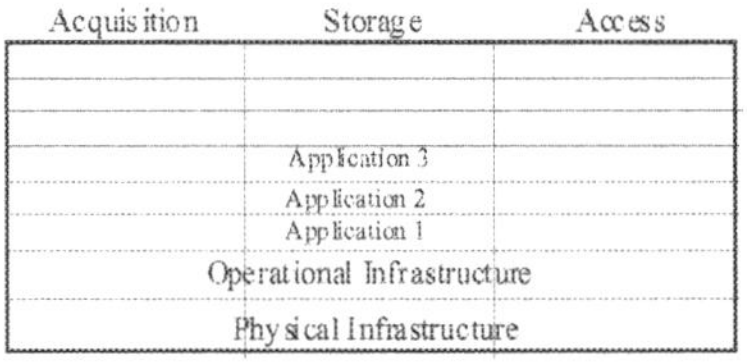

Acquisition	Storage	Access
	Application 3	
	Application 2	
	Application 1	
Operational Infrastructure		
Physical Infrastructure		

Figure 12-13. The warehouse framework

One of the first things we need to do before making specific staffing decisions, is to determine the size and scope of the overall project. This is essential, since the bigger the project, the more able we will be to identify specialized roles and responsibilities. Conversely, the smaller the project, the more we will be forced to blend these jobs and try to identify a few people, with an incredibly rich set of experiences and capabilities.

We will begin our discussion of this topic assuming that the project is relatively large (more than fifteen people working on it simultaneously) and that we will therefore be able to identify many specialized kinds of roles.

As in our other considerations, we will attack the problem of staffing by starting with our data warehouse framework, considering the staff required to address the needs presented by each layer and each component of the system.

Physical Infrastructure Skills

As you may recall, from our chapter regarding the development of the physical infrastructure, there are an almost infinite variety of combinations of hardware, software, and networking components that can be used to deliver a data warehousing solution. Obviously, the staffing requirements are going to depend upon that particular combination.

Experience has shown however, that certain types of skill sets will be required, regardless of the platforms selected. For every unique environment, platform or tool set utilized, there should be resources available who understand what it takes to install and utilize them. In many cases, these support personnel will already be in place, but if (and when) they are not, they will need to be identified. It is amazing how many people will bring in vast quantities of disparate products, and simply forget that each of them will have to be supported in some way. The major categories of products that need to be supported will include:

- Hardware
- Operating system
- Network
- Windows environment
- Programming languages
- Database software
- Data mining tools

Traditionally, this level of support was known as the "systems" or "internals" level. In the good old days of mainframe computers, there were extensive staffs to support each of these areas. In today's environment, this level of support is often overlooked, with disastrous consequences.

Operational Infrastructure Skills

Luckily, in the area of the development and maintenance of the operational infrastructure, our skill requirements are relatively self-defining. To begin with, it is routinely accepted that the physical infrastructure support will need to be in place, if the operational infrastructure is going to function properly. In addition, the main skills required will be:

a) Database Management - The biggest requirement for the development of an operational infrastructure will be the presence of a database administrator who is able to design, build and deliver the core control/tracking tables which drive the operational infrastructure management process.

b) Front End Development - The second need will be for a person able to program the end user' and warehouse manager's interface screens. This screen allows people to check on the status of different data feeds, files and databases throughout the course of the warehouses different load and utilization cycles.

c) Network Connectivity - If the Legacy systems performing data extraction and preparation, or the data chain building and data mining tools, are located on platforms that are not already connected to the main storage area platform; then it will be critical that a person able to initiate those connections is available. If the Legacy systems extraction programs are unable to update the control/tracking tables, then the operational infrastructure will be greatly hindered in its ability to manage.

d) Native Legacy system programming - The final skill required is the ability to place customized control/tracking table calls into the extraction programs themselves. These skills will probably already be part of the skill sets of the people writing and delivering the extraction and preparation programs.

Application Development Skill Requirements

Of course the previous two areas covered represent only a very small portion of the overall allocation of staff to a data warehousing project. The lion's share of this staff will be dedicated to the construction of warehouse applications themselves. We will separate the staffing requirements for this process into three major categories: management, operational and technical support, and then spend the majority of our time considering the technical and analytical skills required.

Management Level of Participation

While clearly the biggest draw of management's time during the process of warehouse development occurs earlier on in the process, during the vision development and planning phases, it is important that everyone understand that management must remain involved throughout the development of the project.

The most obvious level of management participation will be at the level of budget and project status reporting. Management needs to stay apprised of the progress of the warehousing project on a weekly basis, at a minimum.

Not so obvious, however, will be the need to have management available to make policy and judgment decisions when the data discipline process begins to uncover serious problems with the integrity and meaning of the data. Inevitably the data discipline process will uncover many anomalies in the nature of the data within systems. While some of these anomalies may be trivial, occasionally a major revelation about the nature of the Legacy systems, or about the way things get done, comes to light. This might change management's decisions about how the warehouse should be rolled out.

Operational Level of Participation

While management's role in the application development process may be minimal, the same is not true for the people who work within the different operational units that will be using or feeding the warehouse. These individuals will need to have significant time allocated to assist the technical staff in the development of specific solutions.

As far as the skills required of these individuals, the biggest requirement will be that they are familiar with the business area for which the solution is being developed, and are also familiar with the current modus operandi in that environment.

Unfortunately, the usual case is that the people best qualified to serve in the role for the warehousing team are also the most valuable people overall, and consequently are least able to spend the time required. There is no easy answer to this problem. The right business people must be ready to spend the time on development -- if the system is going to work the right way the first time.

Technical Skills for Application Development

The majority of the staff required for application development will come from the technical area. In general, we will consider the skills from the following general areas:

- Data discipline and database skills
- Application development skills
- Warehouse and operational support skills

Data Discipline Skill Sets

We have already talked a lot about the skills required to perform the data discipline skills, but we will briefly review them again, for consistency. The diagram shows the different specific steps involved in the data discipline process, and shows which of the three components they are the most concerned with.

What is important about the tasks specified by this chart is that they represent a combination of skills. The position of a task in one of the three component areas (acquisition, storage or access) implies:

1. Technical Familiarity with the platforms each of those respective components will be built within.

For example, if the warehouse is going to be based upon a mainframe acquisitions component, UNIX-Informix storage component, and a windows-based access component, then people involved in each of these areas will have to be technically competent in their respective areas in order to do their jobs.

2. Business and Operational familiarity with the processes being modeled and the solutions being developed.

For example, those people involved in the access component data discipline tasks will need to be familiar with the business problems that the end users are trying to solve with a particular data mining approach. While people involved in the acquisition component efforts will need to understand the business functions that the Legacy systems are delivering.

3. A core set of skills involving data analysis, modeling, database administration and systems analysis. This includes data modeling, data mapping and the identification and documentation of key data characteristics.

All told, the problems faced by people trying to staff a data warehousing project in the data disciplines area, can be extremely challenging and compromises must often be made.

Application Development Skills

In the area of programming and application development skills, our requirements are a little more straightforward, and more easily specialized. We will need:

- Graphical user interface and windows programmers - to develop user "front end" solutions, others to write the programs and jobs that move data through the warehouse
- Data mining specialists - People familiar with the process of installing data mining tools, hooking them into the warehouse and utilizing them.
- Batch/background job execution- Another set of personnel competent in the development of programs, often in the Legacy system environments, who will be involved in the extraction, cleansing and synchronization of that data.

Warehouse and Operational Support Skills

The final area of staffing concerns in the operation of the warehouse, is the designation and allocation of personnel who will actually run and manage the warehouse after it is built. A warehouse is an extremely complicated and mission-critical system, and there will need to be permanent staff assigned to its "care and feeding." These people will be responsible for ensuring that everything within the warehouse is working well, and they must be available when things go wrong.

The process of budgeting and staffing a warehousing project can be an extremely complicated and critical process.

THE BIDDING PROCESS

Hopefully, by the time the reader gets to this point in the book, it will become apparent that there are a variety of superior ways that the bidding process for warehouse development can be handled.

Acquisition	Storage	Access
		Solution Development
		Data Identification
Data Sourcing		Data Sourcing
Data Integrity Validation		Data Integrity Validation
Data Synchronization	Data Synchronization	
Back Flush Development		
	Storage Topology Mapping	Storage Topology Mapping
Data Transformation Mapping	Data Transformation Mapping	Data Transformation Mapping
Data Metrics Gathering	Data Metrics Gathering	Data Metrics Gathering
	Data Modeling	
	Database Design	

Figure 12-14. Data disciplines

We have partitioned the entire process of warehouse development into a series of discrete phases, each of which should be executed in a serial order. By using this framework as a guideline, it should become easy to determine how to proceed.

The first and biggest revelation about the overall process should be that the development of a warehouse plan is a very different process than the process for developing and delivering specific solutions. In view of this, it might make sense in many situations, to approach the development of the overall warehouse plan as one project, and the delivery of each of the subsequent parts of the warehouse (physical infrastructure, operational infrastructure and each application) as separate projects.

This makes great logical sense, and in many cases, will be the best way to proceed. Unfortunately, there will be times when the simplicity and linearity of the approach will need to be varied, in order to take business or economic issues into account.

WHEN VALIDATION FAILS!

The single biggest reason that we find ourselves needing to vary from our plans will occur when the execution of the validation process uncovers a number of issues which cannot be resolved without the investment of a significant amount of money in the development of prototypes, benchmarks and proof of concept projects. When this occurs, we will have little choice but to vary our plans accordingly. The important things to keep in mind when we decide to vary from this ordered approach to the process are that:

1. We clearly identify the purpose and deliverables expected from the special project being proposed.

2. We not overvalue the reuse value of the solution being developed, and

3. By no means do we allow the development of these validation projects to somehow make it possible for everyone to skip the rest of the steps involved in the process. The execution of a proof of concept project does not eliminate the need for the validation of all of the other warehouse propositions, nor does it eliminate the need to develop an infrastructure and propose an overall warehouse plan. It doesn't even eliminate the need to develop a plan for the real solution that the project has been designed to validate!

If the people preparing to put a warehouse project (or some phase of it) out for bid are aware of the many issues that we have identified, and are familiar with the structure that we have proposed for its execution, then the bidding process should become considerably easier and more accurate.

CHAPTER 13

DATA MINING IS
WHAT IT'S ALL ABOUT

At this point in our consideration of data warehousing we are going to make an abrupt shift. Up until now we have been concentrating on the issues, problems and concerns that people may have when thinking about building and managing a data warehouse, but have spent almost no time talking about what to do with it. More importantly, we have made some rather tall assumption. We have assumed that you, the reader, are fully aware of what data mining tools are, how they work, and why all of our discussions about data warehousing would be next to pointless without them. So, let's correct this gross negligence.

WHAT IS DATA MINING ANYWAY?

The first problem we are facing is to come up with a meaningful definition that the majority of people will be able to accept. Just as the data warehousing marketplace is rife with a plethora of contradictory and complementary definitions of the term, so too is the data mining area.

On the one hand we have the people with the extremely narrowly focused meaning who believe that data mining should be defined as a collection of end user tools and/or applications which perform analytical and statistical analysis of a large pool of data.

On the other hand are those individuals who believe that any product that enables end users to access data directly from a database, without the benefit of customized application programs, should also be included.

We will address the data mining subject to include the broadest and most liberal interpretation of the term. For our purpose we will assume that any product which allows end users direct access and manipulation of data from within the data warehousing environment without the intervention of customized programming activity is a data mining tool.

Why the Fuss?

There is a dizzying array of data mining tools available on the market today. Some of them are relatively new, offering end users capabilities that, until only recently, were considered to be impossible. Some of the products have been around for a long time, but have undergone a recent face lift. All of these products have several things in common, however.

1. They are PC or UNIX Workstation based.

While tools for data mining type operations and customized applications for data mining functions have been around for a long time, the real hoopla about data mining today is a direct result of the widespread acceptance and popularity of personal computers and scientific workstations. As personal computers have continued to increase in power and decrease in price the possibilities for desk top computation have sky rocketing. Personal computers not only make this kind of power affordable, but they make it extremely convenient as well.

Probably the most frightening thing about this trend is that we are only just now beginning to understand and exploit the vast potential it represents. Indeed, data warehousing on its own is practically a meaningless concept. It is only with the kind of power these desktop tools represent that we can begin to capitalize on the information that the warehouse provides.

2. They are Windows or, at least, WIMP driven.

Although we can give some credit to the PC as a desktop computer for making this kind of activity possible, it is not that power in and of itself that makes it attractive. If that were the case, then we would all be busily programming our PCs, using COBOL or BASIC language, and looking at printed green bar reports at our homes and offices. No, it is the power and intuitive usefulness of the Windows style environment that really makes data mining tools work. With these 256 color, graphically pleasing , sound-card squawking WIMP interfaces (Windows, Icons, Menus and Pointers) almost everyone can now get friendly with their computers.

3. They make it possible for end users to gain access to computer data directly.

Most importantly, by delivering this power and ease of use directly to the user, it enables people to grab, manipulate and report on vast accumulations of data. The client/server revolution has served its purpose. Suddenly it is possible for personal computers to be attached to disparate sources of data and to treat them as if they were on the same machine.

THE CATEGORIZATION OF DATA MINING TOOLS

Given this decidedly broad based definition of the subject and this very generalized observation about the products, we next have to develop a scheme to differentiate the various kinds of data mining tools and approaches. Because the field is so broad and complex, we need to categorize these products according to several criteria. Our categorizations will include:

The type of product

The characteristics of the product

- Data identification capabilities
- The media it uses to display results
- Formatting capabilities
- Specification management (the way people tell the product what to do)
- Execution management (the way execution and timing is controlled)

The objectives (what you do with the product)

Developmental participation (the roles of hardware, software and greyware) in the delivery of information

TYPES OF RRODUCTS

The vast assortment of data mining products can be broken down into the following general types.

1. Query Managers and Report Writers

This group represents the biggest collection of different types of products and has the longest history of existence. From almost the earliest days of computers and databases vendors attempted to provide simple tools for end users to query for data and print out the results. In the pre-relational database days, this category of products was represented by FOCUS, EASYTRIEVE and RAMIS. These products allowed users to define data that they would like to see, and then ran against the databases and files that stored the data. Then, with the relational databases came the introduction of products like QMF, ISQL, and a wide range of SQL based query and reporting tools. These products were an improvement, but still left a lot to be desired in terms of ease of use.

The query managers and report writers of today have come a long way since those days. Nowadays it is possible to pull and generate these reports in a fraction of the time it used to take and with a fraction of the effort. The same basic functionality, however, still holds true and still provides value.

2. Spreadsheets

The second most popular data mining tool is the spreadsheet. Typified by MS-Excel and Lotus 1-2-3, these products perform a wide variety of analytical and reporting within one easy to use environment. In fact, spreadsheets have been identified as the most popular data mining tool.

3. Multi-dimensional Databases

The next generation of product actually turned out to be a combination of the first two. Multi-dimensional databases allow users to tie queries to spreadsheets in a way that executes many different kinds of sophisticated multi-dimensional analysis. While the typical spreadsheet is limited to a few dimensions, the multi-dimensional database greatly expands the capacity and, at the same time, works directly with database stored data. In our subsequent chapter on multi-dimensional databases we will explore this type of mining tool in more detail.

4. Statistical Analysis Tools

Another of the "old timers" in the data mining area are the statistical analysis tools, represented by products like SAS or SPSS. With these products users can pull in data and perform sophisticated statistical analysis operations, allowing them to compute regressions and clusters, display graphical relationships, and perform all manner of complex computation to gain new insight into the nature of the available information.

Like the query managers, the statistical analysis tools have undergone a significant GUI (Graphical User Interface) face lift over the past several years, making them also more user friendly and more intuitive than they were in the past. We have also included a chapter on statistical analysis approaches for a more thorough consideration of this category.

5. Artificial intelligence and Advanced Analysis Tools

While artificial intelligence and advanced analytical approaches have been around for some time, only recently has it become possible to bring their computational power down to the level of the typical end user. These products employ extremely complex algorithms and approaches to develop and refine new insights into previously collected data. In this category we include neural nets and other advanced approaches. We have included subsequent chapters to consider neural nets in general and a look at working with specific neural network applications.

6. Graphical Display Tools

Last but not least are the graphical display products. Many products in the previously mentioned categories include graphical display capabilities, but specialized graphics products can fit the bill in situations where really sophisticated graphical representation is desired. We have also include a chapter about this category of product.

CHARACTERISTICS OF THE PRODUCTS

While understanding the basic focus of each of these product groups is helpful, categorizing them by that criteria alone provides us with far too little information to really appreciate what they are and how they work. There are several operational characteristics that all of these products share.

Data Identification Capabilities

No matter what kind of data mining tools you are talking about, they all must provide the users with some way to identify the specific data they want to pull into the program for processing or display. Capabilities in this area are defined by the language the product uses to "call" for the data and by the way the user codes that language gets.

Data Access Languages or DML (Data Manipulation Languages) are either pre-relational or relational. The pre-relational languages consist of a broad range of proprietary languages. In general, each language is specific to a particular platform and a particular database product. Because of this, these languages are cumbersome, complex and far from user friendly.

The relational access language, SQL, put an end to all of that. Suddenly we had one common data access language that could be used to access data from almost any platform or environment. SQL has certainly revolutionized data access. Although SQL is still far from being user friendly, working with only one data access language has simplified data mining tools development. Without SQL the vendors would need to build hundreds of customized user access mechanisms into their products, making it impossible for them to support as many different sources of data as they do.

The second important aspect of data access capabilities is the way the user inputs the query specifications. At the low end of our continuum are products which allow us to input the raw SQL calls ourselves. While this is certainly an improvement over earlier "manual" proprietary data access language entry, it is far from optimum.

Some vendors stop at this level of ease of use, others provide the end user with query building capabilities. These products have screens and menus to select, point and click from options in order to interactively "build" the queries. Those screens provide the user with metadata (data about the data). The user simply selects the desired information from the menus, and the system builds the SQL command automatically.

At the high end of this continuum we find the business object generators. These products actually allow programmers or DBAs to pre-load already organized queries so that the end user needs to do little more than select the particular business object of interest.

Output Media

After we have figured out which data we want the data mining tool to give us, our next issue is to decide how we want that information displayed. Data mining tools can provide output in several forms.

Printed - To this day printed output still represents the vast majority of data processing output. Of course, now we need to worry about things like PostScript, Laser, Plotted or Fully color print outs.

Green Screen - Unfortunately, a large number of end users are still saddled with the old fashioned 3270 type green and black or amber and black two tone screens. Although it is becoming rarer with each new release of personal computers, there is still a need and, therefore, there are data mining tools that can work in this mode.

Standard Graphics - By far the most common form of output for data mining applications these days is the personal computer 256 (or higher) color screens.

Enhanced Full Graphics - In some cases we find that normal PC graphics will not provide the detail and depth that the graphical display requires and special high resolution graphics terminals need to be called into play.

Formatting Capabilities

After we have identified the data we want to look at, and have determined which media will display it, we have to figure out how it is going to look. There are a number of ways data can be displayed.

Raw data format - The data is dumped out to the screen or paper exactly as it is stored in the file

Tabular - This is the standard SQL output form with data organized in columns and rows and headings describing what data is in which column. This form of output also can include what is known as "control break" logic which prints summary lines at different levels.

Spreadsheet form - It not only show us data in column and row form, but also allows us to embed formulae and calculations into the structure of the output itself. This format makes it possible to include complex calculations within a simple framework. While the key to tabular reporting is columns and rows, the key to spreadsheet type reporting is the "cell." Each cell can contain a different calculation and, while tabular reports can only perform calculations on complete columns or rows, the spreadsheet/cell formatting approach allows us to refer to any cell anywhere on the screen and work with all of the data that is available.

Multi-dimensional databases - These tools take the power of data access languages and build them into the column, row and cell structure of the spreadsheet. With a multi-dimensional display tool cells can be tied, not only to cells that are available, but to fields within the database itself, making it possible to add many more dimensions of computational capability from the same screen.

Visualization - At the high end of the formatting capabilities is visualization. Many tools allow you to convert the formatted data into graphical displays.

Computation Facilities

Some computational capabilities are inherent in the way products format data. However, the category of computation facilities itself is really something different. Computation abilities are provided to the user through the following.

Columnar Operations - The standard "control break" or SQL columnar functions perform summarization, addition, multiplication and other operations on the available data on a column by column basis.

Cross-Tab Capabilities - They take the columnar operations one step further by enhancing the product so that it performs those same operations on the individual rows of data.

Spreadsheets - These provide us with the "cell math" approach that we have already talked about. Cell math greatly enhances the usefulness of the tool with the ability to compute any field on the screen.

Multi-dimensional spreadsheets - This is the approach used by multi-dimensional databases, making it possible to build "virtual spreadsheets" that are several layers deep.

Rule driven or trigger driven computation - With these facilities you can pre-store and pre-execute different kinds of computations.

Specification Management

With the ability to go after data in the hands of the users comes a new problem. How will you manage the process of putting your specifications into the machine for what you want the system to do. In the traditional world this was the programmer's job. He or she figured out what the program should do, how it would get done, and then wrote the specifications using a programming language.

In the data mining world we open up a whole new range of possibilities. With the automation of metadata access and the development of query builders, report builders and other forms of automated specification, we suddenly find that it is possible to let end users "write" their own programs.

Execution Management

Directly related to the way some data mining tools allow end users to write and manage their own specifications is the way their execution is timed and managed.

In the traditional I/S world there are only two options:

1. Batch Jobs - Programs are scheduled to run on some kind of regular basis.
2. Real Time / Interactive - Hit a button and the program runs.

Now other options are available. Users can schedule jobs to run at a certain time, to executed overnight, or to run over the next few hours.

At the high end of these capabilities are agents. Agents are software modules that sit out on the system and check for conditions. When the looked for condition is found, they trigger the execution of a program or a report.

For example, an accountant might create an agent that monitors the balance of the corporate checking account. This agent will check the balance every hour and, if the amount drops to a certain level, will trigger the execution of a checking account audit and activity report which is immediately printed and shows up on the accountant's desk.

By using agents to schedule work, the users' and the systems personnel's time and energy are optimized.

OBJECTIVES

Understanding how a data mining tool works gives us one perspective on its usefulness. Another, more puzzling, aspect is understanding how or why these tools are different from the traditional applications programs or simple query writers we have used in the past. One of the easiest ways to develop an appreciation for these differences is to look at what the objectives are for using each of these types of programming tools or approaches.

We can see that all application development programs and data mining tools fall into three operational categories. You use the application for any one or for a combination of these.

1. Data collection and retrieval - the traditional definition of an On Line Transaction Processing or Legacy System, Operational System. Data mining tools apply very little, if at all, to this category.

2. Operational monitoring - the process of keeping tabs on your business operations and making effective decisions to correct or improve its workings. Clearly, better than half of the data mining tools, as we have defined them, fit into this category. They include query managers, report writers, spreadsheets, multi-dimensional databases and visualization tools.

3. Exploration and discovery - the process of taking a look at your business with the objective of trying to discover new things about how it works, or how to make it run more efficiently. It is in this category that we find the rest of the data mining tools, the statistical analysis, artificial intelligence, neural net, advanced statistical analysis and advanced visualization products. The "die hard" definers of data mining would say that only this category holds the "real" data mining tools.

The Operational Monitoring Cycle

Regardless of the technology or tools that are available, business people spend a considerable amount of their time monitoring and maintaining the business's activities. They proceed through three steps.

Step 1. First, there is the actual monitoring of activities and conditions. In the traditional I/S world of the 1960s, '70s and '80's the vast majority of monitoring was done through the use of printed, regularly scheduled reports. These reports allowed the business people to check on the status of whatever they happened to be responsible for. Consequently, dozens and even hundreds of printed reports, showing inventory levels, balance sheet amounts, and other types of activities, were created regularly. The problem, of course, was that people had to actually read all of those reports to make sure things were running smoothly. The second problem was that, once the reports were written, it was difficult to turn them off. It had been so much trouble to get the report in the first place, it was a lot easier to just leave it running just in case it was ever needed again.

Data mining tools have made the monitoring process many times easier. Now, through the use of the on line tools, users can very easily check on whatever it is they want, whenever they want. More importantly, the use of agent technology makes it possible to have the system do the monitoring work for you. This eliminates the menial, tedious aspects of the monitoring process.

Step 2. During this process of monitoring the business person will eventually discover a problem or strange situation. The next step then in the monitoring cycle is the investigation phase. During investigation the users need to dig much more deeply into some aspect of the system's operations. They may need to take a look at historical, operational, and real-time transactional data. It is during this phase that the new data mining technologies and data warehousing approaches can make a significant difference. All sorts of information can now be accessed immediately which, in the past, might have taken days, weeks or even months to figure out.

Step 3. Finally, after discovering what went wrong, the business person makes adjustments to the organization to correct the problem. After that, it is back to the monitoring process.

The data mining tools make the monitoring cycle easier, faster and more efficient and, therefore, provide a significant improvement to the overall operational efficiency of the business people and the organization as a whole.

The Exploration Process

The exploration of data is a relatively new phenomena in the business world, but it is a process that has been extremely popular in the scientific community for some time now. Data exploration entails assembling as much data as possible about a given problem area and then applying analytical criteria to it in order to discover new cause and effect kinds of relationships which can help better predict future activities.

For example, medical researchers use this technique when trying to figure out how a new disease works, or how a plague spreads. Social scientists use the same approach to study attitudes and behaviors in different societies and cultures. Biologists, physicists, engineers and psychologists, all use this technique to help unravel the mysteries of how things work in the physical world.

This is not to say that the application of these same techniques has never been used in business. Underwriters in the insurance industry take a look at the statistical probabilities of how likely a person is to die within a given time frame when deciding upon life insurance rates. Banks have long attempted to use the same techniques to try and get a handle on who is most likely to default on a loan.

Three things have happened relatively recently.

Firstly, business people have discovered that they own a vast wealth of information which often holds useful insights into predicting how to better run their operations, or how to better predict the behavior of consumers. In effect, they are finding that they have a resource which they need only figure out how to tap.

Secondly, the increased ability to manage large amounts of data through a data warehouse makes it possible to get at the data in a convenient form. Let's face it, who would want to do statistical analysis on billions of records that can only be accessed via micro-fiche or tape?

Thirdly, the sophistication, the power, and the ease of use of today's new generation of data exploration tools make it economically and functionally feasible to do things that, in the past, required a team of statisticians and a support staff of dozens of clerks to execute.

We have dedicated a good portion of the rest of this book in offering you some different perspectives and explanations of how this data exploration process is executed and used in practical business situations.

DEVELOPMENTAL PARTICIPATION

The last area of data mining characteristics that we will consider is the developmental participation. It is only through understanding developmental participation and the roles of hardware, software and greyware (the software in people's heads) that we can truly come to appreciate just how powerful the data mining and data warehousing concepts are.

The Traditional Model of Application Development

Under the traditional mode of application development end users gained access only through application programs written by in house programming staff or by the vendor of the application package.

In the process of writing this package, the developer sat down and figured out everything an end user might need to know. Usually, subject matter experts in the area that the application was designed to service (accounting, marketing, etc.) would be called upon to provide input to the process. End users were asked about the functionality they were looking for. Any computational or statistical analysis that the system would provide was researched and built into the software.

The end result of this process was a piece of software that made most of the decision for the user. It was an application that shielded the end user from needing to think about anything but whatever the application had decided. Not only were the business rules and mathematical characteristics of the system built in and automated, but the whole process of finding the requested information was also done for the user.

When you move into the world of data mining tools, however, a large amount of that research, development and other brain work are no longer built into the system.

The provision of data mining tools to the end user is both a blessing and a curse. On the one hand, the business person is now able to gain access to all sorts of data that was never before available, which he or she can then put through almost any kind of computational or statistical regimen imaginable.

On the other hand, the flexibility and power that is now at the users' fingertips requires that they be able to understand the data they are using, the statistical analysis processes they invoke, and the systems they are manipulating, to a degree that was never before required.

We can break this analysis down into its component parts to help explain it better.

We start with the "raw" application. Whether it is programmer written or data mining tool delivered, every application is made up of a series of logical and physical processing steps.

In the traditional environment all of those processes and steps were packaged by the programmer as one application program.

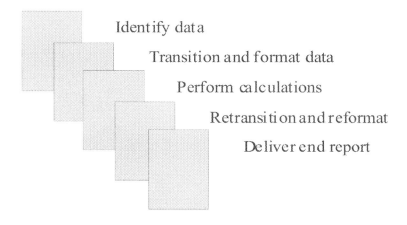

Identify data

Transition and format data

Perform calculations

Retransition and reformat

Deliver end report

Figure 13-1

In the data warehouse/data mining environment we "break up" this "package" into pieces. The data access and identification functions, formally hard coded into programs, are now managed by data warehouse facilities, metadata managers and data mining tools.

The ability to access, manipulate and format that data is now placed under the direct control of end users via the data mining tools themselves.

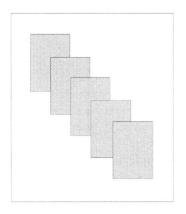

One application
can do it all

User contribution

Figure 13.2

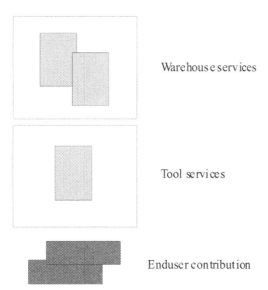

Warehouse services

Tool services

Enduser contribution

Figure 13-3

The brain power necessary for figuring out how to assemble these steps, and what to do with the data recovered, must now be provided by the end users themselves.

Too often, people have undertaken to develop large scale data warehouse and data mining projects without taking these facts into account. The end result has been disastrous. Data mining is not a replacement for application development. You cannot take your existing business processes, procedures and staff and simply replace OLTP and legacy systems with warehouse/mining systems.

No, to capitalize on the capabilities we are talking about requires that the end users themselves change the way they view their jobs and develop a deeper understanding of the "bigger picture" of the problems they are trying to solve. Without this kind of end-user paradigm shift, the effort to move into the data warehouse/data mining universe is a colossal waste of time and energy.

www.ingramcontent.com/pod-product-compliance
Lightning Source LLC
Chambersburg PA
CBHW051044050326
40690CB00006B/587